This book portrays the life and institutions of a great medieval Italian city, Siena, through the surviving records and buildings of the period. Laws, council minutes, records of the commune's revenue and expenditure, wills and other charters from the thirteenth century are among the plentiful material which makes up the picture of the city republic's institutions and those who ran them.

The main themes are the political institutions of the city, and the involvement of the citizens in them. The preoccupations of the Sienese as revealed in their conciliar discussions are studied, as well as their attitudes to government and well-developed bureaucracy, their territorial overlordship in southern Tuscany, and their involvement in diplomacy and war. The religion of the Sienese is also investigated.

This is a portrait of a special, but not untypical, society which was engaged in an experiment in oligarchic self-government. Although the milieu was urban, Siena's bankers and tradesmen, craftsmen and those involved in transport and agricultural labour, were in many cases landowners: the city was dependent on and greatly involved with its rural environment. The precocity of the commune's governmental methods and the wealth of information that has survived mean that the medieval life of this famous and beautiful Tuscan city can be depicted in full and convincing detail.

D1548086

SIENA AND THE SIENESE IN THE
THIRTEENTH CENTURY

Siena and the Sienese in the thirteenth century

DANIEL WALEY

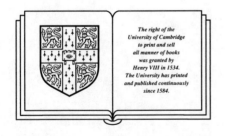

The right of the
University of Cambridge
to print and sell
all manner of books
was granted by
Henry VIII in 1534.
The University has printed
and published continuously
since 1584.

CAMBRIDGE UNIVERSITY PRESS

Cambridge
New York   Port Chester
Melbourne   Sydney

Published by the Press Syndicate of the University of Cambridge
The Pitt Building, Trumpington Street, Cambridge CB2 1RP
40 West 20th Street, New York, NY 10011–4211, USA
10 Stamford Road, Oakleigh, Melbourne 3166, Australia

© Cambridge University Press 1991

First published 1991

Printed in Great Britain at the University Press, Cambridge

British Library cataloguing in publication data
Waley, Daniel
Siena and the Sienese in the thirteenth century.
1. Italy. Siena, history
945.58

Library of Congress cataloguing in publication data
Waley, Daniel Philip
Siena and the Sienese in the thirteenth century/Daniel Waley.
      p.   cm.
Includes bibliographical references and index.
1. Siena (Italy) – History. 2. Siena (Italy) – Social life and customs. 3. Siena (Italy) – History –
Sources. 4. Siena (Italy) – Social life and customs – Sources. I. Title.
DG975.S5W35   1991
945'.58 – c20   90-20127   CIP

ISBN 0 521 40312 X hardback

To the custodians of Siena's historical archive, past, present and future

Contents

Illustrations

Tables

Preface

The intention of this book is to depict the Sienese and their city through the use of records of the period between 1250 and 1310. The extent and nature of these sources – principally laws, minutes of council meetings, financial records and wills – are such that it should be possible to give an idea of how the city was run at that time and what it felt like to live there. My aim has been to portray Sienese institutions – the commune's and others – to explain how they worked and who participated in them, and to link up the people who exercised power in the city with the ways in which they did this. The computer has helped me in attempting some quantitative use of the sources; I hope that this has been cautious.

William Bowsky's Herculean labours on the source material in the Sienese Archivio di Stato began a decade before I set to work, and culminated in his *The Finance of the Commune of Siena, 1287–1355* (1970) and *A Medieval Italian Commune, Siena under the Nine, 1287–1355* (1981). The technique of this book has dictated a different approach from Bowsky's, but we have about a quarter of a century (1287–1310) in common. I have sought to depict Siena as it appears to me without allowing Bowsky's viewpoint to dictate mine either in agreement or reaction, but I have almost certainly acquired more from his writings than I was aware of when writing myself and I acknowledge most gratefully my indebtedness to his many publications. Bowsky emphasizes continuity in the period 1287–1355 and implies a break at the start of that period, whereas my emphasis is on continuity through the preceding half-century and in the early decades of the Nine. A differing view also emerges concerning the *Noveschi*. Bowsky sees the Nine as a 'regime', the *Noveschi* as a 'governing class' or 'ruling oligarchy'. My contrasting interpretation portrays the period after 1287 as a phase in the commune's constitutional development in which the older ruling class accepted a continuous process whereby 'middling merchants' played a more prominent or more formally defined role in government.

It is about twenty years since I began to devote my leisure to collecting material for this book and it is now time to bring together the work done rather than pursue further archival research. Because my aim is to give a realistic picture of Sienese society, the technique employed is to give examples from the surviving records of how things were done and perceived, so the arrangement is topical, dealing in turn with the place, its people, the working of their political and social institutions and their religion. In the last chapter, on continuity and change, I have made an attempt to compensate for the disadvantages of this non-chronological approach. Naturally the records are not equally informative for all aspects of medieval Sienese life and I am aware of gaps through the virtual omission, for example, of the household and domesticity. I have tried, not with total success, to proceed from Sienese sources alone and not to argue or illustrate by analogy with other medieval cities. The lack of discussion of other cities limits the book's usefulness as a contribution to comparative history, but the sacrifice is intentional. I have also sought to avoid the viewpoints and controversies of recent historical research because the book is intended for general readers, not only for scholars and students.

Acknowledgements

My thanks are due most of all to my wife who has, as ever, helped me very greatly with advice, criticism and forbearance. She gave me the microfilm reader which has been a crucial aid and she has constantly and patiently intervened between myself and a word processor which my own ineptitude in such matters would have made it impossible for me to dominate unaided.

I have much enjoyed working in the Sienese Archivio di Stato over a good many years and my gratitude to the staff and present Director, Dr Sonia Fineschi, is reflected, though inadequately, in the dedication of this work.

Westfield College (now Queen Mary and Westfield College), University of London, generously made me an Honorary Research Fellow on my retirement, and for the computer analysis in chapter 2 I am indebted to the college's Computer Unit.

Professor Paolo Cammarosano most kindly gave me a copy of his and Dr Passeri's marvellous *Repertorio delle strutture fortificate* for the region of Siena and Grosseto. I should like to thank him for this well-timed present and for other gifts of his publications. Dr David d'Avray of University College, London, generously read the chapter on religion in an earlier form and made very helpful comments. Dr Edward English of the Pontifical Institute of Mediaeval Studies. Toronto, sent me copies of publications and writings of his; his gift of a copy of his doctoral thesis was an act of outstanding generosity.

I must express also my gratitude to the Leverhulme Foundation for the award of an Emeritus Fellowship which enabled me to spend many weeks working at the Sienese archive in 1986–7.

Some acknowledgements relating to maps and tables are made in relevant parts of this book.

D. W.

Glossary

The purpose of this glossary is to help readers not familiar with the vocabulary of medieval Italian society. The aim has been to provide brief explanatory keys, not precise or full definitions, to help with the comprehension of some words used in connection with institutions in this book.

1. TOPOGRAPHICAL

1. *Burgi* (also *subburgi*): suburbs, i.e. built-up areas outside the city walls.
2. *Contado:* the area of the commune's jurisdiction outside the city and *Masse* (see below). Its inhabitants are styled *comitatenses* in this book, since the Italian form 'contadini' (= peasants) is ambiguous.
3. *Contrade:* neighbourhoods or regions (not necessarily formal divisions), usually within a city or town.
4. *Masse:* the area close to the city of Siena, the subject of special juridical and fiscal arrangements, being more directly under the commune's authority than the contado.
5. *Popoli:* the districts into which Siena was divided, drawing their names mainly from parish churches; they numbered thirty-four in 1318. (Not connected with the institution 'Popolo' described below under 2b.)
6. *Terzi:* the three 'thirds' into which the city of Siena was divided, i.e. Città, San Martino, Camollia.

For further information see *Repertorio* and Redon. The map in the latter work is particularly helpful about the whereabouts and extent of the Masse.

2. INSTITUTIONS

A. Connected with the commune

1. *Balia* (plural: *balie*). An *ad hoc* committee.
2. *Biccherna*. The central financial office of the Sienese commune.
3. *Camerlengo* (Latin *camerarius* = chamberlain). The principal financial official of the commune.
4. *Cavallata*. The obligation to perform cavalry service or tax payable in lieu of this.
5. *Consiglio della Campana* or *Consiglio Generale*. The principal council of the commune.

 6. *Dazio*. Direct tax.
 7. *Dogana*. Fiscal monopoly.
 8. *Emendatori*. Officials charged with revising the statutes.
 9. *Gabella*. Indirect tax; office concerned with indirect taxation.
10. *Lira* (Latin *libra*). Assessment for direct tax; grouping for direct taxation on a topographical basis.
11. *Maggior sindaco*. Non-Sienese official charged with ensuring obedience to the commune's statutes.
12. *Ordini* (Latin *Ordines*). The leading magistracies, comprising the Provveditori, the consuls of the Mercanzia and the consuls of the Knights (alternatively known as Captains of the Guelf Party).
13. *Parlamento* (or *arenga*). General assembly: see chapter 3, excursus 2.
14. *Placitum*. Court of 'pleas', concerned with the wardship of minors.
15. *Podestà*. Principal non-Sienese official of the commune. His own subordinate officials or retainers were sometimes known as his *curia* (court).
16. *Provveditori*. Four principal Sienese officials of the Biccherna.
17. *Radota*. Additional members co-opted to councils.
18. *Savi* (Latin: *sapientes*). Elected advisers, members of *balie*.
19. *Sindacatio*. Process of inspection of accounts etc. of officials on their leaving office.

For the titles of the leading officials at different periods (Twenty-four, Thirty-six, Fifteen, Nine) see table 4.

B. Others

 1. *Anziani* (Latin: *antiani*, literally 'elders'). Elected officials, usually of the Popolo.
 2. *Arti*. Gilds, i.e. merchant and craft gilds.
 3. *Consuls*. Normally applied in this period to officials of gilds, though the 'knights' (i.e. elements not members of the Popolo) also had consuls.
 4. *Mercanzia*. The merchant gild.
 5. *Popolo*. An organization proclaiming an anti-oligarchical programme (see chapter 5). Unconnected with the topographical unit of the same name. Members: *popolani*. The leading official (captain) from the 1250s was the *Capitano del Popolo*.
 6. *Priors*. Office-holders sometimes enjoyed special powers during that part of their period of office when they served as seniors or 'priors'.
 7. *Tallia* (literally: 'share'). An alliance embodying an agreement covering military contributions made by its members.

3. MISCELLANEOUS

1. *Balitori*. Messengers.
2. *Bannum*. Judicial ban or outlawry (*rebannimentum*: release from the ban).
3. *Carroccio*. The ceremonial waggon of the commune.
4. *Casato* (plural *casati*). Family; specifically family formally identified as of magnate status, i.e. aristocratic or powerful.
5. *Fondaco* (Latin *fundacus*). A complex of buildings possessed by a leading family; a trader's store; or premises of traders resident in a town or land which is not their own.
6. *Masnadieri*. Followers, retainers.

Abbreviations

ARCHIVAL

ASS   Siena, Archivio di Stato

Series in ASS:
B   Biccherna (printed volumes cited as *B.*)
Capitano   Capitano del Popolo
Concistoro
CG   Consiglio Generale
Dipl.   Diplomatico
AGC   Archivio Generale dei Contratti
Rif.   Riformagioni
Spedale   Spedale di S Maria della Scala
Lira
Notarile
Podestà
Statuti

PRINTED SOURCES

AA SS   Acta Sanctorum Bollandiana (reprinted Paris-Rome, 1863–)
Astuti   G. Astuti, *Il Libro dell'Entrata e dell'Uscita di una Compagnia mercantile senese del sec. XIII (1277–1282)* (Doc. e Studi per la Storia del Commercio e del Diritto commerciale italiano, 5) (Turin, 1934).
B.   Libri dell'Entrata e dell'Uscita della Repubblica di Siena (Siena, 1903–70)
'Breve, 1250'   'Breve degli officiali del comune di Siena . . . 1250', ed. L. Banchi, *ASI*, s. 3, 3, 2 (1866), pp. 3–104
CV   Il Caleffo Vecchio del comune di Siena, eds. G. Cecchini and others, 4 vols. (Siena, 1932–84)
Const. 1262   Il Constituto del comune di Siena dell'anno 1262, ed. L. Zdekauer (Milan, 1897: reprinted Bologna 1983)
(Cont.   continuation in *BSSP*, 1–3)
Cost. 1309–10   Il Costituto del comune di Siena volgarizzato nel MCCCIX–MCCCX, ed. A. Lisini (Siena, 1903)

Const. CdP   *Il Constituto dei Consoli del Placito del comune di Siena*, ed. L. Zdekauer (Siena, 1890= *SS*, 6 (1889), pp. 152–206)

P. and P.   *Lettere volgari del sec. XIII scritte da Senesi*, eds. C. Paoli and E. Piccolomini (Bologna, 1871 reprinted 1968)

Reg. Urb. IV   *Les Registres d'Urbain IV*, ed. J. Guiraud (Paris, 1901 ff.)

RIS, CS   *Cronache Senesi*, eds. A. Lisini and F. Iacometti in *Rerum Italicarum Scriptores*. n.s., 15, 6 (Bologna, 1931–39)

Statuti . . . giudici e notai   *Statuti senesi dell'arte dei giudici e notai del sec. XIV*, ed. G. Catoni (Rome, 1972)

Statuti senesi   *Statuti senesi scritti in volgare nei sec. XIII e XIV*, eds. F.–L. Polidori and L. Banchi, 3 vols. (Bologna, 1863–77)

PERIODICALS

ASI   *Archivio Storico Italiano*

BDSPU   *Bollettino della Deputazione di Storia Patria per l'Umbria*

BSSP   *Bollettino Senese di Storia Patria*

JWCI   *Journal of the Warburg and Courtauld Institutes*

MAH (later *MEFR*)   *Mélanges d'Archéologie et d'Histoire de l'École française de Rome*

Misc. St. S.   *Miscellanea Storica Senese*

QFIA   *Quellen und Forschungen aus italienischen Archiven und Bibliotheken*

RSDI   *Rivista di Storia del Diritto Italiano*

RSI   *Rivista Storica Italiana*

SM   *Studi Medievali*

SS   *Studi Senesi*

WORKS OF REFERENCE

DBI   *Dizionario Biografico degi Italiani*

Repertorio   P. Cammarosano and V. Passeri, *Città borghi e castelli dell'area senese-grossetana. Repertorio delle strutture fortificate dal medioevo alla caduta della Repubblica senese* (Siena, 1984)

SECONDARY (PUBLISHED)

Balestracci Piccinni   D. Balestracci and G. Piccinni, *Siena nel trecento. Assetto urbano e strutture edilizie* (Florence, 1977)

Bortolotti, *Siena*   L. Bortolotti, *Siena* (Rome/Bari, 1983)

Bowsky, *Commune*   W. M. Bowsky, *A Medieval Italian Commune, Siena under the Nine, 1287–1355* (Berkeley/Los Angeles/London, 1981)

Bowsky, *Finance*   W. M. Bowsky, *The Finance of the Commune of Siena, 1287–1355* (Oxford, 1970)

Braunfels   W. Braunfels, *Mittelalterliche Stadtbaukunst in der Toskana* (Berlin, 1953)

C. Econ. H.   *Cambridge Economic History of Europe* (Cambridge, 1941–)

Cammarosano   P. Cammarosano, 'Le campagne senesi dalla fine del sec. XII agli inizi del trecento: dinamica interna e forme del dominio cittadino' in *Contadini e proprietari nella Toscana moderna. Atti del convegno di studio in onore di G. Giorgetti* (Florence, 1979), 1, pp. 153–222.

Ciacci   G. Ciacci, *Gli Aldobrandeschi nella Storia e nella 'Divina Commedia'* (2 vols., Rome, 1934: reprinted 1 vol. Rome, 1980)

Ciampoli   D. Ciampoli, *Il Capitano del popolo a Siena nel primo Trecento* (Siena, 1984)

Davidsohn   R. Davidsohn, *Storia di Firenze* (8 vols., Florence, 1977–78: German original, 1896–1927)

Davidsohn, *Forschungen*   R. Davidsohn, *Forschungen zur älteren Geschichte von Florenz* (4 vols., Berlin, 1896–1908: reprinted Turin, 1964).

English   E. D. English, *Enterprise and Liability in Sienese Banking, 1230–1350* (Cambridge, Mass: 1988)

Epstein   S. R. Epstein, *Alle origini della fattoria toscana. L'ospedale della Scala di Siena e le sue terre (metà '200-metà '400)* (Florence, 1986)

Marrara   D. Marrara, 'I magnati e il governo del comune di Siena dallo statuto del 1274 alla fine del XIV secolo' in *Studi per Enrico Fiumi* (Pisa, 1979), pp. 239–76

Mondolfo, *Populus*   U.G. Mondolfo, *Il Populus a Siena nella vita della città e nel governo del comune fino alla riforma antimagnatizia del 1277* (Genoa, 1911)

Pazzaglini   P. R. Pazzaglini, *The Criminal Ban of the Sienese Commune, 1225–1310* (Quaderni di *Studi Senesi*, Milan, 1979)

Pecci   G. A. Pecci, *Storia del Vescovado della città di Siena* (Lucca, 1748)

Prunai   G. Prunai, 'Carte mercantili dei Piccolomini nel diplomatico fiorentino' in *Studi in onore di Amintore Fanfani* (vol. 2, Milan, 1962), pp. 547–637

Redon   O. Redon, *Uomini e comunità del contado senese nel duecento* (Siena, 1982)

Roon-Bassermann   E. von Roon-Bassermann, *Sienesische Handelsgesellschaften des XIII. Jahrhunderts* (Mannheim/Leipzig, 1912)

Rubinstein   N. Rubinstein (ed.), *Florentine Studies* (London, 1968)

Waley, 'Project'   D. Waley, 'Project for a computer-assisted analysis of Sienese tax payments in 1285' in *Florence and Italy. Renaissance Studies in Honour of Nicolai Rubinstein*, ed. P. Denley and C. Elam (London, 1988)

Zdekauer, *Mercante*   L. Zdekauer, *Il mercante senese nel dugento* (Siena, 1899: edn 2, 1925)

Zdekauer, *Vita privata*   L. Zdekauer, *La vita privata dei senesi nel dugento* (Siena, 1896: reprinted Bologna, 1973)

Zdekauer, *Vita pubblica* L. Zdekauer, *La vita pubblica dei senesi nel dugento* (Siena, 1897: reprinted Bologna, 1973)

Secondary (unpublished)

English, '5 magnate families' E. D. English, 'Five magnate families of Siena, 1240–1350' (PhD, Toronto, 1981)

Chronology of principal political events and developments

1250	(death of Frederick II)
1251–54	war against Florence
1253	Capitano del Popolo (first reference)
1255	council of Popolo (first reference)
1259	oath of fealty to King Manfred
1260	victory at Montaperti
1262	secession of Guelf bankers
1266	(Benevento, Angevin victory over Manfred)
1268	(Tagliacozzo, Angevin victory over Conradin)
1269	defeat at Colle
1271	Guelfs return, Ghibellines go into exile; leading officials the 36
1274	Guelf constitution
1277	list of *casati* issued
1280	pacification; leading officials the 15
1287–90	leading officials the 9
1288–92	wars with Florence against Pisa and Arezzo
1290–91	leading officials the 18
1291–92	leading officials the 6
1292–	leading officials the 9 again
1310	(Henry VII enters Tuscany)

Events external to Tuscany are in brackets.

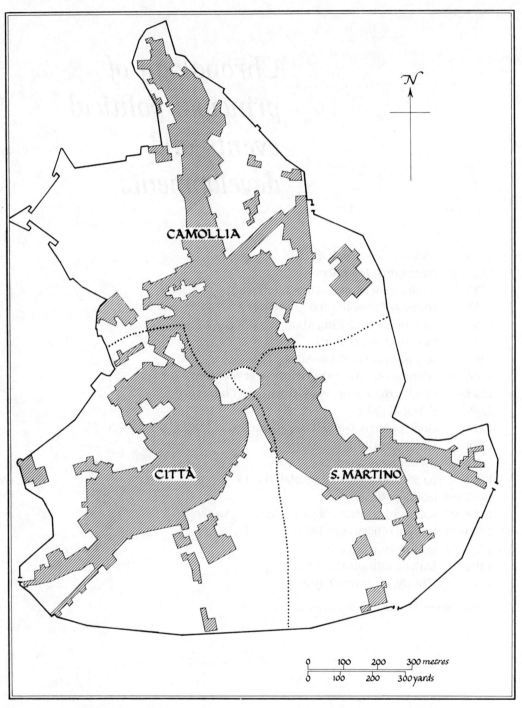

1 SIENA.

1 Setting

This book is concerned with the Sienese rather than their city, but as a preliminary something must be said about the setting within which they lived.[1]

Medieval Siena was an extremely small urban zone in the wide expanse of a predominantly rural Tuscany. The appearance of the place was to strike a French traveller in 1580 as already one of great antiquity ('son visage la tesmoine fort ancienne'). This visitor, Michel de Montaigne, saw Siena as an 'uneven' (*inégal*) town, 'situated along a ridge where most of the streets are. . . Some of these continue onto the facing slopes of other hills'. The built-up area, rapidly growing in the middle decades of the thirteenth century, sprawled along two principal roads. The chief route from the north to Rome, the 'Via Francigena', bifurcated at the very centre of Siena, where the main road bore on, as the Via Cassia, towards Rome, and other routes led away to the south-west, towards Massa Marittima, Grosseto and the other towns of the Maremma. The city – Siena had a bishop and hence ranked as *civitas* – extended in fact along a series of ridges, from which housing had already begun to overflow onto the quite steep slopes and valleys which separated them. To walk from one end to the other of this site would have required no more than some fifteen minutes, unless the streets were exceptionally crowded, and to cross from east to west would have been the work of five minutes or less, despite the contours. Crowded into this urban microcosm were, around the middle of the thirteenth century, some 30,000 people, a number which was rapidly and continually increasing through immigration.

Siena's inhabitants lived in a great variety of dwellings all of which would now be considered appallingly uncomfortable and almost all dreadfully crowded. With little space indoors, life was lived as much as possible in the street, though from October till May this was often a cold and windy alternative to the cramped rigours of existence within the home. For most the house was probably a wattle and daub construction, sometimes with a brick facade, though a good many could afford a small house partly of stone. Often the building comprised a shop at

---

1 On the topography of thirteenth-century Siena, see Balestracci Piccinni (excellent, but concerned with a later period); Braunfels (see 'Siena' in index); Bortolotti, chapter 2; P. Nardi, 'I borghi di S. Donato e di S. Pietro a Ovile', *BSSP*, third series, 25–7 (1966–8), pp. 7–59. M. Montaigne, *Journal de Voyage en Italie*, ed. M. Rat (Paris, 1942), pp. 89–91 (and, for the 'collines fertiles' of the region, p. 214).

ground level with dwelling apartments above reached by a narrow internal stairway or steps outside. The external approach was characteristic also of the towers and houses of the wealthier citizens, which would have the advantage of possessing upstairs loggias and balconies. The grandest families, who derived their riches both from widespread landed estates and financial transactions, inhabited extensive blocks of buildings, sometimes styled 'palaces' or 'castles', ownership of which was complicated by the system of *consorzeria*, the joint 'consorts' being relatives who had shares in the family building.

An older Siena, going back to the eleventh and twelfth centuries, was beginning to seem swamped by the expansion of the mid thirteenth. Land near the centre was already a valuable commodity and the speed of change must have been bewildering for the older inhabitants. The isolated remnants of the early medieval city from which the new mercantile city had originated were primarily ecclesiastical. Besides the cathedral, sited at the centre of old Siena ('Castelvecchio'), there was a small number of monastic foundations nearby, among them the Benedictine house of S Eugenio, the abbey 'at the archway' (all'Arco), S Vigilio (Camaldulensian) and the Vallombrosan house of S Michele. Among the many developments which were transforming the city the churches of the new orders of friars were perhaps the most imposing. With much financial assistance from the city, ambitious building schemes were launched by the religious innovators of the century, Dominicans, Franciscans, Carmelites, Servites and Augustinian Hermits, and the crusading Orders, Templars and Hospitallers, representatives of an older tradition, were also building. Of the great families, the Tolomei already had a 'big palace' (*palatium magnum*)[2] and in general extensive private building kept pace with ecclesiastical building. Secular public work was a necessity, in particular the hilly site set urgent problems of water supply and the most crucial undertakings of the thirteenth century were the reconstruction of one fountain (Fonte Branda) and the addition of three others, Fonte Nuova, Fonte Ovile and Fonte Follonica.

The lie of the land and the rapidity of the city's expansion militated against a neat system of ring defences. Although the necessity for city walls was a commonplace and Siena possessed a body of officials whose responsibility was to strengthen these defences, the reality was a series of *ad hoc* arrangements. By 1257 the watchmen had thirty-six gates to guard, many of which must have been situated within the city rather than on any outer perimeter. If in some parts building had outgrown walls, in others there were still green expanses within them; inside the walls were vineyards and vegetable gardens, also to be found in the environs of some of the religious foundations.

---

2 G. Prunai, 'La famiglia Tolomei' in Prunai, G. Pampaloni, N. Bemporad, *Il Palazzo Tolomei a Siena* (Florence, 1971), pp. 9–58.

The gardens are a reminder that the land and its activities dominated Siena. The rhythm of the judicial year was that of the harvests. Agricultural instruments, both wooden and iron, were excluded from those possessions which might be confiscated on account of debt,[3] not surprisingly, since a high proportion of the population earned their living by tilling the soil. Medieval Siena had originated as a stopping-place on the road to Rome: by this time it had become a market and financial centre on the road.

ROUTES

Proper guard and protection of the highway was a normal function of government in the Middle Ages and it was natural that the oath taken by Siena's leading official, the Podestà, on assuming office, should include the promise 'to govern the highway throughout the territory of the city, to the honour of God'.[4] The duties of the commune were indeed defined more closely: 'clerks (clerici), pilgrims, merchants and others travelling on the highway or other roads of the city or its sphere of jurisdiction must be defended and protected', and any one harming them must be punished, whilst a special legal protection prevailed for those travelling to the market or fairs.[5] The didactic frescoes by Ambrogio Lorenzetti in the Palazzo Pubblico emphasize vividly the significance of these clauses. The horrors of bad government include robbery on the highway by an armed band, and a man lies murdered just outside the city gate: the entire countryside is dominated by the figure of Fear. In the contrasting scene of good government the corresponding figure of Safety (Securitas) carries a gibbet whereon hangs the body of a malefactor.

The road to Rome from France and the north, the Francigena, ranked in a special category. Robbery on such a frequented route may have been relatively uncommon – though a Sienese merchant lost his gold on it in 1255 and some Florentines a valuable load of iron in 1257[6] – but its upkeep was essential to the city's well-being. A clause in the 1262 statutes begins with the lament that 'the main roads near the city are in such a state of disrepair and the bridges so broken-down that travellers cannot pass without great danger and in consequence the market suffers great disadvantage and foodstuffs cannot be brought to the city'.[7] The aim was to maintain the Francigena as a pilgrim route, not merely as a way for pack animals and carts; a duty of officials of all places between Siena and Torrenieri, thirty kilometres to the south, was to provide chained cups in

---

3 Const. 1262, p. 128.
4 Ibid., p. 25.
5 Const. 1262. Cont. BSSP, 2, pp. 318–19.
6 B.17, p. 67.
7 Const. 1262, p. 297.

wells by the roadside.[8] The travellers themselves appear in Sienese legislation in other ways. When a pilgrim or merchant died in Siena itself, the owner of the hostel or inn where he was lodged was responsible for handing over his possessions, normally to the city; if he died intestate, however, and had been with companions who were willing to take an oath that they would pass on his property to his children or heirs, then these companions would receive it.[9] The numerous hostels were thickest along the main road, particularly close to the northern entrance, Camollia.[10] Naturally transport and communications were important sources of employment for the Sienese. However, analysis of the occupations of Sienese taxpayers in 1285 shows 'carriers' as numerically seventh in the list of trades given (with thirty-four names), keepers of hostels or lodgings ranking a good way below them (with seventeen).[11]

The market was Siena's heart and access to it Siena's arterial flow. If its business was interrupted by warfare the consequences were extremely serious for the city's finances and for those who farmed the indirect taxes. On such occasions the city officials would receive petitions explaining that receipts from the customs would be inadequate to repay the 'farmers' for the advances due from them. As one set of tax-farmers explained, the normal situation thus interrupted was that 'many merchants from Pisa, Lucca, Florence, San Miniato, Volterra, Figline, Colle, San Gimignano and the Elsa and Arno valleys and places north of Siena and its territory came to buy animals for their farms – sows, swine, piglets, sheep, oxen, cows'.[12] Trade in oxen was particularly lively since these beasts constantly needed replacement, having a working lifetime of only two to three years. The principal Sienese hospital, which had big estates, had to purchase between 100 and 150 of them each year.[13] No doubt most of the transactions at the market were on a small scale, such as that of Francuccio from Quercegrossa (a village five miles to the north on the Castellina in Chianti road) in 1306, who sold two oxen in the Campo for 33 l. but had the misfortune to be attacked on his way home by the armed band of Mastro of Poggibonsi, and robbed of all his money.[14]

If the arrival of grain was most crucial of all to the city's well-being, that of raw wool for the local textile industry was also of great importance. Wool-dealers

8 'Breve 1250', pp. 72–3.
9 *Cost. 1309–10*, 1, p. 409; *Const. 1262*, pp. 218–19.
10 Balestracci Piccinni, pp. 150–1, carta n. 9 (locates thirteen hotels in 1318–20). See also G. Venerosi-Pesciolini, 'La strada francigena nel contado di Siena nei sec. XIII–XIV', *La Diana*, 8 (1933), pp. 116–56.
11 Computer analysis of B 88, ff. 77–165v and 90, ff. 61–84v. Only one payer in five gave an occupation.
12 Bowsky, *Finance*, p. 138.
13 Epstein, pp. 220–4, 289.
14 CG 69, ff. 81v–3v (1306).

(*lanaioli*) rank numerically immediately after carriers among the 1285 tax-payers, while more specifically industrial textile occupations (carder, dyer, comber, shearer, fuller) are cited by twenty-five of them. The upkeep of the main road northwards to 'Lombardy' (i.e. the Francigena) was the subject of routine discussion by councils,[15] but the major route for commerce may have been that to the nearest port, Pisa. The most commonly used road for this journey branched off the Francigena only a few miles out of Siena and bore north-west through San Gimignano. With Rome the main links were financial rather than industrial. Whether the papal court and its innumerable ecclesiastical visitors were in that city or nearby in the Alban hills, or at Viterbo or Orvieto, they constituted the most promising nucleus of potential borrowers for Siena's bankers. Viterbo was the only significant commercial centre on the way to Rome, while Siena also had links with Umbrian towns such as Perugia, Foligno and Todi.[16]

That legislation concerning Siena's roads was extremely frequent is in part a testimony to its inefficacy.[17] Outside the city the principle of local responsibility for the upkeep of roads and necessary works prevailed, and on the chief roads boundary stones marked the limits of the areas of responsibility of the various localities. In 1306 twenty-nine authorities contributed sums ranging from 55 l. to 16 l. to the maintenance of the main road to Asciano and fifty-one shared the costs of the 30-kilometre stretch of the Francigena further west. Nine roads were regarded as 'principal' or 'public' ways, and those within two miles of the city walls ranked with those in the city itself. These were the special charge of three *ad hoc* officials (*pretori*), but after the 1270s they were reinforced by the office of six 'good men' appointed to act as general supervisors of roads, bridges and fountains. Later on it was decided that these functions were so sensitive that a high-grade official was appointed who was not to be Sienese; the problems presumably arose over local financial responsibility, since only fountains were maintained from the city's general fund. This *iudex viarum* held office for a period of six months and his duties included both inspection and decision-taking. He supplemented and regulated but did not supplant the existing Sienese supervisors.

---

15 E.g. CG 31, ff. 15 ff. (1286).
16 See D. Bizzarri, 'Trattati commerciali del comune di Siena nel sec. 13', *BSSP*, 30 (1923), pp. 199–216. On the itinerary of the thirteenth century papal Curia see A. Bagliani Paravicini in *Società e Istituzioni dell'Italia comunale: l'esempio di Perugia (sec. XII-XIV)* (Perugia, 1988), 1, pp. 225–46.
17 T. Szabò, 'La rete stradale del contado di Siena. Legislazione statutaria e amministrazione comunale nel duecento', *MEFR*, 87 (1975), pp. 141–86. Szabò counts 339 clauses in the Statutum Viarium (1290s).

PROMINENT BUILDINGS

The predominant impression within the city must have been one of social inequality. The homes of the wealthy towered above the dwellings of ordinary citizens, were much more numerous than churches and other religious buildings, and indeed in the thirteenth century had no secular rivals. Giovanni Antonio Pecci, an immensely learned eighteenth-century antiquary, noted that original sources known to him contained references to fifty-six towers as being in existence in the thirteenth century. This provides a minimum figure for the towers but it is also relevant that the list of *casati* or 'magnates' compiled by the commune in 1277 comprised fifty-three families.[18] The date at which leading families constructed 'palaces' or extensive towers cannot be established nor is it clear whether towers were features of all early magnatial palaces. Quite commonly the earliest reference that now survives to such a building is an account of its destruction by the commune following a 'rebellion' or family warfare or feuding. The rarity of specific reference before the middle of the thirteenth century is due merely to the poverty of surviving manuscript sources, the exceptionally early reference (1212) to the castle block *castellare* of the Ugurgieri family being the result of a freak (and indirect) survival.[19]

A rubric in the Sienese statutes proclaimed the right of any citizen to build 'in the city or *burgi* (suburbs) a house or tower or any other building of any height, size or nature' − with the proviso that this applied unless the council should decide to establish fixed maxima. Nor should a citizen be deprived of his house or tower unfairly; any confiscation must be general, i.e. applied not just to an individual but to his co-owners also.[20]

The high towers characteristic of the towns of northern and central Italy in the Middle Ages had a parallel in the watch-towers of the countryside and were probably modelled on them, though there is insufficient evidence to establish any clear priority.[21] The purpose of the towers was primarily to serve as a place of safety, but they could also be used as bases for offence. 'If anything is thrown for the purpose of inflicting harm (*ad iniuriam*) or to begin or carry on warfare', the 'lord' or principal owner of the tower where the offence occurred had to pay a fine of 100 l., in the case of a *casatorre*, palace or other fortified building, or 25 l., in that of an unfortified building (1262). By the early fourteenth century the penalties had been increased and varied from a 400 l. fine for both the lord and

18 For Pecci's figure see *Misc. St. S.*, 2 (1894), pp. 18–25. Eleven torri in the terzo of Camollia are mentioned in Lira, n. 5 (1260).

19 P. Cammarosano, *La famiglia dei Berardenghi* (Spoleto, 1974), pp. 210–13.

20 *Const. 1262*, p. 403.

21 For a contrary view see A.A. Settia, 'L'esportazione di un modello urbano: torri e case forti nelle campagne del nord Italia', *Società e Storia*, 12 (1981), pp. 273–97.

the giver of the relevant command in the case of a tower (the thrower himself was to pay 200 l. and to lose the offending hand by amputation if payment was not made within a month) to a 50 l. fine for the thrower from an unfortified house.[22] In time of emergency the commune would commandeer and garrison and if necessary repair strategically situated towers.[23]

Tenure in common must have been liable to a continuing process of subdivision. In 1254 ownership of the Tolomei palace was divided into nine fractions, one half share being fragmented into four shares and the other into five. Even these nine shares were subject to co-ownership, so that at least twenty-four members of the family were part-owners at that date. This situation is revealed in the terms of an agreement that every ten years all the occupants would change their place of habitation within the palazzo. The principal aim was presumably to secure fair treatment for all concerned.[24] The process of subdivision was of course continuous: in the early fourteenth century one Francesco di Luccio owned a 1/192 share in the same palazzo or complex of buildings.[25]

Why did the possession of an imposing tower become a major social aspiration? The word 'aspiration' in itself helps (surely) with the answer. It would be hard to invent any achievement more illustrative of conspicuous consumption and conspicuous ownership. Not everyone could hope to achieve the status of those powerful men who 'began or carried on warfare', but possession of such a lofty launching-pad was an evident sign of having 'made good', of having become at least a potential aggressor. Ambitions to tower over others expressed social ambitions, to do so was to have strength and status: towerlessness was humility in the worst and best senses.

For a long time municipal building lagged behind. Throughout the thirteenth century, as before, the normal places for council-meetings were churches, most commonly the very central S Pellegrino or S Cristoforo, occasionally the cathedral.[26] More rarely secular palazzi were pressed into service, among them the palaces of the Ugurgieri, the Tolomei and Jacobus Pieri.[27] The rent for such scattered premises came to comprise a normal though not very considerable item in the commune's expenditure. At times the Podestà resided in the palaces of the Piccolomini, the Ugurgieri and Guglielmus Benachi, the Captain in that of Jacobus Pieri. In 1281 the normal meeting-place for councils was the palace 'formerly of the Alessi', while the leading office-holders (the Fifteen) met at the palace 'of the sons of Mariscotto', but by the following year the Fifteen had moved

---

22 *Const. 1262. Cont. BSSP*, 3, p. 89; *Cost. 1309–10*, 2, pp. 235–7.
23 B 36, f. 58 (1263); 39, ff. 3, 19 (1266); 44, f. 14v (1270).
24 Dipl., Tolomei, 19.3.1254 (text in English, '5 Magnate Families', pp. 237–40).
25 Balestracci Piccinni, p. 131.
26 CG 15, f. 43v (1272).
27 CG 5, f. 7v (1255); 17, ff. 45–8 (1273); 20, f. 33v (1275).

on to the Gallerani palace. Tax officials sometimes met at the house of the Templars.[28] A building near the principal square, the Campo, which housed also some fiscal and other offices, was occasionally styled the 'palazzo del Podestà'.[29] Although rented premises continued to be required by the commune well into the fourteenth century, in the 1290s the great task was at last undertaken of clearing and extending the Campo with the intention of constructing a majestic public palace on the north side. Henceforth public wealth and might were to be proclaimed and private architecture would no longer predominate in grandeur.

HOUSING

Towers and palaces were for a minority, but they tended to cluster near the centre, which made a quite different impression from that made by regions closer to the walls. This disparity is evident from tax assessments and payments. The surviving fiscal material from 1260 relates only to the terzo of Camollia, the northern third of the city, but it is noticeable that the sums due from taxpayers in a libra (fiscal parish) near the gate (S Bartolomeo) average only one-sixtieth of those due in the central libra of S Cristoforo *a lato dei Tolomei*.[30] The figures of payments made in 1285, which are from the whole of Siena, show a very clearly marked pattern, the nearer to the centre, the greater the sum paid. The wealthiest libre of the terzo of Città were Galgaria, Incontri and Manetti, all close to the cathedral. In Camollia the highest payments – as in 1260 – were from S Cristoforo, followed by S Pietro ad Ovile *sopra*, S Egidio and S Andrea *a lato della piazza*, all of them quite central, whilst in the terzo of S Martino too the rich libre were the central ones of Pozzo S Martino, S Pietro alle Scale and S Vigilio *dentro*. In contrast the poorest libre of Città were S Agata and S Marco, those for S Martino the similarly placed Badia Nuova and S Maurizio *fuori*. Even within particular regions this pattern normally prevails: the payments from Stalloreggi *dentro* were larger than those from Stalloreggi *fuori* (the proportion of those paying above 5 l. was eight times as high) and the same was true of S Andrea *a lato della piazza* and the less central libra of S Andrea itself. At the time of the major fiscal survey of 1318–20, for which there are fewer gaps in the surviving evidence, the same generalization held, as it did in other cities. Grohmann's study of Perugia in 1285 presents an identical picture and in particular emphasizes the poverty of those who lived immediately outside the walls.[31] Many of these, at Siena also, must have been recent immigrants living, surely, in roughly constructed shanties.

---

28 CG 25, Alleg. D; B 79, ff. 29–31; 82, ff. 155–6; Zdekauer, *Vita pubblica*, p. 88n.
29 An early reference (1248) is *B*. 8, p. 173.
30 Calculation from Lira, n. 5 (the sums are 1s. 3d. and 3 l. 16s. respectively).
31 Balestracci Piccinni, maps 5 and 6: A. Grohmann, *L'imposta diretta nei comuni dell'Italia centrale nel XIII sec. La Libra di Perugia nel 1285* (Rome/Perugia, 1986), pp. 63–106.

An indication of comparative wealth was the possession of a loggia or balcony, but these desirable features had disadvantages for the population as a whole. Extending over the narrow thoroughfares (only the main street was reasonably wide), they blocked the way and made the streets and passages dark and greatly increased the danger from fire. That hazard was one of the reasons for the policy of encouraging the construction of fountains. Crafts involving the use of ovens and kilns were seen as particularly perilous: potters were not permitted to have kilns inside the city, glass manufacture was prohibited within a zone of some fifteen miles,[32] and inspectors were sent out to search for potentially dangerous ovens. Despite these precautions fires were fairly frequent and it was difficult to confine the damage to the immediate neighbourhood of the outbreak. At least sixty-four major fires are known to have occurred in Siena during the fourteenth century.[33] Sometimes the damage was so widespread that nearby towns sent messages of condolence, as happened in May 1279 when more than 300 houses were burned to the ground. After a severe fire in 1292 it was decided to appoint a corps of eight paid fire-fighters (appropriately they were to be chosen from Siena's carpenters) while it remained the duty of all to assist in fire-fighting within their own region.[34] Checking fire from spreading often involved the destruction of property and it was not easy to reach decisions about this. Accusations of over-zealousness were inevitable because 'sometimes people suffer greater damage from human agency than from the fire itself'.[35]

'If it should happen that a house in the city of Siena is destroyed by reason of fire – which God forbid! – I [the Podestà] shall cause compensation to be paid by the commune according to the valuation made by three good and law-worthy craftsmen' runs a clause in the city statutes. This sworn estimate covered damage as well as total destruction.[36] The compensation could be an expensive matter for the commune and this may explain the failure to extend the provision to the Masse (the areas beyond the walls) where housing must have been tightly packed and mainly of timber.

In 1305 a fire caused much damage to the palazzo and houses of the Scotti and Saracini families. This proved a particularly costly occasion, largely because those who came to the rescue were numerous and their expenses considerable. At least 540 people helped over a period of two days, apart from 149 carpenters who gave skilled assistance. Many claimed for water-carrying pots which had been broken and one potter lost more than 1,000 vessels of various descriptions (767 oil jars at

---

32 *Const. 1262. Cont., BSSP*, 2, p. 138.
33 Balestracci Piccinni, p. 169.
34 Davidsohn, *Forschungen*, 2, 213; *RIS, CS*, pp. 76–7, 225.
35 *Cost. 1309–10*, 2, p. 166.
36 Ibid., 1, p. 302; *Const. 1262. Cont., BSSP*, 2, p. 140.

16d. each, 374 water jars at 1s., 145 pots at 4d.). At a quite early stage more than 1000 l. was paid out by the commune (619 l. in compensation for damage, 402 l. in expenses and 41 l. in other payments to helpers). The bill continued to mount. When a member of the Tolomei family returned from a business visit to France he found that he and his 'consorts' had lost a house and a roof as a result of destruction undertaken to prevent this fire from spreading.[37] This disaster was by no means totally exceptional. In 1292 compensation totalling over 700 l. had been made to fifty-two houseowners, and a fire in 1307 involved the payment of over 1000 l. to twenty-nine owners and 138 l. to water-carriers.[38]

With buildings packed tightly together the policy of destroying houses to check fires from spreading must have created widespread damage. Towers which had been destroyed for this reason, others destroyed as a political punishment, and those which had collapsed from decay all constituted a danger and their debris sometimes blocked the streets. In 1271 the church of S Cristoforo was damaged by the destruction of the Salvani family's palace, and when the tower of the Incontrati fell in 1300 it caused havoc in the surrounding area. Nine members of the family died and the total death roll was over seventy.[39]

The very large volume of legislation concerned with building is also a reminder that lack of intervention by the commune in this matter would have brought about a very dangerous form of chaos.

CONCERN FOR THE APPEARANCE OF THE CITY

That the commune, the community of the city, should be concerned with Siena's appearance as a matter of self-respect and pride was taken for granted. No doctrine of the rights of the individual hampered this assumption. A Sienese could not, for example, destroy his own house except to rebuild immediately on the same site. Any dwelling demolished by its owners without consent had to be rebuilt within three months. This did not mean however that an all-powerful commune was totally ruthless in dealing with private property: if an owner suffered through schemes of clearance such as those designed to extend piazze, compensation was paid.[40] The prevailing attitude is well introduced by the words of a law proclaiming the need for a public garden in Siena: 'Among the cares and responsibilities that pertain to those who undertake the government of the city is especially that which regards the beauty of the city; and in any noble city one of the principal beauties is that it should have a meadow or place for the recreation and delight of citizens and strangers; and the cities of Tuscany and also certain

---

37 B 117, ff. 333–7, 339 ff; CG, 67, ff. 159–60v.
38 B 107, ff. 174v–5v; 121, ff. 301, 336 ff.
39 *RIS, CS*, p. 257; CG 59, ff. 76–8v.
40 *Cost. 1309–10*, 2, p. 264; B 83, ff. 111v, 117; Zdekauer, *Vita pubblica*, pp. 118–19.

other towns and cities are provided and adorned with such meadows and pleasure grounds.'[41]

A more basic requirement than fine public buildings, squares and gardens was a decent degree of cleanliness. A rubric in the statutes concerned 'the election of the inspectors of streets which have not been cleaned'. Four officials were to be chosen in each terzo and it was their responsibility to inspect the streets and the brick-paved piazze every Saturday. If these were found to have been neglected the local inhabitants were to be warned to clean them up. Should they fail to obey, a fine of 1s. a day was to be levied – on the area rather than on each individual, though the wording is ambiguous – for each offence. Each house-holder or shopkeeper was answerable for the street outside their own building.[42] Such ambitious measures needed the support of realistic legislation dealing with the filth which threatened to swamp any medieval city. From these clauses one could compile a list of Siena's unofficial public privies and litter dumps. Rubbish was not to be thrown into the public street or the Campo in daytime or at night 'up to the third ringing of the bell' and excrement was not to be thrown into the street at any time. Refuse and in particular human excrement was banned on the road along 'the ditch between Porta S Giorgio and Porta di Follonico since the route (which had presumably become an open-air public lavatory) is a most useful one for women and men'. Refuse was not to be thrown onto the property of religious foundations or churches, including cemeteries, and smelly leather products were prohibited from the same areas. Householders might not have privies which issued into the territory of their neighbours. Privies and wells could be cleaned out only at night (this applied also to the refuse of butchers' shops), and those who cleaned them were exempted from the curfew; they were not to throw away the resultant refuse within the city or into the roads just outside the walls leading to fountains. Bodies of animals were not to be flung into the ditch near S Domenico.[43]

Various textile and leather trades were prohibited from using the streets and water used in dyeing could not be thrown into the street. The intestines of animals were not to be stored in the street or used for industrial purposes anywhere in the city. Timber was not to be stored in the street either, nor mules saddled there. There is perhaps a tendency for such legislation to become increasingly realistic and specific, directed at keeping filth from certain streets and areas, including the squares in front of churches and particularly that outside the bishop's palace. The ban on lepers from living within the city or nearby, except in

41 Quoted from *Cost. 1309–10* by Braunfels, p. 208n.
42 *Const. 1262*, pp. 300–1; *Cost. 1309–10*, 2, p. 304.
43 *Const. 1262*, pp. 277–8, 286, 329; *Cont., BSSP*, 1, pp. 283–4; 2, p. 137.

recognized leper hospitals, was another measure designed to protect health and appearance.[44]

Such sanitary legislation was dependent on the activity of special officials appointed, for example those whose responsibilities included the cleanliness of streets and the throwing of refuse from balconies. Among them were some whose paid task was to denounce their neighbours. Versatile, all-purpose denouncers had to enquire into 'thieves and thefts, the cleaning of paved streets, women spinning in the streets, girls wearing long trains to their dresses, people throwing water or rubbish from balconies into the street, people mourning loudly after burials' or otherwise breaking the sumptuary laws concerning funerals. By the early fourteenth century sixty people were being paid a small wage of 5s. (probably for a six-month period) to act as 'secret accusers of those who throw away refuse in public places and those who wear pearls and superfluous ornaments'. An accusation against a man of 'having refuse in front of his workshop' would lead to a light fine, but a heavier one of 3 l. awaited the miscreant who bathed in a public fountain.[45]

In a category of its own, surrounded by a special protection verging on that accorded to a religious site, was the Campo, the *campum fori* as it was called, the classical vocabulary conveying a special dignity. There were officials appointed 'pro custodia campi fori', their duties being to keep the Campo clear of stones, bricks, timber and dirt and to prevent such activities as slaughtering and skinning animals. ('Committing a nuisance' was an offence only for those aged over fourteen.) The wardens' functions extended to the streets immediately adjoining the Campo. Grain, straw and hay could not be sold there or stored nearby – though marketing of most commodities at stalls was permitted – and barbers could not exercise their craft in the open Campo, presumably since this was messy and was felt to lack dignity. An ambitious law even sought (1297) to establish uniformity in the appearance of windows in the buildings round the square.[46]

The last measure coincided with a programme already mentioned, to extend greatly the area of the Campo and to erect a superb municipal palazzo on its northern side. This was the genesis of the Campo as we know it today. Though earlier extensions had been undertaken, until the late thirteenth century it was essentially the open space on which stood the customs office (dogana delle gabelle) and the church of S Paolo. As early as 1257 the lower end of the Campo had been seen as a possible site for the commune's palazzo, but discussion of the building of an ambitious new structure began only in 1281 and the site was not

44 *Const. 1262 Cont.*, *BSSP*, 2, pp. 137–8; *Cost. 1309–10*, 2, pp. 297–8.

45 *Const. 1262*, p. 183; *B.* 8, p. 135; 9, p. 143; B 82, f. 93v; 116, ff. 41, 383–4.

46 *B.* 15, p. 193; 'Breve 1250', pp. 86–8; *Const. 1262*, pp. 287–92; *Cost. 1309–10*, 2, p. 29 (printed in Braunfels, doc. 1).

definitely settled till 1288. The necessary purchase of nearby housing began in 1293.[47]

Although many cities of Lombardy, Emilia and the Veneto had purpose-built public palazzi by the start of the thirteenth century, this development occurred rather later in Tuscany. Volterra's palace, contemplated early in the century, was completed in 1257, probably the first in a Tuscan city. It was one consequence of their comparative tardiness that the Sienese felt that they could and must build on a spectacular scale. One factor was the need to outshine the Florentines, who were at work contemporaneously (1299–1314) on their Palazzo Vecchio. In Siena the work of clearing was still under way in 1299, but most of the palace was constructed between 1300 and 1310. The immensely high tower, designed to rise above that of the cathedral, followed in 1326–48. Meanwhile the inconveniently sited church of S Paolo had been demolished (*c.* 1308) and paving of the Campo begun. The paving of the central part was completed by 1346, when the activities of the cattle market were moved to the area behind the palazzo.[48]

A great deal of money was expended on Siena's impressive urban nucleus. Although labour and building materials were cheap by modern standards, the total cost was swollen by large payments of compensation to the dispossessed, such as the 2,700 l. paid in 1293 to Bartolomeo Saracini and Meo Nastasii for their houses and courtyards, and 900 l. for a house to Tuccio Alessi.[49] At the period when the building process began to achieve its busiest rhythm, in 1297, it was decided to set aside 2,000 l. in each six-monthly financial period for work on the palazzo and more than 10,000 l. was spent in the years 1309–10.[50] Deficiencies in the sources, however, make it impossible even to estimate the total sum spent on the palazzo.

Thenceforth the great brick Gothic structure dominated Siena, its tower visible from afar, and the finished work stood up well to comparison with its Florentine rival. Some of the frescoes inside were soon damaged by fire, but after restoration their appearance was judged 'a delight to the eye, a joy to the heart and a pleasure to all the senses. And it is a source of great honour to a commune that its rulers and leaders (*rectores et presides*) should live well, handsomely and honourably (*bene, pulcre et honorifice*).'[51] This reflection expresses clearly the motives which dictated the great public works of the Sienese at the end of the thirteenth century.

---

47 For purchases in 1293–94 v. *CV*, 4, docs. 994–5, 999.

48 E. Guidoni, *Il Campo di Siena* (Rome, 1971); Braunfels, chapters 3 and 5, especially pp. 121–2, 193–8; see also J. Paul, *Die mittelalterliche Kommunalpalasten in Italien* (Cologne, 1963).

49 B 109, f. 166

50 *Cost. 1309–10*, 1, pp. 98–9; Balestracci Piccinni, p. 103n (and at least 16,900 l. in all in 1307–10: A. Cairola and E. Carli, *Il Palazzo Pubblico di Siena* (Rome, 1963), pp. 20–5).

51 Quoted by Braunfels, p. 198.

Nor was this pride demonstrated in secular building only, as the subsidies paid to the Dominicans and other mendicant religious orders prove. The purpose of one grant of 100,000 bricks for the continuation of work at S Domenico was to make possible the construction of 'the crossing of the church at the upper end, towards Fontebranda, using the columns which are there already, so that the length of the church, when the altars are sited there, should be more beautiful, more extensive and more spacious for housing the multitude of people which often gathers to hear sermons and the divine service'. Intervention could take the form of instructions as well as aid, and the Dominicans received orders to demolish a wall which impeded church-goers and blocked the view.[52] The mendicants were the main recipients of assistance, but older orders were not neglected: in 1306 the Camaldulensian abbot of S Donato successfully appealed for legislation in support of the abbey's intention of buying up and demolishing the buildings facing the abbey and its hospital. He wanted to open up a piazza 'for the adornment of the city and the convenience of neighbours'.[53]

A more ambitious scheme for opening up the area around the cathedral dated back to the middle of the thirteenth century. The commune had contributed to work on the interior and facade over a long period, but the principal development planned was the reconstruction on a new site of the baptistery, S Giovanni, which was to be below and to the north-east of the cathedral.[54] The next stage was to be a vaster cathedral, of which the earlier building was to be a mere apse, but that ill-fated plan falls outside the period covered by this book.

It is harder to trace work on Siena's walls and gates, though this must have been more or less continuous. Six official *superstantes murorum et operationum* had the task of employing masons to undertake regular repairs and improvements. Statutes sought to prevent people from making a passage-way through the city walls or otherwise weakening their defences.[55]

Water supply was a matter of far greater moment to the Sienese than fortification and, in view of the possibility of a siege, more crucial as a military requirement. The city's supply depended on an elaborate system of aqueducts and channels excavated in the rock, which brought water from quite distant streams. The main duct feeding Fonte Branda, with its tributary inflows, was some 1,600 metres in length, and the work of excavation had to be undertaken between compact clay and the porous sandstone stratum above, with one man working at a time with pick or axe in a narrow channel. Such was Siena's anxiety about

---

52 *Cost. 1309–10*, 1, pp. 77, 336–7.
53 CG 68, ff. 61–5v.
54 Braunfels, pp. 156, 257–8 (docs. 15–17); CG 4, f. 47; 47, ff. 32 ff.
55 CG 80, ff. 104 (payment to the mason Andrea Albertini who had agreed to repair a section of wall 'at his own risk'), 105v, 107v, 109v, 112; *Const. 1262*, pp. 275–7.

water that in 1267 a project was considered – though eventually abandoned as too expensive – for drawing water from springs at Ciciano, beyond the Val di Merse, which would have involved channelling a total distance of about sixty-five kilometres.[56] The discovery of any spring had to be reported to the authorities, and sometimes false hopes were raised, as in the notorious case of the Diana, that non-existent river over which the Sienese were mocked by Dante.[57] The maintenance and extension of fountains was a considerable item in the city's expenditure: the Biccherna volumes for 1293–96, for example, record sums amounting to over 5,000 l. spent on work at seven different fountains, one of them the particularly prized Fonte Branda where water spouted out of the mouth of a lion.[58] Sculptural work on fountains was considered no less appropriate than figures for the cathedral facade for an artist of the calibre of Giovanni Pisano.

Before work on the great municipal palace had started, the palazzo of Sugio Iuncte degli Arzocchi was bought as a stopgap (1294), at the considerable price of 4,600 l. It was characteristic of the Sienese authorities that they were not content to take over that building as it was. Within a few days of purchase a payment was made to an artist for his work of 'painting in the palace of the commune, which was formerly Sugio's'.[59] Public buildings and public objectives were constantly kept in the forefront of interest. There was a sort of dialogue between the architecture of the commune itself and the proud display of the palace-owning patricians.

---

56 F. Bargagli Petrucci, *Le Fonti di Siena e i loro Acquedotti*, (Siena, repr. 1974), especially 1, pp. 33–46.
57 *Const. 1262*, p. 350; *Purgatorio*, XIII, 151–3.
58 B 109, f. 171; 110, ff. 152 ff; 111, f. 132v; 113, ff. 244v ff. (for a further 1,600 l. spent in 1298, B 114, f. 218). These figures omit much expenditure on roads leading to fountains.
59 B 110, ff. 120v, 125.

2 *People*

OCCUPATIONS

To start on the true topic of this volume, Siena's people, it is convenient to begin with their work. Lists of inhabitants citing their employments are hard to come by for the Middle Ages, though there were men (and some women) who seem to have habitually added their occupation when giving their name. Since the normal form of nomenclature in thirteenth-century Italy was merely a personal name followed by a patronymic, the addition of an occupation must quite often have been necessary to avoid errors of identity.

The Biccherna Revenue and Expenditure series[1] records each payment made in 1285 towards a direct tax (*dazio*) of one-twentieth levied in Siena in that year. Payments totalling 5,256 are noted and in 1,236 cases an occupation is given, so that the trade or profession of nearly 25 per cent of the payers is known. What follows is a table setting out in numerical order the twenty-six occupations which occur at least ten times in the list: see table 1 (p. 17).

It is interesting to set out beside this table another in which the same information is augmented and presented in a different order, arranged according to the average amount of tax paid: see table 2 (p. 18).

To use a list of tax payments as an indication of wealth is to take a very short cut indeed, and requires discussion. If the assessments were inequitable, if the sums paid do not reflect the assessments accurately, if a sizeable proportion of the population did not pay – to raise some of the difficulties – the figures in table 2 will not constitute an unbiassed representation of the wealth of the various occupations. It will be necessary to return to these questions later, since they are most relevant to the 'shape' of Sienese wealth as shown in the revenue yielded by the dazio, hence their discussion must be postponed to the section of this chapter in which the derivation of that revenue is analysed.[2] At that stage it will also be necessary to make use of other levies of direct taxation for comparison.

---

1 B 88, ff. 77–165v and 90, ff. 61–84v: computer analysis. In reality various factors complicate this sum in minor ways. Some payments were made on behalf of more than one person. Sometimes the dividing line between name, occupation and status is not totally clear. The occupations of those no longer living have been excluded.
2 See below, pp. 22–4.

Table 1. *1285 taxes: occupations*

Shoemaker (*calzolarius*)	119
Agricultural labourer (*laborator*)	104
Notary (*notarius*)	97
Butcher (*carnifex, carnaiolus*)	62
Grocer (*pizzicaiuolus*)	43
Smith (*faber*)	36
Baker (*fornerius*, etc.)	35
Carrier (*vecturalis*)	33
Clothier (*lanaiolus*)	29
Tailor (*sartor*)	27
Doublet-maker (*farsettarius*)	25
Porter (*portator*)	25
Furrier (*pelliparius*)	24
Messenger (*nuntius*)	23
Stall-keeper (*treccholus*)	22
Miller (*mugnarius*)	21
Doctor (*medicus*)	17
Barber (*barberius*)	16
Judge (*judex*)	15
Locksmith (*clavarius, accorarius*)	15
Saddler (*basterius*)	15
Donkey-driver (*asinarius*)	14
Spicer (*spetialis*)	13
Hotel-keeper (*albergator, asbergherius*)	11
Brooch-maker (*fibbiarius*)	11
Water-carrier (*qui fert aquam*)	10

A few general points can be made about tables 1 and 2 before discussing some of the occupations. Table 1 does not provide a full list of the occupation which gave employment to large numbers of Sienese in 1285: at least two forms of work which must have been very common are missing from it – there are no domestic servants (though a few payers are described as *famulus*), and no merchants or bankers or office-workers (clerks etc.). That the list may offer a distorted view of Sienese employment seems confirmed by comparison with the lists (relating to the Camollia terzo only) which record payments still due in 1262 towards a dazio levied two years earlier.[3] Here 'agricultural labourer' ranks far ahead of any other occupation (33); then come 'shoemaker' (14) and 'smith' (11). Although these three trades stand high in the 1285 lists and though Camollia may well have been untypical in the large number of its labourers and the paucity of notaries, the

3 Lira, n. 5.

Table 2. *1285 taxes: size of payments*

Place in table 1	Number	Occupation	Average tax payment
19=	(15)	Judge	5 l. 8s. 8d.
23=	(13)	Spicer	4 l. 6s. 9d.
17	(17)	Doctor	3 l. 12s. 9d.
24=	(11)	Hotel-keeper	2 l. 13s. 4d.
3	(97)	Notary	2 l. 11s. 6d.
19=	(15)	Saddler	1 l. 19s. 7d.
5	(43)	Grocer	1 l. 14s. 4d.
9	(29)	Clothier	1 l. 13s. 1d.
7	(35)	Baker	1 l. 6s. 6d.
10	(27)	Tailor	1 l. 6s.
1	(119)	Shoe-maker	1 l. 3s. 8d.
4	(62)	Butcher	1 l. 1s. 1d.
6	(36)	Smith	1 l. 0s. 7d.
19=	(15)	Locksmith	1 l. 0s. 2d.
24=	(11)	Brooch-maker	19s. 1d.
14	(22)	Stall-keeper	17s. 3d.
11=	(25)	Doublet-maker	15s. 6d.
13	(24)	Furrier	14s. 5d.
16	(21)	Miller	14s.
18	(16)	Barber	11s. 4½d.
8	(33)	Carrier	9s. 1½d.
2	(104)	Agricultural labourer	6s. 11d.
22	(14)	Donkey-driver	6s. 6d.
14	(23)	Messenger	5s. 10d.
11=	(25)	Porter	5s. 10d.
26	(10)	Water-carrier[4]	1s. 6d.

disproportion between these two sources of information suggests their unreliability as mirrors. The vagaries of calculations of this sort are also illustrated by an isolated list of Sienese cross-bowmen paid in 1254, sixty-two of whom gave an occupation: twenty were shoemakers and seven were smiths while no other trade appears more than four times.[5] Since the proportion of payers giving an

---

4 All the water-carriers recorded here were women. Of the stall-keepers, six were women and the average payment by them was 10s. The average payment by male stall-holders was nearly 1 l. 13s. Certain difficulties of vocabulary complicate the picture presented here: thus the average payment of the nine furriers styled *pelliciarius*, at 36s., is more than twice that of the twenty-four *pelliparii* and it would have been misleading to merge the two to produce an average payment of 21s.

5 *B*. 15, pp. 51–4.

occupation was quite low (about 23 per cent) and they may not constitute a representative sample of those following the trades named, it would in any case be rash to present table 2 as reflecting the structure of Sienese wealth by occupation in 1285. It does nevertheless give a general notion of the economic standing of the twenty-six occupations most frequently cited.

Moreover various points emerge from it incontrovertibly. Of the five highest-paying categories, which stand well above the rest, only one (the spicers) are engaged in commerce in the normal sense. There is a marked bunching in the middle of the table between average payments of 2 l. and of 14 s. which covers fourteen occupations, most of them crafts. Had the list extended to trades appearing nine times (rather than ten and above) this middle category would have been reinforced by the more prosperous furriers (*pelliciarii*: 1 l. 16s.) and inn-keepers (*tabernarius*: 1 l. 0s. 9d.). Far below all craftsmen are the manual occupations, agricultural workers, messengers and porters (bracketed together rather below these) and the women water-carriers.

In many medieval Italian cities gilds achieved a powerful constitutional position when the 'popular' element gained a share in the regime; indeed the popular party (the groups excluded from the earliest forms of oligarchic control) was often constituted from gild components. In Siena the craft gilds won no such authority or standing in esteem, though on some occasions their officials played a consultative role. The oath taken by the commune's officials committed them to investigate thrice yearly any sinister agreements and ordinances, written or verbal, made by gilds. If any were detected the deeds recording them were to be destroyed. The rectors of the two major gilds i.e. merchants and *pizzicaiuoli* (grocers) also had to swear that they would remove such clauses.[6] In general terms, as Professor William Bowsky has put it, 'Sienese policy . . . contradicts assertions that it was the government's duty to further and improve the positions of the city's guilds.'

The *pizzicaiuolo* was a versatile trader – the closest English equivalent is 'grocer', though Bowsky suggests they should be styled 'large-scale retail merchants' – who dealt in spices, wax, parchment and paper, among other things. The high standing of their gild is confirmed by its having been linked with the 'merchants' as the *due mercanzie*, the major gilds whose consuls ranked as important officials frequently summoned to assist in discussions of the affairs of the commune.[7] The officials of the cloth gild (Arte della Lana) ranked only a little below this and their duties also were such that during their tenure they were not allowed to hold any

6 'Breve 1250', pp. 83–6. On the commune's policy *vis-à-vis* gilds, see Bowsky, *Commune*, pp. 209–24.

7 *Cost. 1309–10*, 1, p. 311.

other office.[8] Only citizens were eligible for membership of the gild, a condition which made life difficult even for prosperous clothiers if they were not Sienese by birth.[9] No doubt most of them were in the solid middle ranks of tradesmen, like the Bonamico di Giovanni of the *popolo* of S Giovanni whose will of 28 February 1274 distributed 260 l. in specific religious and lay bequests before assigning the residue to his two sons and two daughters.[10] Bonamico may have been untypical only in his apparent lack of rural property. Another clothier, Bartolomeo di Ildibrandino Vincentii, made a will ten years later which mentions both a textile factory or warehouse (*ubi lanificium exercetur*) in the city and a good deal of land at Chiarenna (to the west of Siena).[11]

With butchers and bakers we come to tradesmen whose gilds were treated with suspicion by the commune's authorities. Many historians think that butchers were on the whole prosperous, but in the 1285 dazio they paid less than bakers.[12] Legislation about the malpractices of butchers was voluminous and often repeated and revealed such tricks as selling meat from diseased animals and under misleading descriptions, and inflating carcasses by blowing air into them.[13] At two successive meetings of the General Council in October 1284 it was even proposed that butchers should not be permitted to have a gild or that their gild should have no rector. The outcome was an anticlimax – no alterations were made.[14] Ten years later a councillor suggested that the Podestà should send for the butchers and order then 'to make and cause to be made good meat' (*quod ipsi faciant et fieri faciant bonas carnes*).[15] The expression of indignant opinions about butchers in council meetings was something of a commonplace. The price of bread was also a subject for legislation. In the mid thirteenth century the normal baking charge was 1d. in summer and 1½d. in winter, when fuel was scarcer and demand greater.[16] Bakers were forbidden to have a gild, but this measure (of 1287) turned out to have disadvantages for the commune. It seemed a desirable arrangement

---

8 The nature of the membership of the merchant gild in this period is not clear. It seems unlikely that the major bankers were involved. There are useful remarks in M. Ascheri. *Siena nel Rinascimento* (Siena, 1985), pp. 113–23.

9 CG 68, f. 156 (petition for citizenship, 1306).

10 Dipl., AGC 28.2.1274.

11 Ibid., 23.4.1284.

12 Table 2. See Bowsky, *Commune*, pp. 210–11 and cf. A. I. Pini, 'Gli estimi cittadini di Bologna dal 1296 al 1329. Un esempio di utilizzazione: il patrimonio fondiario del beccaio Giacomo Casella', *SM*, s. 3, 18 (1977), pp. 111–59.

13 *Cost. 1309–10*, 2, pp. 384–5; 'Statuto de' carnaiuoli' (1288) in *Statuti Senesi*, 1, pp. 76–9, 97–8; many other examples could be given.

14 CG 28, ff. 20–2.

15 CG 47, ff. 27 and v.

16 'Breve 1250', § 25. Early in the following century the prices authorized were higher (*Cost. 1309–10*, 2, pp. 411–12).

that the *gabella* (indirect tax) on baking should be farmed by the bakers themselves, but this was not feasible so long as they were not even permitted to have a rector or to hold meetings.[17]

A number of other crafts ranked somewhere near the butchers and bakers. The will of a timber-merchant (*magister lignaminum*) shows well the way an urban trade could be linked with rural property. Grimaldo di Ventura had a house and workshop (*apotheca*) in Siena and possessions in the country round Ampugnano and Sovicille (a little to the south-west of the city) which included houses, a vineyard and a good deal of woodland probably acquired for his timber business.[18] In other instances the agricultural property of craftsmen is likely to date back to before they moved into the city: Matteo di Trogio, a stone-mason (*magister lapidis*) had arable and vineyards out at Chiarenna and Tressa as well as four sheep and four goats at Petriccio.[19]

'Labourer' is an occupation which ranks high in numbers and low in wealth in tables 1 and 2. Cities inhabited by agricultural workers may seem paradoxical to twentieth-century 'western' man, not corresponding to the ideas of nineteenth-century scholars who propounded so many of our accepted notions of the past. But an article published as long ago as 1906 pointed out that those 'rustics' who went to live in towns continued to pay dues to their lords and to cultivate the same land as before.[20] Luzzatto was writing about the March of Ancona, but his generalization holds for the rest of central and northern Italy. The land close to Siena – good soil, rich in vineyards and financially valuable – was largely owned by citizens, and those who worked the soil were normally tenants of the owners, holding by *mezzadria*; in other words they were share-croppers, sharing both the costs of production and the crop. It is difficult to be sure whether the man who styled himself *laborator* when paying his tax was implying anything about his status. Some may have been *mezzadri* – in a sense, after all, their labour was hired and their share of the product was their wage[21] – but it is likely that most belonged to the class of men whose precarious living depended on being hired by the day. These were the 'labourers' who were forbidden by law to gather in the morning at the Croce del Travaglio, the city's central crossroads, because their presence there obstructed the traffic.[22]

---

17 CG 61, ff. 40 and v (1302: special authority was given for the holding of such a meeting). See also Bowsky, *Commune*, pp. 209–10.
18 Dipl., AGC, 6.2.1292.
19 Ibid., 10.8.1281.
20 G. Luzzattto, 'Le sottomissioni dei feudatari e le classi sociali in alcuni comuni marchigiani' reprinted in *Dai servi della gleba agli albori del capitalismo* (Bari, 1966); the passage quoted is on p.383.
21 See P. J. Jones in *C. Econ. H.*, 1 (edn 2), p. 414.
22 *Cost. 1309–10*, 2, p. 381.

SOCIAL STRUCTURE

The recorded tax-payments of 1285 cannot of course be a precise record of the ability to pay of those whose names appear. Many complicating factors have to be taken into account, most of all those concerned with the determination and ability of the assessors to learn the full truth about the wealth of the assessed. Nevertheless an analysis should at least assist in answering certain questions. Was most of the revenue from direct taxation derived from the wealthy, as the preference for direct rather than indirect taxation among the popular parties in the Italian communes seems to indicate? Was there a sizeable contribution from the middle ranges of tax-payer? What do the different shares contributed by the various ranges of payers suggest about the distribution of wealth among the people of Siena? We can begin to answer these questions by setting out in tabular form a breakdown of the payments made in 1285 towards two direct taxes, one of 'one-twentieth', the other the 'twenty-fifth' analysed above in tables 1 and 2. For this purpose payers have been divided into deciles, ten groups of equal numbers, the division being made according to the sums paid.

Table 3. *Cumulative percentage of total contributed, by deciles in ascending order of size of payment*[23]

	One twentieth	One twenty-fifth
Number of payments	5,256	3,785
Total sum received:	15,439 l. 10s. 8d.	10,860 l. 13s. 1d.
Average payment		
(arithmetic mean):	2 l. 18s. 10d.	2 l. 17s. 5d.
Median payment:	13s. 4d	11s. 3d.
Deciles		
1	.4	.2
2	1	.8
3	2	1.6
4	3.3	2.7
5	5.2	4.3
6	8	6.8
7	12.5	10.9
8	20	17.5
9	34.5	31
10	100	100

23 Computer-assisted analysis of B 88, ff. 77–165 and 90, ff. 61–84v (twentieth) and B 90, ff. 85–235 (twenty-fifth). These data could also be analysed for presentation in the form: 90 per cent of the yield from 3,785 payments was achieved by the 1,843 highest payments; 80 per cent of the yield by the highest 1,051 payments etc.

Perhaps the most striking fact to emerge from table 3 is that the 'top' decile, i.e. the 10 per cent of highest payments, provided some two-thirds of the revenue yielded by each tax (65.5 per cent for the twentieth, 69 per cent for the twenty-fifth). That proportion is so large that it is logical to divide the top decile itself, and when this is done the result shows that the 5 per cent of largest payments produced about 50 per cent of the yield of the twentieth and about 55 per cent of that of the twenty-fifth. The top 1 per cent (some fifty and forty payments respectively) accounted for about 25 per cent and 28 per cent. The largest single payment was so considerable in each instance that it accounted for about 6 per cent and 7 per cent of the totals. Those who failed to make their payments by the due date were condemned to pay one-third extra (the *tertium plus*) and rather more than one in three of the payments towards the twentieth (1,919 of 5,256) included this element.[24] Inevitably those who could not achieve prompt payment were by and large the poor, since money was not difficult to borrow in Siena for those whose credit was good. The *tertium plus* fines account for only about 3 per cent of the yield of the twentieth, which confirms further that although the number of payments by poorer people was very considerable, their contribution towards the total receipts was extremely low.

The yield of the tax was principally dependent on about a thousand payments, without which it would have amounted to no more than one-fifth of the sum actually raised. Of those who contributed, 10 per cent provided two-thirds of the yield, and a comparatively small element remained in the middle, between the poor payers of very little and the rich payers of a great deal. We can examine this stratum by distinguishing from the rest those who made payments of between 1 l. and 5 l.; these people probably stood clear of the poverty line but had not attained a comfortable degree of wealth. About 28 per cent of the payments fell between these limits in the case of the twentieth, 27 per cent in that of the twenty-fifth. These seem low proportions, particularly in comparison with the equivalent proportion in a modern industrialized society, and are only about double the percentage of those who paid more than 5 l. (respectively 13 per cent and 11 per cent).

Does this mean that medieval Siena lacked a numerically substantial middle class? In the sense that the numbers do not present a graphical curve of conventional form, increasing steadily in proportion to diminishing economic means, but rather taper away with a lower proportion of moderate payers, this certainly appears to be the situation.[25] The rich held a social and political

---

24 In the case of the 1/25th only 59 payments of the *tertium plus* fine are recorded, i.e. only about 1 per cent of payers were fined for late payment.

25 The Gini coefficient for the curve is .766549, which represents a very wide gap between these statistics and the 45° line which might have been expected. P. Earle, *The Making of the English Middle Class* (London, 1989), pp. 80–1, suggests figures of 20 to 30 per cent in pre-industrial

authority which extended to fiscal matters, and if the fiscal bill, at least as far as direct taxation was concerned, was met by them rather than being forwarded to the middle elements, this also suggests the lack of a really large and prosperous stratum between landed financiers and those who carried messages and tilled the soil. The way of life of the comfortably off involved a supporting cast of craftsmen and shop-keepers – butchers and bakers and doublet-makers – but these were in general not particularly well-to-do nor so numerous as to outnumber vastly the richer elements themselves.

The fact that the numerous poor paid their small sums in direct taxes and also endured hunger and squalid surroundings is not surprising. Taxation was for all. What seems to require more explanation is the very substantial sums paid by the powerful. To some extent this must have been due to pressure from those who ranked immediately below them in power and wealth. There may also have been a need to demonstrate that they were bearing their share of the common burden. It was understood that indirect taxation bore least heavily on the rich, and direct taxation gave them an opportunity to show that they were not shirking their contribution to the costs of war and government. This was underlined, presumably, by the realization that the dazio, whose administration was a complicated and expensive matter, would bring in little if the wealthy did not contribute in proportion to their means. And 'the wealthy' may be a misleadingly generic description. Those who paid most heavily may have been not so much 'the rich' as the rich who lacked political clout at the time, or those seeking popularity. It is striking that a huge contribution by one family, the Salimbeni, stands at the head of the payments for each of these 1285 dazi.[26] This is a point to which we shall have to return.

THE POOR

The people most difficult to investigate and count are the very poor. A decision of 1289 defined as poor (*pauperes*) those whose direct tax assessment was below 2 l.[27] This would have implied a payment of less than 2s. towards the 1285 dazio of 1/20th, and as about one payment in five fell below that level (1,208 out of 5,256) 20 per cent of the taxpayers at that period were categorized as paupers.

London and Paris for those coming between the 'upper class' and 'wage-earners or self-employed artisans', but use of my criteria would probably increase this percentage as I would class many self-employed artisans in the intermediate category.

26 A payment by the same people of the same very large sum (978 l. 14s.) was also the highest, by far, made to another *dazio* of 1/20 levied later in 1285 (B 90, f. 320). They also contributed the largest payment to a 1/25th in the same year (782 l. 19s. 2d.: B 90, f. 185).

27 Bowsky, 'Medieval Citizenship: the individual and the state in the commune of Siena, 1287–1355', *Studies in Medieval and Renaissance History*, 4 (1967), p. 227n.

These included water-carriers, washerwomen and street-cleaners (such as Grazia *qui lavat Campum*) and those involved in similar occupations, and there must also have been many *nichils*, particularly among the old, assessed as unable to make any fiscal contribution at all.

Material about the aged and infirm at this time is hard to come by. A good many must have been resident in hospitals. Recent immigrants, often unemployed and probably living in shanties outside the walls, helped to swell the numbers of the poor. The low fine (10 l.) levied on those found guilty of exposing infants is a reminder of the struggles of the unfortunate,[28] and so is the fate of prisoners who were ordered to march round the city and beg for food because the gaol could provide none (March 1291).[29] The assumption that they would not take the opportunity to escape must have been based on the belief that escape might condemn them to even greater hunger.

The commune was indeed mindful of the very poor and from time to time allocated money to them, the provision of alms from the commune's funds being a matter of routine even if the sums allotted were often small. Occasionally the contrast with the donations to religious institutions was most striking: in 1275 5 l. was set aside 'for alms to the poor at 12 d. per day', whereas the gifts to religious houses, mainly for building projects although an element of contribution to social welfare was not completely lacking in such grants, totalled over 700 l.[30] Even if a gift of 25 l. was more normal (1252), the occasions on which a larger sum was given were rare and presumably denoted widespread suffering. This may have been the situation in 1284 when at least 2,000 l. was assigned, but the circumstances were considered unusual and the money was spared from the commune's budget only in a series of small grants.[31] Moreover the poorest elements were objects of suspicion as well as charity. In 1308 the gild of the Virgin Mary sought powers to pursue its intention of succouring the poor of the city and contado. Its members had undertaken to beg help throughout the city for the poor and all who were 'wretched and needy modest persons' (*personis miserabilibus et indigentibus veruccundiosis*). The assistance could take the form of bread, money, clothing or anything else, yet the communal authorities expressed doubts about the confraternity's charitable plans and voted to refer them for legal opinion.[32]

With a rapidly increasing city population largely reliant for its sustenance on local grain supplies much depended on the harvest. There were years of famine, for instance in 1302 and 1303. In 1302 the number of paupers was assessed at

28 Zdekauer in *BSSP*, 7 (1900), p. 251.
29 CG 41, f. 69.
30 CG 20.
31 *B*. 13, p. 137; B 85, f. 43.
32 CG 73, ff. 162–5; see also below, p. 153.

15,000, perhaps one in three of the city's inhabitants.[33] In better times many of these were doubtless able to subsist on a very simple diet, but the horrors of 1302–03 are a reminder that many who in a good year were just above the subsistence line would starve when shortage brought about even a small rise in the price of bread.

FINANCIERS: THE WEALTHY

Whereas the structure of crafts, shopkeeping and agricultural employment was common to almost all medieval Italian cities, the rich Sienese may have been untypical of the wealthy class in the cities generally. Those who on account of their activity as financiers had to deposit a security with the consul of the Mercanzia were defined as 'argentieri o vero banchieri, volgarmente chiamati, e li cambiatori'.[34] These financiers or bankers had been prominent in Siena since the beginning of the thirteenth century or even earlier. Some of the families were very wealthy indeed and the greatest of them were the owners of widespread lands in the contado. Wealth from land no doubt provided the initial capital for the bankers, and success in finance was followed by the acquisition of more land. Siena's bankers were not merely specialists in finance, but were landowners who had learned the elementary analogies of breeding from money as well as from stock, and of 'ploughing in' financial profits as they ploughed the land for the seed which was to provide the grain harvest.

The banking companies gave Siena its special individuality, and their members were at the centre of the city's social and political life. Though their ill-documented origins belong to the twelfth century, the period of their rise to greatness is the first half of the thirteenth. The chronology is particularly difficult to establish because contemporary documents which illuminate the subject – such as papal letters and letters written to and from the merchants themselves – only survive in appreciable numbers from the early thirteenth century. The unbroken series of papal registers of letters, for instance, begin in 1198. It is easy, but not necessarily correct, to assume that the role of the bankers only became important at the time when the evidence first makes it possible to study them. Traces of activity at the fairs of Champagne provide the earliest glimpses of the Sienese as international financiers and traders. They were present at the fairs by 1216 and from the early 1220s were involved in textile purchases there as well as in banking. Loans to prelates elsewhere in France are recorded by 1217 and to the English crown in 1228. In the following year the collector of a papal tenth to assist the war against Frederick II operated in England with Sienese help, and

---

33 CG 61, ff. 133 ff; *RIS, CS*, pp. 231, 272, 278.
34 *Cost. 1309–10*, 1, p. 427.

by that time German and Hungarian prelates were also clients of the bankers.[35]

The Sienese were closely connected with rise of the papacy as an 'international' fiscal power. The first general papal tax on the clergy was levied in 1199 and this was renewed in 1225 and 1228. It was essential to the success of this innovation that the task of conveying considerable sums across vast distances should be undertaken by those who commanded or could acquire the necessary expertise. Churchmen themselves were not ideally equipped, and a technique was required which would obviate the moving of currency in *specie*. For all this the fast-growing network of the Italian banking companies was eminently suitable.[36] Nor was the growth of papal control in the west merely a fiscal matter. As the Church became increasingly centralized, prelates and ecclesiastical bodies involved in the operations of Roman authority needed loans to see them through the costs of travel and litigation. For the bankers themselves the papal link was also an important element in securing repayment, since the Roman weapons of excommunication and interdict were powerful forms of pressure in persuading ecclesiastical and other debtors to pay up.[37] Meanwhile potential borrowers, lay and ecclesiastical, became aware of the deficiencies and lack of capital of local lenders.

The spirit of financial enterprise – which needed no inculcation by Calvin, whatever some historians and sociologists have implied – breathes in the letters of the Sienese bankers. 'We tell you that the kingdom of France has never been so good for making profits (*guadagnare*) as it will be as soon as this peace has been made' explains a letter to the Sansedoni from Paris in June 1305.[38] Account-books bore headings (such as 'In nomine Domini amen e di buonaventura che Dio ne dia')[39] linking God's name with the achievement of prosperity.

Banking firms with representatives in the key cities of western Europe were able to evolve contracts whereby drafts on the various branches could be sold to

---

35 For this phase of Sienese banking see English, *Sienese Banking*, with good bibliography (pp. 116–25). Particularly useful are Q. Senigaglia, 'Le compagnie bancarie senesi nei sec. XIII e XIV', *SS*, 24 (1907), pp. 149–217 and 25 (1908), pp. 3–66; C. Paoli, *Siena alle fiere di Sciampagna* (Siena, 1908); M. Chiaudano, *Studi e documenti per la storia del Diritto commerciale italiano nel sec. XIII* (Turin, 1930), pp. 1–44; R.-H. Bautier, 'Les foires de Champagne: recherches sur une évolution historique', *Recueils de la Soc. Jean Bodin*, 5: *La Foire* (Brussels, 1953), pp. 97–147; Prunai, pp. 547–637. The essays by M. Tangheroni, M. Cassandro, G. Cherubini, G. Pinto and F. Cardini in the lavishly illustrated *Banchieri e mercanti di Siena* (Rome, 1987) provide an excellent summary of the present state of knowledge.

36 See E. B. and M. M. Fryde in *C. Econ. H.*, 3, pp. 448–9.

37 See for example the case brought to the papal court by Sienese financiers in 1258 concerning their failure to secure repayment of 4,600 marks by the archbishop of Cologne (A. Schulte, *Geschichte des mittelalterlichen Handels und Verkehrs zwischen Westdeutschland und Italien mit Ausschluss von Venedig* (Leipzig, 1900), 2, pp. 175–6).

38 P. and P., pp. 71–83.

39 Astuti, p. 255.

transfer funds between Italy and, for example, Flanders or England.[40] The evolution of what became prototypes of the bill of exchange, efficient book-keeping and the conduct of business by correspondence rather than personal contact, all combined to give the Italian financiers great advantages in technique. The organization of regular postal services, particularly between Italy and the Champagne fairs, gave them also the opportunity to act on news not yet available to potential rivals. In later times the dealings in bills of exchange and stocks which depended on differences of price in markets distant from each other became known as 'arbitrage'. Merchant banking was revolutionized in the nineteenth century by the advent of the telegraphic cable: in the thirteenth century Italians were in the position of men operating with cables when their rivals lacked this advantage. A surviving letter of 1260, in which a partner in Champagne is told to borrow there rather than in Tuscany where Siena's military crisis has put up the rate of interest, contains advice based on arbitrage, and the same is true of one of 1265 in which a correspondent (this time from Champagne) urges purchases of French currency and letters of exchange in Italy in view of the expenditure proposed there in connection with the Angevins' forthcoming campaign.[41]

The Sienese and other Italian businessmen were not specialists in finance who disdained to trade in commodities. Commerce implied either food or clothing and the latter meant, above all, wool. The Champagne fairs were centres for dealings in textiles as well as in money and bankers could use money received from ecclesiastical taxes to purchase wool in Champagne, the cosmopolitan gatherings at the fairs facilitating the fixing of dates for settlements and making 'clearing houses' of the banks. Wool, often from England, would be shipped south from France by sea (Nîmes was a favoured port) to Pisa for the manufacture of cloth in Tuscany, and the products of the Italian cloth industry could then be exported to other Mediterranean lands, including the Levant.

Papal financial needs increased notably during the pontificate of Innocent IV (1243–54), the energetic opponent of Frederick II, and this seems to have been the period of the rise to greatness of the Sienese firm of Bonsignori, as papal bankers. The position of papal banker was not an easy one as the political developments of the 1260s were to show. A letter written to the Bonsignori representative at the Provins fair in the crucial year 1260 illustrates some of the difficulties. Orlando, the head of the firm, was absent with the Sienese army at Montepulciano, the correspondent explained, hence a delay in authorizing loans.[42] More seriously, the army in which Orlando was serving was fighting for

---

40 R. De Roover in *C. Econ. H.*, 3, p. 67.
41 P. and P., pp. 13–24, 49–58. Comment in A. Sapori, *Studi di Storia economica medievale*, edn 2 (Florence, 1946), pp. 320–3 and in R. S. Lopez and I. W. Raymond, *Medieval Trade in the Mediterranean World* (NY, 1955), pp. 392–4.
42 P. and P., p. 18 (trans. in Lopez and Raymond, pp. 390–1).

the Hohenstaufen cause, an awkward situation for a prominent papal banker. A few years later the dilemma had worsened: some of the Sienese bankers were backing the papal-French enterprise which was to win the Neapolitan kingdom for Charles of Anjou while others were assisting the 'wrong' (Hohenstaufen, or Ghibelline) side, and the pope threatened them by ordering their debtors not to make repayments. Florence was supporting the Angevin cause, and this was at a time when Florentine bankers were already tending to supersede the Sienese at the papal Curia.

Orlando Bonsignori himself was sufficiently sure-footed in the difficult terrain of the 1260s, and having made a considerable loan to Charles of Anjou he was exempted from the interdict proclaimed by the pope against those bankers who gave assistance to the Ghibellines. The seriousness of the menace of papal hostility is well illustrated by a letter from Andrea Tolomei to his cousins and partners in Siena, written in Champagne on 4 September 1262.[43] It would not be sensible, Andrea says, to deposit money with the Cistercians; 'they are so much afraid of the Church that in no way would they be willing to act against the conscience of Christians, and there is now money which they owe to us and others which they will not pay through fear of being excommunicated'. Altogether the Angevin conquest of the Sicilian kingdom proved a disastrous development for the Sienese companies, confirming conclusively the Florentine supremacy at the Curia of which there had already been strong indications. Even though the 1250s and 1260s had been prosperous years for many of the Sienese companies, this was a fateful tilting of the balance.

It was essential to the scale of the operations of the Sienese bankers that they should trade as companies. Legislation and some surviving early contracts throw some light on the nature of these entities. On the formation of a company, the period for which men entered into a contract would be stated and might be as brief as one year, and any agreement about prolongation would have to be unanimous. During the lifetime of the company the participants could not withdraw their capital; profits had to go back into the company; the partners could not join other companies or trade on their own account and they also had to be prepared to disclose their financial position (i.e. accounts could not be kept secret from partners). A certain share in the capital normally – but not invariably – implied the same share in the profits; the partners promised each other this proportion (*lucrabitur quilibet pro rata sua* and *promittimus . . . dare vobis rectam et equalem partem indivisam*). The participants might be numerous and not all of them were related. A company formed by some Bonsignori in 1289 had as many as twenty-two partners, not all of them Bonsignori, who brought in capital of

43 Ibid., pp. 25–48 (p. 28).

amounts which varied between 6,800 l. and 1,200 l.[44] The nature of the banking companies is a reminder that the great Sienese dynasties were not tightly knit units.

Factors, juniors and other employees of the companies had contracts, such as the one which bound Ugo di Ugolino to serve Alessandro and Giovanni Salimbeni (1282) in Tuscany, Lombardy, France and England 'and anywhere else required' for four years.[45] A good deal of legislation was concerned with the responsibilities of such employees *vis-à-vis* the companies. On returning to Siena they had to hand over their accounts and copies of contracts made as well as money received. Partners in the companies were subject to similar rules and had to pay over to the heirs in full all sums due to partners who had died. Other statutes dealt with frauds by partners and factors.[46]

Few account-books have survived from the early Sienese banks. The Ugolini 'book of the fairs of Champagne', of 1255–62, and a volume recording receipts and expenditure for an unidentified company in 1277–82 are the only thirteenth-century survivals, followed by the accounts of the London and Paris branches of the Gallerani for 1305–08.[47] So much attention has been paid to the 'international' nature of the companies' business that there is a danger of forgetting that much of their money was made in the Italian peninsula. The bank whose accounts for 1277–82 have been published (which had at least twenty-nine partners or factors) had branches at Florence, Pisa, Massa, Perugia, Ancona, Orvieto, Viterbo, Rome and Naples.[48] Those parts of north-eastern Italy where there was little local competition – the Veneto and Friuli – were also an important field for the Tuscan bankers.[49]

Outside the peninsula incomparably the most important sphere of operations was France. A law required that thirty-six *boni homines* should be consulted on disputes concerning commercial reprisals 'of whom at least two-thirds must be from those who have business in France or elsewhere', while another statute refers to those merchants 'e' quali vanno in Francia o vero in altre parti'. It was assumed that the merchants' gild would need to send embassies to France where they dealt with the authorities of the Champagne fairs concerning defaulting

44 Chiaudano, *Studi e Doc.*, pp. 31–4; Senigaglia in *SS*, 25, docs. 4–5 (Gallerani contracts, 1255, 1259), 6. For a company formed in 1321 for a period of nearly six years, see P. and P., p. 112.
45 ASS, Ms B 5, ff. 101–2 (calendar of charter now apparently lost).
46 *Const. 1262*, pp. 229–34; *Cost. 1309–10*, 1, pp. 439–44.
47 Chiaudano, *Studi e Doc.* (text of accounts is pp. 164–208); Astuti; G. Bigwood, *Les livres des comtes des Gallerani*, 2 vols. (Brussels, 1961–62).
48 Astuti's Introduction, pp. i–xxiv.
49 Senigaglia in *SS*, 24, pp. 150–1; Prunai, pp. 549–64.

debtors.[50] 'France' was perhaps almost a synonym for 'abroad', though 'beyond the mountains' (*oltremonti*) is another common phrase. Residence outside the Italian peninsula was so common an eventuality that a statute dealt with the case of merchants requiring special fiscal assessment in view of their return after a long absence.[51] Since writers have sometimes implied that the distance and times involved were immense, as though the journey was the medieval equivalent of a sea voyage to Australia, it needs to be emphasized that from Tuscany a man could travel to Avignon in ten days, to Champagne in twenty. It was not difficult for an intelligent Italian to master French (even the 'Languedoil' of the north), and Sienese bankers cannot have felt more alien in Champagne than they did in Piedmont or Friuli. When a Sansedoni wrote to say that his wife and family were to join him in France he was making a perfectly reasonable request, even if it was an uncommon one.[52]

The Low Countries, though industrially precocious, were less advanced in finance, and the Sienese found willing borrowers among the powerful of that region, such as Countess Margaret of Flanders and the Duke of Brabant in the 1270s, and the Counts of Namur and Artois in the following decade. In 1306 the Gallerani were involved in a loan of some 18,000 l. (of Paris) to various lords, among them the Counts of Flanders, Namur and Zeeland.[53] Papal taxation established the Sienese in England from the 1220s and kept them occupied there on several occasions later in the century. The English crown also became an important client at the same period, and bishops, deans and priors were not slow to follow.[54] The Rhineland was another region rich in ecclesiastical borrowers: a particularly large loan to the archbishop of Cologne is mentioned elsewhere.[55] Further afield in central Europe there was perhaps less scope, but operations in Hungary are recorded as early as the 1230s.[56] Siena's links in the eastern Mediterranean were commercial rather than financial; the wool which came from England and elsewhere was often exported to Greece and the Levant.[57]

The account-books and correspondence which have eluded the waste-paper basket bear witness to the versatility of the Sienese businessmen but are

---

50 *Cost. 1309–10*, 1, pp. 234, 510–11; 2, p. 197; Zdekauer, 'Documenti riguardanti le fiere di Sciampagna, 1294', *Nozze Sanesi-Crocini* (Siena, 1896).
51 *Cost. 1309–10*, 1, p. 336.
52 P. and P., pp. 87–95.
53 *C. Econ. H.*, iii, p. 494; Senigaglia in *SS*, 24, pp. 157–8; Bigwood, *Les Livres des comptes* (cited above), pp. 49–65, 137–220.
54 Senigaglia, pp. 158–60; F. Patetta, 'Caorsini senesi in Inghilterra nel sec. XIII', *BSSP*, 4 (1897), pp. 311–44; N. Denholm-Young, *Collected Papers* (Cardiff, 1969), pp. 293–5.
55 Above, p. 27.
56 Senigaglia, pp. 161–2.
57 For links with Chiarenza in Greece see Astuti, p. 545 (index).

inadequate as testimony to the comparative contribution to their wealth of their various activities. Deposit, credit and exchange were all closely connected, and dealings in money at both the French and the Tuscan end were also involved with the trade in wool. The bankers acted as brokers (*sensali*) and it was an assumption of their calling that credit involved interest. Whatever the theories of the theologians, a loan was normally a transaction bearing interest. There were ways in which this interest could be disguised – frequently through repayment in a different currency – but it was understood by all, popes included, that he who forwent the use of his money because he had loaned it would normally receive compensation. A Bonsignori loan to the Angevins made 'without burden of usury or gain' (*absque omnium usurarum seu lucri onere*) was an altogether unusual arrangement. Financiers' consciences plagued them over excessive rates, but they would not have expected to operate as 'bankers' lending free of interest.

Banking began at home, though little attention has been paid to this aspect of the subject. A manuscript survival, incomplete and partly illegible, happens to preserve a list of Sienese debtors to the wealthy Aldobrandino del Mancino (*c.* 1289).[58] Nine names appear, two of them indebted for sums over 200 l., and the total must have been above 1,000 l. Apart from loans to the commune of Siena itself, to which we shall return, transactions within Tuscany are less well documented than those made farther afield. The Ugolini's Champagne accounts reveal that the company's French office at Bray-sur-Seine lent to counts (Nevers), bishops (of Toul), several abbots, burghers and artisans. The loans were normally for a short term, the conditions being renegotiable when – as was usual – repayment had not been received.[59] A letter from a Tolomei representative in Champagne (1269) mentions sixteen exchange transactions, gives news of a big loan (30,000 l. of Provins) to Charles of Anjou from the Bonsignori and Salimbeni as well as from Florentine and Lucchese bankers, and seeks authority to travel to Flanders to buy English wool.[60] The Tolomei's business in France included dealings in wax and spices (pepper, ginger and cinnamon) imported from the Levant via Italy, as well as textiles (with which was connected a lively trade in Italian dyes, such as woad). A letter from Provins (1294) records the acquisition of more than 200 pieces of cloth, rather over half of them originating from Champagne and elsewhere in France, the remainder from Artois and Flanders.[61]

58 Notarile (Antecosmiano), n. 3 (Orlando di Guglielmo), binding.
59 Chiaudano, *Studi e Doc.*, pp. 143–208.
60 Text (abbreviated in P. and P., pp. 58–9) and discussion in Chiaudano, 'Contratti di cambio in una lettera mercantile senese inedita del 1269', *Atti d. r. Accad. d. Scienze di Torino*, 66 (1931), pp. 627–50. See also R.-H. Bautier, 'Les Tolomei de Sienne aux foires de Champagne', *Recueil de travaux offerts à M. Clovis Brunel* (Paris, 1955), pp. 106–29.
61 Bautier, 'Marchands siennois et "draps d'outremonts" aux foires de Champagne (1294)', *Annuaire-Bulletin de la Soc. de l'Hist. de France*, 1945 (1947), pp. 87–107; CG 45, ff. 35v ff. (Tolomei company's purchase of 2,000 l. worth of woad at Cortona, 1293).

From the viewpoint of the city authorities the most important activity of the bankers was the provision of loans to the commune. Evidence for earlier periods is sparse, but it is clear that by the 1250s the companies were lending on a considerable scale. The Biccherna volume (no. 26) for the second half of 1257 records big loans from the Bonsignori (1,000 l.), Salimbeni (700 l.), Tolomei and others. In volume 35 (second half of 1262) loans total some 16,000 l.; four firms then providing large sums are Ranieri Bistugi (about 3,000 l.), the Bonsignori (about 2,000 l.), the Scotti, and Uguccione di Bartolomeo Rugerotti (both over 1,000 l.).[62] The dramatic tale related by a patriotic chronicler of the fourteenth or fifteenth century, repeated by many subsequent historians, that Salimbene Salimbeni granted an immediate loan of 118,000 florins in 1260 to pay the German cavalry just before the battle of Montaperti is surely a myth.[63] It bears no relation to the sums of money actually expended at the period, yet it is probably based on the reality of a substantial Salimbeni loan. This was indeed a time of significant loans from the Salimbeni: in 1271, for instance, they lent 2,000 gold ounces (equivalent to over 16,000 l.) to assist in payment of the fine levied by Charles of Anjou for Siena's imperialist role in the previous decade.[64]

The Salimbeni dazi payments of 1285, amounting to nearly 3,000 l., were possibly sums set against the commune's large debt to that family. Not all Biccherna entries record payments in currency and if these tax contributions were in fact merely means of lowering the commune's indebtedness this would explain their exclusion from the normal framework of payment within libre. The Salimbeni might also have accepted the doubtless very high tax assessment involved more readily if it was not to lead to payment by them in specie. It is even possible that the tax was in this instance administered by the Salimbeni bank (the companies occasionally undertook this function), though for that there is no evidence. In any event these large tax payments, particularly if they were notional rather than real, indicate the Salimbeni's considerable financial hold over the commune in the 1270s and 1280s. At that period Siena came rather closer to being in the pocket of a single banking dynasty than at any other time, yet this seems not to be mirrored by any Salimbene dominance in political control.[65]

The commune had already experimented with the appointment of a firm as its

62 *B.* 26, pp. 1–50; 35, ff. 1–9v.
63 *RIS, CS,* p. 57 (and in varying forms in many other late chronicle sources). See E. B. Garrison, 'Sienese historical writings and the dates 1260, 1221, 1262 applied to Sienese paintings', in his *Studies in the History of Medieval Italian Painting,* 4 (Florence, 1960–62), pp. 23–58. On the chronicle sources see also Anna M. Chiavacci Leonardi, 'Gli "Annali Senesi di Anonimo" del Muratori' in *Studi sul Medioevo Cristiano offerti a R. Morghen* (Rome, 1974), 1, pp. 293–304.
64 Dipl., Rif., 21 and 25.4.1271, 15.10.1272.
65 See Bowsky, *Finance,* pp. 101–2 and below, p. 82.

own banker, or so it would appear from the dominant position of Ranieri Bistugi, the lender of some 10,000 l. in the first half of 1267 and of 12,000 l. in the first half of 1268.[66] As Ranieri's position also involved his farming sources of direct and indirect revenue it is not easy to distinguish loans from the commune's many other transactions with him. Though the Gallerani were big lenders in 1286 and the Bonsignori in 1288,[67] the tentative experiments with a sort of prime banker were never pushed so far as to become a near monopoly. When a loan of 30,000 l. was negotiated in January 1291 there were four *ad hoc* syndicates involving fifteen or more names and these participants included Gallerani, Tolomei and Piccolomini.[68]

The rates of interest offered to such lenders were often around 20 per cent, but they could be a good deal higher and a stated rate of 15 per cent sometimes concealed an actual one (the capital was fictitiously halved) of 30 per cent. On occasions loans were secured by the pawning of communal lands, as happened in 1287 with the woodland of the Pian del Lago.[69] Terms such as these have been described as 'attractive' to lenders, but it seems more accurate to speak of 'fiscal arrangements . . . based on the constant indebtedness of the commune to the mercantile and banking class and the chief magnate families'. These indeed enjoyed direct control of financial administration and the revenues from farming direct and indirect taxes offered them 'a secure and regular source of profit and control'.[70]

The Bonsignori were a firm which certainly achieved their greatness through acting as papal financiers. The adroit leadership of Orlando saw them through the 1260s, but he died in 1273 and four re-organizations in the years 1289–95 may be indicative of difficult times. By 1298 it was clear that the Bonsignori were in serious trouble. The partners then (9 August) submitted a petition to the ruling officers (the Nine) in which they asked, among other things, for a moratorium, limited liability (proportionate to capital invested) of each partner, and assistance in negotiations with the papacy.[71] The decision to make a special case of one particular company, however illustrious, would have constituted an embarrassing precedent, and so the Bonsignori went to the wall, the lengthy conciliar

---

66 B 40, ff. 1–21v; 42, ff. 1–18. The latter volume uses the term *bancherii communis*, etc. (ff. 7, 13v) but does not apply it to Ranieri Bistugi and it seems clear that the formula does not imply an official appointment.

67 B 93, f. 1v; 97, ff. 79v, 81v, 121, 125.

68 Dipl., AGC, 15.1.1290 (Sienese style).

69 Bowsky, *Finance*, pp. 191, 210–11.

70 Ibid., pp. 223–4; Cammarosano, review of Bowsky in *SM*, s. 3, 12 (1971), p. 322 (for the view accepted here).

71 For the failure of the Bonsignori, the detailed treatment in English, *Sienese Banking*, pp. 55–78, supersedes the earlier accounts.

discussions of the following years being concerned mainly with the question of whether the firm's Sienese creditors should be granted priority.[72] One pressing creditor, a particularly powerful one, was the French king.[73] Complaining that he was owed 54,000 l., Philip IV eventually set about the confiscation of Sienese property in France (1307).

The main underlying difficulty for the Bonsignori was perhaps the tendency of the popes at this period, particularly Boniface VIII (1294–1303), to make use chiefly of Florentine bankers, and the same factor was involved in the contemporary failure of Pistoian and Lucchese companies. It has been suggested that the Bonsignori would have done well to diversify; untypically, they seem to have been putting all their eggs into the banking basket. In any case the leadership of Orlando was no longer available when things started to go wrong in the 1280s. The bankruptcy of the Bonsignori was followed, in the early fourteenth century, by some less spectacular failures among the Sienese banks. The practice whereby companies were re-formed at intervals of a few years served to diminish the seriousness of such crashes. Philip IV's confiscations in France had the 'knock-on' effect that the Sienese authorities compensated sufferers from them with property confiscated by Siena from the Bonsignori.

LANDHOLDING

In the mid fourteenth century the Bonsignori still possessed enviable slices of territory near the city, in the Montagnola, and further afield in Val d'Orcia. Each of the great banking families had a firm foundation in rural landholding. The resistance of the Sienese to categorization will be reiterated, perhaps *ad nauseam*, in this book. Those whose capital was invested in banking were likely to be owners of lands and lordships in Siena's subject-territory with all that that implied in involvement with policy and administration in the contado. They were also concerned in manifold ways in the commune's affairs, for instance as cavalry soldiers or even military leaders. Some were engaged in wider spheres, for example as Podestà of other cities.

In 1284, relates a chronicler, *xiiii cavalieri di casa Salimbeni si fenno in Siena con gran triunfo per Santa Maria d'agosto*:[74] fourteen Salimbeni were triumphantly knighted on the feast of the Assumption. Clearly the Salimbeni were much more than bankers, moreover the large number involved (all, presumably, young men) is a warning that some of the great families (Tolomei and Piccolomini, for example, as well as Salimbeni) were so numerous that generalizations about the

---

72 E.g. CG 60 (1301), ff. 106 ff.
73 CG 71, ff. 102 ff; 73, ff. 167 ff.
74 *RIS, CS*, p. 226.

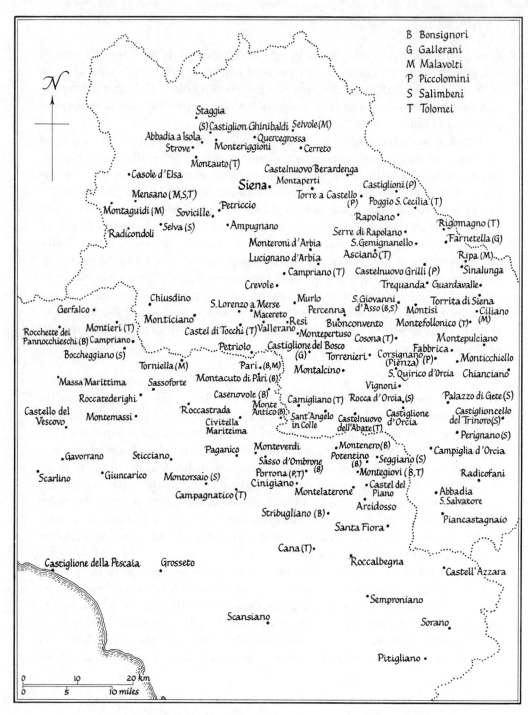

B Bonsignori
G Gallerani
M Malavolti
P Piccolomini
S Salimbeni
T Tolomei

Staggia
(S) Castiglion Ghinibaldi Selvole (M)
Abbadia a Isola Quercegrossa
Strove Monteriggioni Cerreto
Montauto (T)
Casole d'Elsa
Castelnuovo Berardenga
Siena Montaperti Castiglioni (P)
Mensano (M,S,T) Torre a Castello Poggio S. Cecilia (T)
(P)
Montaguidi (M) Sovicille Petriccio Rapolano
Radicondoli Selva (S) Ampugnano Rigomagno (T)
Serre di Rapolano Farnetella (G)
Monteroni d'Arbia S. Gemignanello
Lucignano d'Arbia Asciano (T) Ripa (M)
Sinalunga
Campriano (T) Castelnuovo Grilli (P)
Crevole Trequanda Guardavalle
Chiusdino Murlo S. Giovanni Torrita di Siena
S. Lorenzo a Merse Percenna d'Asso (B,S) Montisi Ciliano
Gerfalco Macereto Resi Buonconvento Montefollonico (T) (M)
Monticiano Castel di Tocchi (T) Vallerano Montepulciano
Montieri (T) Montepertuso Cosona (T)
Rocchette dei Petriolo Castiglione del Bosco Fabbrica
Pannocchieschi (B) Campriano (G) Torrenieri Corsignano (P) Monticchiello
Boccheggiano (S) Pari (B,M) Montalcino (Pienza)
Torniella (M) S. Quirico d'Orcia Chianciano
Massa Marittima Sassoforte Montacuto di Pàri (B) Vignoni
Roccatederighi Casenovole (B) Camigliano (T) Rocca d'Orcia (S) Palazzo di Gete (S)
Monte Castiglioncello
Castello del Roccastrada Antico (B) Sant'Angelo Castelnuovo Castiglione del Trinoro (S)
Vescovo Montemassi Civitella in Colle dell'Abate (T) d'Orcia
Marittima Perignano (S)
Monteverdi Montenero (B)
Gavorrano Sticciano Paganico Potentino Seggiano (S) Campiglia d'Orcia
Sasso d'Ombrone (B)
Scarlino Giuncarico Montorsaio (S) Porrona (P,T) (B) Montegiovi (B,T) Radicofani
Cinigiano Castel del Abbadia
Campagnatico (T) Montelaterone Piano S. Salvatore
Stribugliano (B) Arcidosso Piancastagnaio
Santa Fiora
Cana (T)
Castiglione della Pescaia Grosseto Roccalbegna
Castell'Azzara
Sempronìano
Scansiano
Sorano
Pitigliano

0   10   20 km
0   5   10 miles

2 MAGNATE LANDS IN THE CONTADO.
The initials are indications of holdings by these families at some period between 1250 and 1318.

economic interests and means, political sympathies and so on of 'a family' are almost bound not to apply to all branches or members. It would indeed be interesting to trace these great clans back to their origins and, in particular, to know whether each once possessed a rural territorial base whence they moved into the city, but lack of sources frustrates attempts to investigate their genealogies in periods earlier than the thirteenth century. By the end of that century the major banking dynasties had firm territorial footholds in each part of the contado. A map[75] shows that Salimbeni, Bonsignori, Tolomei and Piccolomini all had considerable holdings in the Maremma, a very extensive region where such comparative latecomers as the Bonsignori may have found it easier to buy land. The same families and the Malavolti also had estates closer to the city, the Salimbeni especially in Val d'Orcia and around S Giovanni d'Asso, the Tolomei further east, near Asciano, Poggio S Cecilia and Rigomagno, the Piccolomini above all in the region of Corsignano. If only the Salimbeni and Tolomei are known to have had important holdings between Siena and the city's northern border it must be remembered that this was a comparatively small area. That there were no larger zones constituting family territorial empires is a further indication that these families can only be regarded as 'units' if that word is taken with its loosest implications.

It is perhaps unsurprising that the picture which emerges is one of an untidy patchwork quilt. As the 'families' often consisted of numerous branches there was no reason why they should continue to be concentrated in particular regions – if indeed they ever had been. In any case their acquisitions were the result of purchase of what chanced to appear on the market or else came through inheritance or marriage or alienation by the Sienese commune when under financial pressure. Opportunities for accretion had to be accepted as they occurred and most of these arose in the areas south of the city.

Payments of taxation made by banking companies on behalf of contado communities are likely to be a sign of the further involvement of the family in question. A tax levied in the contado in 1278 was paid by the Tolomei on behalf of Torrita, Monticiano and Abbadia a Isola, by the Salimbeni for Montauto (near Monteriggioni), the Piccolomini for Poggio S Cecilia, the Malavolti for Asciano and the Gallerani for Corsignano.[76] Such arrangements were common; the Gallerani, for example, paid for S Gemignanello in 1281. Payment of fines suggests similar links, as when the Tolomei paid up on behalf of Rapolano in 1293.[77] It was also normal for the more important contado communities to have

---

75 Map 2 (p. 36) based on information contained in *Repertorio*.
76 B 71, ff. 9v–13.
77 B 80, f. 9v (see also *Repertorio*, p. 152); B 109, f. 24v.

Podestà from leading Sienese families. At the sizeable town of Chiusdino, for example, there were Tolomei Podestà in 1288 and 1295, followed by a Mala-volti.[78] Such posts did not always mean residence *in situ*, regular visits being regarded as sufficient.

Service as a Podestà might also be undertaken beyond Sienese territory. Volterra had a Tolomei Podestà in 1288 and another, in succession to a Malavolti, in 1301. Such appointments were not limited to Tuscany either. Dino de' Tolomei was Podestà at Reggio Emilia in 1304, in 1307 Guccio de' Malavolti held office first in Brescia and then immediately after in Parma.[79] The military command of the Guelf cavalry *tallia*, a senior post normally held by a Frenchman from the Regno or by a feudal magnate, fell in 1278 to a Malavolti, Guicciolino, a man whose transactions figure prominently in the Sienese banking account-book of 1277–82[80] and is quite possibly identical with the 'Guccio' just mentioned.

It was natural that these families should produce energetic political men and administrators as well as bankers and generals, poets and bohemians. In the first half of the 1270s Scozia de' Tolomei was the most frequent of all speakers in the commune's councils. Angioliero, a papal banker and a Salimbeni son-in-law, was another frequent office-holder at the same period, while his son Cecco was outstanding among the gilded youth of the city, notorious as a gambler and breaker of the curfew. Now Cecco's poems are still read and his father is remembered only in his son's unfilial sentiments:

> If I were death, I would call on my father,
> If I were life, I would flee from him.[81]

The acquisition of lands and lordships in the contado by the great Sienese families proceeded rapidly in the last decades of the thirteenth century and the early years of the fourteenth. By the time the fiscal Tavola delle Possessioni was drawn up (begun in 1318) the share of the four major families in the recorded landed values of the city and contado, in the twenty-seven libre analysed by Giovanni Cherubini and his team, was a follows:

Salimbeni	6.5 per cent
Tolomei	5.9 per cent
Gallerani	4.5 per cent
Bonsignori	3.3 per cent[82]

---

78 B 35, f. 128; 47, f. 27.
79 B 35, f. 128; 59, f. 21v; 65, f. 24: CG 70, ff. 26–9; 71, ff. 15–30.
80 Astuti, pp. 48, 51, 420.
81 Cecco Angiolieri, sonnet 86.
82 G. Cherubini, *Signori, contadini, borghesi* (Florence, 1974), pp. 231–312, especially pp. 249–51; see

Thus the share of these four dynasties alone was some 20 per cent of the total landed wealth.

If the predominance of these banker-landowners by that date seems extraordinary it must be recalled that the outlets for investment were very limited. What could a Sienese banker do with his profits other than purchase fields and castles? He could put them back into the bank, in the sense of offering more loans to bellicose monarchs and extravagant prelates, but these were the very categories of debtors from whom it was most difficult to extract debts. Conspicuous consumption, much of it in the form of donations to charitable and religious causes, was another outlet. The only one in which prudence could be combined with display was the acquisition of agrarian property and lordships in southern Tuscany.

The phenomenon of mixed sources of wealth was indeed common to most of those who can be said to have had 'wealth' and some examples of this routine combination of urban and rural possessions have already been given from the evidence of wills. Another may be mentioned, from the will of Giacomo di Angioliero, *civis senensis*, a man much troubled by a career of usury and of ill-gotten and illicit gains.[83] Giacomo (his will is dated 21 June 1259) was a banker on a fairly considerable scale in Siena and central France. His company had a separate account-book for its French transactions and he would appear to have been recently on a business trip to the area between Champagne and Paris, where he had made twenty-five loans to the value of some 1,500 l. of Tours, and he had made another important loan to the commune of Trequanda, in the western contado. Giacomo's interest, or share, took the form of a very considerable quantity of grain,[84] and this was a transaction about which his conscience was particularly perplexed. In Siena itself Giacomo had two houses and part-holdings in some other houses and shops (including 5/16th of two spicers' shops, half a cobbler's shop and a share in some butchers' shops near the Campo). In the country he had two vineyards, one of which had a house attached, together with part-shares in various mills and other houses, these rural possessions being in four different localities. This looks like the accumulation of someone who was liable to find himself a part-owner in the property of a debtor unable to meet obligations rather than the result of purchasing bits and pieces. He had also a quantity of silver plate and jewellery, two rather grand horses and some armour, and naturally a store of grain at home. Perhaps Giacomo di Angioliero was merely a

---

also A. K. Isaacs in *I ceti dirigenti nella Toscana tardo comunale* (Florence, 1983), pp. 84–7. On the general theme of growing control of the contado by citizens Cammarosano, especially pp. 191–2.

83 Zdekauer, *Mercante*, pp. 36–40.

84 Sixty *staria*, the amount in question, was about one ton (calculation with the assistance of the table in Epstein, p. 6).

Salimbeni 'writ small' or a Tolomei *manqué*. Certainly the pattern of his property is similar to theirs.

Many other occupations were of course compatible with activity as a financier, just as landownership was. A good deal of business, including trading in textiles, was conducted through the landlords of inns, the form of transaction whereby the host acted as middleman in such sales being known as *casaticum*. The account-book of 1277–82 records at least fifteen transactions of this nature with one Scotto *albergatore*.[85] It is no surprise to meet Saladino, another prosperous hotel-keeper, as farmer of a lucrative toll in 1273.[86] Some years earlier a loan of 100 l. to the commune was made by Lombardo the furrier *et sua societate*.[87] No doubt there were numerous instances of other forms of versatility, since 'financiers' were merely men dedicated to creating money from money and 'land-owners' men who invested their gains in the only existing form of capital. The occupations cited earlier in this chapter should probably not be seen as sole occupations, though this would have been less true for agricultural labourers and carriers of water.

CONCLUSIONS

Much more information has been offered in this chapter about the wealthy than about the poor, largely because their lives are far better recorded, though it can also be pleaded in justification of this imbalance that Siena's rich, the financier–landowners, were highly distinctive, whereas the Sienese poor were much like the poor elsewhere. More striking even than the social and political hegemony of the banking farmers and than the very general combination of city residence with rural possessions is the pattern of wealth suggested by Sienese tax payments. In the absence of comparable material it is not easy to know whether that pattern is characteristic of the medieval Italian cities in general, but it seems unlikely that the role of craft industry and commerce in Siena differed greatly from that prevailing elsewhere. Considerable elements of the population made their living from the manufacture and sale of clothing and the essentials of domestic existence and from involvement in building. In most cases the rewards for such activity were low, placing these craftsmen and shopkeepers far below the money-lenders and big landholders in terms of wealth. Above all the absence of a considerable textile industry was a very considerable difference between Siena and Florence and must account in part for the lack of a really flourishing Sienese commercial class.

---

85 Astuti, pp. 75, 267, 287, 300, 378 (and see index, p. 559).
86 B 53, f. 3v.
87 *B.* 36, p. 18 (1257).

The theme of the weakness – financial certainly, perhaps numerical also – of the industrial craft element in Siena's population will be returned to elsewhere in this book.[88] It explains the comparatively small constitutional role of the gilds. The Sienese Popolo's lack of achievement surely reflects the same weakness: some gains were made at the expense of the group which had formed and controlled the early commune, analogous to that dilution of the original patriciate which was general in the Italian cities and indeed in most of the towns of medieval Europe. Yet the authority of the families which had dominated Siena from the earliest days – Tolomei, Piccolomini, Ugurgieri and others, established in their formidable palazzi and castellari – survived, and with it their glorious and arrogant way of life. The legislation which banned them from one principal office, the Nine, did little to weaken their control.

88 Below, p. 209.

3 *Institutions*

THE PRINCIPAL OFFICES

The senior official of the commune of Siena was the Podestà (Latin *potestas* = power); this had been the case, as in most of the Italian cities, since the early thirteenth century. The matter of his election had to be raised each year before the end of the first week in September, to allow time for the new Podestà to take up his annual office in November. The selection was the responsibility of three electors drawn by lot from the members of the Council, who proceeded to put forward four names; their choice required confirmation by the Council. The electors were not allowed to leave Siena between the presentation of their list and the receipt of an acceptance by one of the candidates proposed. These arrangements, which applied in mid century and in the 1260s, had been modified by the early fourteenth century, when the Sienese governing officials, the Nine,[1] sent an emissary four months before the choice had to be made to places selected by them to seek out 'buoni e sufficienti e convenevoli huomini e amatori de la santissima romana Chiesa e del prosperevole stato della città'. At the next stage the choice was made by the Nine themselves, reinforced by the consuls of the merchant gild, the consuls of the knights and sixty men chosen for the purpose. The individual named (at this period for a six-month tenure) had to be aged at least thirty and to have been knighted by the time of assuming office, if not previously.[2]

In 1262 the possibility of the choice of a Sienese rather than a 'foreign' (*foretaneus*) Podestà remained, in theory, open, but in practice the position had already become virtually the monopoly of an experienced cadre of men trained in the law, mostly from Lombardy and Emilia. The duties of the Podestà, which varied considerably from time to time, included summoning and presiding over gatherings of the Council, judicial functions and, occasionally, military command. He had to preside, with 'collateral' judges, at the sessions of his own court and was responsible for the promulgation of the decisions of all the commune's courts.[3]

---

1 See below, pp. 47–8.
2 'Breve 1250', pp. 9–10; *Const. 1262*, pp. 56–9; *Cost. 1309*, 1, pp. 138–42. On *podesteria*, Bowsky, *Commune*, pp. 24–34. For some elections, CG 14, f. 68v; 16, f. 63; 18, f. 105; 20, ff. 12, 57–8; 21, f. 81v.
3 *Cost. 1309–10*, 2, p. 281.

There was plenty of room for disagreement, in the absence of clear constitutional definition, about the borders between the Podestà's jurisdiction and that of the commune's local officials – the Nine and their predecessors – and the Captain of the Popolo. He had to reside in a different terzo of the city from his predecessor – other measures designed to shield him from involvement in Siena's domestic disputes forbade him to receive gifts from Sienese citizens or even to eat with them – and he was not to move more than one day's journey from the city. Only in the rare circumstances of his being entrusted with personal military command could a longer absence be permitted. Such military duties also entailed a special financial allowance above the agreed rate of pay, which itself differed according to the standing of the individual.[4] The salary was high, but from it the Podestà had to pay his own body of retainers, his *familia*. Count Guido 'Salvatico', a feudatory of the Tuscan dynasty of Guidi, received a totally exceptional salary of 8,500 l. for a year's service (1282), very nearly double that of the Podestà two years earlier. After Count Guido's final tenure (1288) the rate remained much lower, normally between 3,000 l. and 3,700 l., till it rose again in the 1320s.[5] Though it was normal for the man selected to serve in person, his place was sometimes taken temporarily by a judge.[6]

The provision that at least four names should be suggested was necessary since the man first invited might not be free or willing to serve. Four was sometimes considered too short a list; in 1271 eight names were proposed.[7] In the course of the thirteenth century the cities of Lombardy and Emilia lost their commanding position as suppliers of Podestà. Siena then recruited mainly from the the Guidi counts and other prominent Guelf feudatories, thus linking the city to the Guelf military alliance. Thereafter, though many Podestà still came from northern Italy, there was a shift towards the March of Ancona and Umbria as recruiting grounds, and by the 1290s these regions were providing Siena with more Podestà than the north. Favourite places for recruitment in the Marche were Camerino (a tradition founded with the appointment of Giovanni di Accorimbone in 1290), Fermo and S Elpidio, in Umbria Gubbio and Spoleto.[8]

The Podestà was accompanied by an extensive staff of judges and other

4 *Const. 1262*, pp. 68–9, 74, 80–1, 85–7; *Cost. 1309–10*, 1, pp. 174–5; B 92, f. 110.
5 B 78, f. 51v; 82, f. 103v. On pay see also Bowsky, *Commune*, p. 30 and *Finance*, p. 316.
6 *Const. 1262*, pp. 78–9; CG 25, f. 34v and 35, ff. 35v–6v; *Const. 1309–10*, 1, p. 177.
7 CG 14, f. 68v. For letters conveying invitations to act as Podestà, see Concistoro 1773, nn. 20, 50.
8 Lists of Podestà in *Archivio di Stato di Siena. Archivio del Consiglio Generale del comune di Siena: Inventario* (Rome, 1952), pp. 101–7. The shift towards the appointment of central rather than north Italians was characteristic of the Umbrian communes at the same time: see A. I. Galletti, 'Note sulla mobilità d'élite nell'Umbria comunale: le magistrature forestiere' in *Orientamenti di una regione attraverso i secoli: scambi, rapporti, influssi storici nella struttura dell'Umbria* (Perugia, 1978), pp. 567–74.

officials who were usually from his home city or a neighbouring one. In 1295 Berardo of Varano brought with him seven judges, three knights (*socii*), two notaries, six squires and sixty police (*berruarii*); all these, except one judge, seem to have been from his own province, the Marche. A decade later the *familia* had grown, and Angelo of Rieti had nine judges, four knights, three notaries, six squires and ninety police, most from Rieti or nearby places in Umbria. Since there was an equivalent body of retainers with the Captain of the Popolo and a certain number of unattached 'foreign' judges and other officials, the total force of non-Sienese officials and armed men recruited as a matter of routine was a considerable one. In 1305 (Angelo of Rieti's year) this numbered fifty-four without counting police, 166 with.[9] Judges liked to bring their own notaries and servants or squires, which was one reason why this corps of administrators tended to expand. Part of the Podestà's household was recruited locally, among them six more notaries, four messengers and a reserve of sixty *balitori* who had to hold themselves in readiness for any mission for which they might be required (and they were only paid for services actually performed). Twice each month a parade was held to ensure that the city's foreign officials and police were actually present.[10]

After completing his term of office the Podestà remained at Siena for at least a week (the period had been prolonged to ten days by the early fourteenth century) while a full investigation (*sindicatio*) of his regime was undertaken, with particular reference to the financial aspects of his tenure. Five men were named for the enquiry and the Podestà had to deposit 500 l. as a surety until cleared by this board.[11] The investigation was no mere formality: Giovanni da Camerino had to forfeit 225 l. of his salary in 1291, 200 l. because he had brought a smaller force of police than was due, 25 l. 'on account of damage done by his household in the commune's buildings'. Later the commune claimed 325 l. from him, and the dispute went to the papal court. Cante de Gabriellis, Podestà in 1297, had 500 l. held back from his salary for seven months until he was eventually cleared by the investigating syndics. Quarrels of various sorts about the Podestà's pay were not uncommon. A particularly serious dispute concerned Tommaso de Anzola, who was deprived of office in 1291 after condemning a priest for murder, an infraction of ecclesiastical privilege which caused a quarrel with the bishop of Siena.[12] Tommaso's salary was to have been 6,000 l. for a year's service, but only half of

---

9 CG 49, ff. 7 and v; 66, ff. 17–23v. On the familia, Bowsky, *Commune*, pp. 26–7.

10 *Const. 1262*, pp. 104–5, 113–14; *Cost. 1309–10*, 1, 211, 348–9.

11 *Const. 1262*, pp. 84–5; *Cost. 1309–10*, 1, pp. 137, 225–7; 2, pp. 538–41. On *sindicatio* see V. Crescenzi, 'Il sindicato degli ufficiali nei comuni medievali italiani' in *L'Educazione Giuridica. IV. Il pubblico funzionario: modelli storici e comparativi*. Tomo 1 (Perugia, 1981), especially pp. 433–41.

12 B 104, f. 28; CG 41, ff. 62–3v. See also below, p. 131.

this was paid when his tenure was terminated. Five years later a dispute arose with a man from Rieti whose appointment was revoked on the grounds of his Ghibelline affiliations.[13]

The possibility of disagreements between commune and Podestà is mentioned in the code of 1309–10 and the instances just described must have served as a reminder of the difficulties inherent in this official's status. The ambiguity goes back to the office's origin. Around the beginning of the thirteenth century many of the communes had begun to recruit a sort of 'city manager' who was to govern without involvement in the factionalism characteristic of the period when the commune's leading officers were local men, the 'consuls'. However, the standing of this new official, the Podestà, lacked juridical definition, and the troubles of Siena's Podestà in the 1290s showed how a man who had been hired could also be fired. Later, the Podestà's functions tended to be more limited, with emphasis on his judicial capacity, but that development is not detectable before the fourteenth century. Meanwhile the gild of judges and notaries still thought it a necessary routine that its representatives should lecture each new Podestà on his duties.[14]

Such was the authority of the Podestà's position that one is bound to ask whether he was considered to be the superior of all other officials of the commune and Popolo, both local and foreign. In other words, where did sovereignty lie? The ambiguity of the position of the Popolo itself makes the enquiry a difficult one, nevertheless the arrangements laid down in the 1262 code for the settlement of any dispute between Podestà and Captain of the Popolo provide a partial answer. If the priors of the twenty-four and the consuls of the merchant gilds (i.e. the Mercanzia and Pizzicaiuoli) agreed that such a dispute had arisen, the matter had to be settled in a special meeting of the Council of the commune and Popolo at which neither the Podestà nor Captain could be present. Since the Council was also the only body which could grant citizenship, it would seem that it was envisaged as a supreme authority ranking above all the officials.[15]

GOVERNORS OF THE POPOLO AND COMMUNE

The doubtful standing of Podestà and Captain of the Popolo was a particular case of a more general constitutional ambiguity. In Siena, as in many other Italian cities, the commune itself had by the middle of the thirteenth century undergone a process of constitutional and institutional change as a result of which its own officials and councils had come to share power with those of a new organization, the Popolo (people). To summarize so complicated and varied a process in a single

13 Bowsky, *Commune*, pp. 31–3.
14 *Cost. 1309–10*, 1, pp. 209–10; *Statuti . . . giudici e notai*, p. 55.
15 *Const. 1262*, pp. 72–3; *Cost. 1309–10*, 1, p. 166.

sentence is to over-simplify greatly, but the crux of the situation was that
elements in the population which had been excluded from the early regime of the
consuls elbowed their way to the fore and ensured that they shared in the power
of the landholding elements which had formed the dominant class in the original
commune.

Thus by the mid century many of Siena's local-born officials were representatives of the 'people', at least notionally, rather than of the Sienese 'commune'
itself. The Popolo as an organization within the Sienese city-state will be treated
later,[16] but it is necessary at this point to say something of those of its officials who
served alongside the Podestà as Siena's principal administrators and came to
supersede him as the city's supreme authority. The 'foreign' Capitano del Popolo,
the 'popular' equivalent of the Podestà, can also be discussed later, partly because
his office was an intermittent one, partly because it did not achieve the degree of
power enjoyed by the native priors and governors.

Between the middle of the century and the 1290s the experimentalism
characteristic of the Italian city-republics prevailed to such an extent that
institutional developments are best set out in the form of a chart. The changes
which occurred between the time of the Sienese Popolo's first officials, the
twenty-four *anziani,* and the eventual installation of a more enduring institution,
the Nine 'governors and defenders of the people and city', were as follows:

Table 4. *Titles of signorie, 1235–1355*

Dates	Number of officials	Formal title
1236–71	24	antiani populi
1271–79	36	gubernatores et difensores civitatis et communis
1280–87	15	gubernatores et difensores communis et populi
1287–90	9	gubernatores et difensores communis
1290–91	18	domini ad gubernandam civitatem
1291–92	6	gubernatores et difensores communis et populi
1292–1355	9	gubernatores et difensores populi et civitatis[17]

Throughout these permutations the number of office-holders was divisible by
three; this is because each terzo of the city had always to have equal representation. The interesting point about the changes in nomenclature is the disappearance of the 'popular' label between 1271–79 and again in 1287–91, these
being periods in which emphasis on a Guelf regime led to temporary suppression

16 Below, pp. 101–4.
17 Sources: volumes of CG for the years in question: see also Mondolfo, *Populus* and Bowsky,
   Commune, pp. 34–6, 58–9.

of the Popolo. At other times after 1280 the use of the word is an indication of a claim to inclusiveness rather than of any popular or anti-oligarchic tendency.

In Siena all these organs have in common their topographical basis. The structure of the Popolo's organization in the Italian communes was either corporative (i.e based on gilds) or else topographical, or occasionally some combination of the two. In many cities representatives of the craft gilds served as the officials of the Popolo, but in Siena the *arti* never achieved this position. The formal nomenclature of the officials is not easy to establish since it was usual to refer to them as 'the Twenty-four', the 'Thirty-six', and so on; the list given above is derived from the occasional use of a fuller title in the proceedings of the Council, the Consiglio Generale. The Twenty-four were chosen to hold office for six months, within which time three of them served as priors for each of the eight *priorie* into which the six-month period was divided.[18] The Thirty-six were elected for three months, and three of them at a time served as priors, each priorate lasting one week.[19] The criterion for choice naturally depended on political circumstances. During the Guelf regime of the 1270s the *gubernatores* had to be merchants (*de numero mercatorum*) zealous for the honour of the city and its Guelf party. Members of the magnate families and knights were ineligible, as were judges, notaries, doctors and, of course, Ghibellines.[20]

The task of the Nine (as it was defined in the code of 1309–10) was to bring the city, commune and people (popolo) to 'true and right and loyal peace and unity, *communalmente e singularmente*', to maintain them 'in unity and *buono stato pacifico e riposato*', and to stand for 'reason and equality and justice'.[21] At that time the choice of the Nine was made by a cautious process designed to secure continuity within the controlling oligarchy. The election was carried out in a meeting of the Nine in office, with the consuls of the merchant gild (Mercanzia), the Podestà and the Capitano del Popolo. Ten favourable votes were required (of the fourteen or fifteen present), but close relatives and business partners of the voters themselves were ineligible. There was a period of twenty months before holders of the office themselves became eligible again. It was necessary to be literate and aged at least thirty to qualify. The tenure of various other important offices was also incompatible with membership of the Nine: these were the Provveditori of the Biccherna, the Signori of the gabella (indirect tax) and the Chamberlain of the Consuls of gilds,[22] as well as any ambassador.

18 CG 6, ff. 2v, 183; 8, f. 83v; 12, ff. 45, 54. See also Bowsky, *Commune*, p. 54n. Some writers have referred to the 24 and their successors as 'priors', but this is incorrect.
19 CG 15, f. 111v; 16, f. 10v.
20 Statuti 3, f. 45v (quoted by G. Martini, *Siena da Montaperti alla caduta dei Nove* (Siena, 1961), pp. 25–6).
21 *Cost. 1309–10*, 2, p. 498.
22 Ibid., pp. 490–2; Bowsky, *Commune* , pp. 59, 62.

The Nine had to be, in the terms of the statute, *de' mercatanti de la città di Siena o vero de la meza gente* (the middle people). These 'middling sort of people', or those of them interested in sharing in oligarchical authority, were not very numerous, and some families were represented on the Nine many times. Professor Bowsky's analysis (for the period 1287–1355) shows that nearly half of those in this office held it more than once, while one in ten held it three times or more, and there were men who served on the Nine as often as eight times. Although a payment was made, this was compensation for time lost from business rather than a full salary, amounting to a mere 5s. per day.[23] The Nine were appointed for a two-month period, the office of prior or chairman being held by each for a single week. Throughout their service – and this must have precluded conduct of their normal business, hence the payment for 'broken time' – the Nine were insulated from contact with the social life of the outer world. They had to live and feed together, separated from their families.[24] Strict conditions were laid down for the granting of leave. The Podestà could grant this for a maximum period of twenty-four hours. The prior could authorize overnight absences for a maximum of two members at one time. Fines for unauthorized absence were high: 5 l. was the minimum, 10 l. the penalty for anyone 'going to his vineyard or land or any other place'.[25]

The Nine could not issue new ordinances unless these were backed by a two-thirds majority in council and they possessed, on their own, no fiscal powers. They were however empowered to order the Podestà to call a Council meeting and to call one themselves in the event of his refusing. They were the body normally authorizing all expenditure and also the arbitrators in cases of apparent contradiction between statutes. Various officials, such as the *maggior sindaco* and notaries employed for the commune's correspondence, were chosen by them. Each Thursday they had to hold a session 'in a public and open place' in order to hear petitions.[26] Much of their work was done in smaller meetings, some of which involved discussions with the Podestà and Captain, other officials or inner councils, but records of these and of their own gatherings have not survived. There were certain officials, styled the *ordini*, whose authorization was necessary for action by the Nine in some matters. These were the four Provveditori, the four Consuls of the Mercanzia and the three Consuls of the Knights (known alternatively as the Captains of the Guelf Party).

---

23 *Cost. 1309–10*, 2, pp. 492, 498; Bowsky, *Commune*, p. 73.
24 Ibid., p. 58. A proposal for the reclusion of the Nine was considered, but eventually rejected, in 1291 (CG 41, ff. 17 and v).
25 *Cost. 1309–10*, 2, pp. 495–7.
26 Ibid., Dist. VI.

COUNCILS

The Podestà and the Sienese officials operated to a large extent through and in conjunction with the commune's General Council, the Consiglio della Campana ('of the Bell'). This was basically composed of 300 citizens, 100 from each terzo, to whom were added the consuls of the merchant gild and the cloth gild. Members were chosen for one year. In 1262 the electors were the Podestà, the Twenty-four (or perhaps their priors only), the Chamberlain and four Provveditori and the judges. Some slight alterations had been made by 1309–10, when the electors, for a six-month period, were the four *ordini*, which meant the inclusion of the consuls of knights or Captains of the Guelf Party, at the expense of the Podestà and judges.[27]

The councillors had to be the 'best, most useful and most discreet' and the wisest that could be found. In 1262 at least half had to be members of the Popolo. To be eligible it was necessary to be a tax-paying citizen resident in the city for at least ten years, and the minimum age was twenty-five. Office-holders could not be councillors, nor could two brothers at the same time; heretics and suspected heretics were naturally banned. Those elected had to accept membership and swear an oath on doing so.[28] As circumstances inevitably arose in which men elected proved ineligible or had good reason for absence, the number present at meetings often fell well below 300 – about 150 seems to have been a normal attendance in the 1250s,[29] but later, when nominal membership neared 400, the numbers often rose above 250 and even as high as 350. Even then there were occasions when they were much lower. In 1285 the Council had 390 nominal members, yet at a meeting on 5 March of that year only 146 turned up.[30] Absence might be sanctioned on as many as three occasions in any month, but the fines for unauthorized absence (commonly 5s.) could be as high as 10s., and they were levied frequently.[31] Excuses for absence were manifold: 'he was away', 'he had been excused attendance', 'he did not hear the bell', 'he was hunting', 'they had gone to the woods'. These were among the explanations offered when forty-four councillors on one occasion, and thirty-seven on another, were fined for non-attendance (September 1270). In September 1275 a scandalous number of absences resulted in 256 (considerably over half) of the councillors being fined 20s. each.[32] This was a very exceptional occasion, a more normal number of fines

---

27 *Const. 1262*, pp. 145–7; Bowsky, *Commune*, pp. 85–7.
28 B 71, ff. 2v, 104 (fines for failure to take the oath).
29 E.g. CG 4, ff. 6 and v.
30 CG 29, ff. 3–10. See also *Archivio del Consiglio Generale . . . Inventario* (above, n. 8) p. 2.
31 B 71, f. 5.
32 CG 14, ff. 3–4; 20, ff. 137–9v.

for absence being about 24, while often a mere handful of councillors paid what for them amounted to a very low fine indeed, the equivalent to a contemporary parking fine. The member of the Gallerani family who made a payment for two absences had presumably chosen what for him was a routine option hardly amounting to a status symbol.[33] Late arrival and premature departure also occasioned fines.[34]

It was normal for the Podestà to summon meetings of the Council though, as already mentioned, the Nine and certain other officials could do so in an emergency.[35] The business of the Council meeting came to it from the main *signoria* (i.e. after 1292, the Nine) or from the other leading officers, the *ordini*, or else by way of the very numerous petitions brought to it by individuals or, more rarely, corporations. A request to the Council was the routine procedure for seeking any exemption or privilege, including requests for reduction or cancellation of fines or other judicial punishments, as well as for applying for citizenship. The annual review of the commune's constitution by the thirteen *emendatori* also culminated in consideration of their recommendations by the Council.[36] It was not very common for the Nine (or their predecessors) to pronounce a formal corporate opinion to a council meeting, but this could happen. In March 1275, for instance, Ugo Matteo proposed on behalf of the Thirty-six (*pro parte xxxvi consuluit dicens*) that the military crisis should be dealt with by ordering 200 citizens to provide cavalry service and by recruiting 100 mercenaries.[37] Traffic in the other direction, that is reference from the Council to the signoria or other office, was the normal route, as will be seen.

One important factor in determining conciliar business was the list of subjects discussion of which at regular intervals was compulsory under the terms of the constitution, varying from the broadest economic and military concerns to very specific considerations. Many were intended as a sort of strategic *aide-memoire*, for instance the question 'concerning the construction of a castle on the hill at Monte Corio'.[38] The list was a lengthy one, but the routine way in which the institution functioned must have blunted its impact; frequently the decision was 'no action this year'. The topics thus given a compulsory airing were too varied and numerous to be summarized. They included many aspects of rule in the contado (the building of new fortresses and defences, taxation, markets, the assertion of

33 CG 46, f. 9; 71, f. 5; 83, f. 13v; 95, f. 9v; 114, f. 43 (Gallerani).
34 CG 27, ff. 10 and v; B 53, f. 1.
35 Above, p. 48. *Cost. 1309–10*, 2, pp. 505–6. On the summons and chairmanship, Bowsky, *Commune*, p. 87.
36 These topics are very well treated in Bowsky, *Commune*, pp. 89, 92.
37 CG 20, ff. 33v–4v.
38 CG 1, f. 20 (1249); *Const. 1262*, p. 373, for this as a compulsory agenda item.

existing rights and acquisition of new ones, and so on), also domestic questions (food and water supply, the watch, sumptuary legislation, citizenship, the *palazzo del comune*).[39]

The rules of debate restricted the number of speakers on any topic to five (at times, four) and forbade councillors – ineffectively – to say exactly the same as a previous speaker.[40] Fines were specified for speeches which were irrelevant, for rudeness to other councillors (speaking *villaniam* or *verba iniuriosa*), for failing to listen diligently, and for speaking after the Podestà had ordered silence.[41] These were not mere threats; early in 1277 fines were levied on nine councillors for speaking 'against the orders of the Podestà' (*quia fecit locutionem contra mandatum potestatis*).[42] One very specific (and admirable) rule was that any councillor speaking in favour of military action was obliged to serve in the campaign himself.[43] Consideration of any proposal which contravened an existing statute required a previous vote that discussion of the proposal was necessary and useful. A special and rather strange role was played in the Council's sessions by the *maggior sindaco*, a non-Sienese official chosen by the Nine whose duties required him to express opposition to any constitutional innovation proposed. The practical effect of this automatic and compulsory disagreement with any change to the statutes was small. As with the list of the compulsory topics, this was a weapon blunted by the automatic way in which it functioned, hence it tended to be discounted, rather as though it had been a perpetually red traffic light, and failed to fulfil its purpose. However the *maggior sindaco* had a miscellany of other duties, among them those of reviewing the statutes of the gilds and of contado communities, enquiring into accusations against judges and notaries, and checking the presence of the Podestà's retinue.[44]

The constitution of 1309–10 provided that any measure to which the *maggior sindaco* had stated his opposition required a three-quarters majority and the presence of 200 councillors. A similar majority, on three separate occasions, was also required for a decision to go to war; normally these three meetings were to be held on different days (so that the clause implied a two-day delay before launching a campaign), though there was provision for special exemption from this rule.[45] Certain types of conciliar decision required a two-thirds majority, including election of the Podestà, any reversal of a previous vote and the grant of

---

39 CG.
40 *Cost. 1309–10*, 1, p. 199; Bowsky, *Commune*, pp. 89–90.
41 CG 27, ff. 10 and v (1283).
42 B 67, ff. 3v–4 (for fines for speaking *contra bannum*,B 53, f. 1 (1273)).
43 *Cost. 1309–10*, 1, p. 172.
44 Ibid., pp. 93–4, 348–9; 2, pp. 424–5, 541–7; Bowsky, *Commune*, pp. 42–5, 90, 96 (and his article in *SS*, 80 (1968)).
45 *Const. 1262*, p. 88.

authority by the Nine to ordain a measure contrary to the current constitution.[46] This left only comparatively routine or minor matters for decision by a straight majority. Provision existed, in principle, for taking an open vote, but a clause in the 1309–10 statutes treats the secret vote as compulsory and it seems that in practice voting was always carried out by placing a ball in either the white (favourable) or the black box.[47]

A special notary had the task of compiling the official record of the Council's debates and decisions (*riformagioni*). Arrangements about the performance of this very responsible duty varied. One clause in the 1262 statutes implies that a Sienese notary was elected to this post, another that there were two notaries *pro consiliis scribendis*. By 1309–10 there was a single notary and later the post was always held by a non-Sienese, usually a Tuscan who was in office for many years consecutively. The notary's record had to be agreed by the Council before the conclusion of the meeting, obviously a necessary precaution against subsequent controversy, and he was forbidden to consult speakers about the terms in which their contributions to debate were recorded.[48]

A summary of the discussions in some Council meetings may give more illumination than prolonged generalizations. I have selected more or less at random meetings separated from each other by a decade. The first period is from 19–26 August 1275. During that week five meetings were held of which the record has survived.[49] None was a full gathering of the 'Council of the Bell', all were meetings, called by the Podestà, of the Thirty-six and other officials and selected 'wise men' (*savi*) and took place in the Podestà's residence in the Tolomei palazzo. On 19 August there were present the Thirty-six, the Podestà, the captains of the Guelf party with that party's councillors, the Chamberlain and the four Provveditori of the Biccherna, and certain other *savi*. Four topics were on the agenda: a petition from a cardinal's servant who had been the victim of a robbery in or near Sienese territory; another robbery, at Giuncarico in the southern contado (concerning which there was a letter from the Count of Elci); trouble about a reluctant garrison at Accesa ('Castello del Vescovo'), in the same area; and, most seriously, the excommunication by the bishop of Siena of some officials of the commune. There was one speaker only, and it was agreed, on his proposal, that twelve emissaries should be sent to reason with the bishop, and if he refused to withdraw the excommunication the matter was to be reconsidered by the Council. A small commission of enquiry was to be sent out about the Giuncarico robbery and further

---

46 Ibid., pp. 57–8; *Cost. 1309–10*, 1, p. 206; 2, p. 487. The role of the *maggior sindaco* should have made a 3/4 majority requisite in such instances.
47 *Cost. 1309–10*, 1, pp. 206–7. On voting, Bowsky, *Commune*, pp. 93–4.
48 *Const. 1262*, pp. 104–5, 147, 149–50; *Cost. 1309–10*, 1, p. 205; Bowsky, *Commune*, pp. 95–6.
49 CG 20, ff. 94–99v.

action taken if it was concluded that a family of feudatories, the Pannocchieschi, were involved. The recalcitrant garrison was to be replaced, and the matter of the cardinal's servant was referred to the consuls of the merchant gild.

On the 21st the same body met again, this time to consider a request from Charles of Anjou's treasurer that Siena should contribute its share towards the financial and military resources of the Guelf alliance, together with a proposal for terms of alliance from Pisa's Guelf exiles. There was also news of more trouble in the southern contado, and it was decided to send for representatives of Porrona, the place involved, to come to Siena 'to promise obedience'. There were three speakers at this meeting, but decisions were deferred on the main diplomatic topics.

At the meeting of the same body on 22 August there were eight speakers. The topics this time were various problems in the contado, in particular trouble with the important town of Massa (Marittima), which was to be ordered to send emissaries to promise obedience. Fifty French mercenaries were to be recruited, and a new garrison hastened to Accesa. There was still no decision about the Pisan Guelfs. Later on the same day a second meeting was held at which two councillors spoke. Massa was discussed again and a yet more important subject, the line to be taken by Siena at the forthcoming meeting (parliament) of the Tuscan Guelfs. It was decided that Siena's representatives should encourage a pacific policy and in particular oppose the notion of a campaign against Volterra. The last meeting of this series, on 26 August, was a larger occasion with sixty *savi* co-opted to those who were present *ex officio*. Five topics were discussed, only one of them totally new – a letter from the Podestà of Città di Castello (in Umbria) giving political news from northern Italy – the other subjects being the Guelf alliance (on which views had been expressed by a recently arrived embassy from Florence) and the various troubles of the southern contado. Two councillors spoke: the news from Lombardy was to be discussed later, and the main conclusion was to reaffirm the recommendation to recruit fifty mercenaries.

It should be evident from the preceding paragraph that Sienese councillors received a versatile political education through the variety of problems with which they were faced and which they discussed or (if of passive temperament) heard discussed. The range of their concerns brought a wide acquaintance with the affairs of their city's sphere of influence and its involvement in the diplomatic interplay of the entire Italian peninsula. Far from the Council's concerns being local or municipal, curiously little of what would now be thought of as local government matters came under discussion at these meetings of 1275.

A dip into the *riformagioni* of 1285, this time for meetings of the 'Council of the Bell', provides a partial corrective to that impression.[50] The Council met on

---

50 CG 29, ff. 34–5.

Saturday, 25 January of that year, with four items on the agenda. One, a matter for routine repetition, was the requirement to consider before the end of January any money payments owing to Sienese citizens from inhabitants of the diocese of Volterra and of the seigneurial estates of the Aldobrandeschi and Pannocchieschi lords. The second (again a topic dictated by the constitution) was the need to fix salaries for those wishing to come to Siena to teach 'in any subject, science or art' (*facultate, scientia vel arte*) or to practise medicine. The controllers of the city's prisons could not raise the normal 10,000 l. caution-money asked of them, and they petitioned to offer a smaller amount. Finally, there was a proposal that for convenience the butchers of Siena should be required to so arrange their locations that there should be no more than three butchers' shops in any contrada. There were four speakers, and it was agreed that the first routine proposal be referred to the Podestà and the consuls of the merchant gild; the teachers' salaries were referred to the Chamberlain and Provveditori; the gaol managers' surety was referred to the Podestà and his court (judges). The radical suggestion about the siting of butchers' shops was to be re-considered in mid February when the Council would hold an *ad hoc* meeting, and for the present the butchers might stay where they were. The tendency of this meeting to 'pass the buck' or at least to postpone decisions is very obvious.

A sample from the minutes a decade later still widens the conspectus of subjects coming before the Council. The general Council met four times between 10 December 1294 and 22 January 1295.[51] On two occasions there was only one speaker, once there were two and once three. At the first meeting the topics were the city's walls, the election of a rector for Chiusdino in the contado, and the iniquities of the city's butchers. The second discussed street paving, the provision of guards for the city, the supply of fish for purchase in the city, and the levying of a new direct tax. The third considered the fabric of the cathedral (a routine topic), the new religious order of the 'Frati Gaudenti' (this was left to the Nine), the obligations of cavalry service (another compulsory topic), and the need to encourage people to settle at Monteriggioni, a strategic castle-site, rather than desert it in favour of the plain. The last Council meeting discussed two subjects only, a dispute with Bologna over commercial reprisals, and a petition concerned with the danger of fire in bakers' shops. A proposal had been made that bakers should not be permitted to keep in store more than one *salma* of firewood. The bakers counter-petitioned that a stock of at least three *salme* was a necessity, and this obtained the necessary two-thirds majority. After the discussion at this meeting two clauses from the constitution received formal readings; they related to compensation owed in certain circumstances by the commune, and to the ineligibility of magnates to plead in the commune's courts.

51 CG 47, ff. 27–43v.

With many of the topics of 1294–95 one is back in the realm of civic domestic affairs, but here too there are 'imperial' preoccupations with Monteriggioni and Chiusdino, both important Sienese possessions. Concern with the domestic market in fish involved the wider world, for most of Siena's fish came from Lake Trasimene, outside the city's territory; the matter of the religious order and the dispute with Bologna imply yet wider horizons.

The council-meetings described above, particularly those of 1275, are characteristic in that a question was rarely debated and settled in a single session, and it was normal to refer matters either to another council or office or to an *ad hoc* committee (*balia*), or a combination of these. Common techniques were reference to the Nine (or whatever the current *signoria* was styled) or to the consuls of the merchant gild or to a *balia* of twelve. An initial reference to the Nine was quite often followed by them in turn handing on the matter to a *balia*. Often the process is difficult to trace because minutes of the *balie* have survived in the archive much less well than those of the main Council.

It would be superfluous to pile up examples illustrating the endlessly varied formulae of Sienese conciliarism. The usual title for a gathering comprising numbers much smaller than the main Council was 'secret'. Any project entailing innovation in the contado had to be discussed by the Nine with a 'secret council of a hundred' before it could go to the Council of the Bell.[52] 'Secret' councils could easily imply numbers of this sort, though on other occasions there might be as few as a dozen members.[53] If a small council was reinforced by *ad hoc* members, as often happened, it might grow until it approached the General Council in size. These gatherings often went under very generic titles, such as the 'secret council with the addition of certain *sapientes de casatis* (wise men from magnate families) and others'.[54] When the main Council itself was reinforced, a common occurrence, membership became very numerous. A routine body of added names, the *radota*, was often added to the General Council's basic strength of 300. The number of the *radota*, which had earlier been sixty and then 120, achieved 150 (fifty per terzo) in 1290, and the prohibition against brothers serving together did not apply to its membership, so it could magnify the authority of leading families.[55]

The insistence that a controversial matter should be discussed openly and on more than one occasion is symptomatic of an important facet of the commune's philosophy. This explains the references to decisions reached after discussions 'by the Fifteen and a council of the consuls of the knights, with the addition of many

52 *Cost. 1309–10*, 2, p. 503.
53 E.g. CG 13, ff. 5v. 34v, 52v.
54 CG 16, f. 75 (analogies in CG 17, ff. 5–6v).
55 On the *radota* see Bowsky, *Commune*, pp. 86–7.

nobles and magnates of the city of Siena', which might in turn require confirmation 'by the General Council of the Bell with the addition of the following men of the city, in great number and quantity . . . the consuls of the knights and their council, the consuls of the merchant gild and their council, the consuls of the cloth gild and their council, the lords of the gilds of the city and forty good men from each terzo'.[56] After all that it would be difficult indeed to raise the complaint that 'we were never consulted'.

A distinction which was partly but not entirely a matter of nomenclature was that between councils 'of the commune', 'of the Popolo' and 'of the commune and Popolo'. There were occasional periods of conflict when the Popolo sought to assert itself as an organization of equal strength with the commune, and at such times the Popolo tended to reach its decisions through its own council.[57] Yet in as far as the Popolo gained success its institutions merged with those of the commune itself and indeed reshaped them. When half the commune's councillors had to be *popolani*[58] there was less need for the Popolo to have a separate council. But there were times in the 1250s – and occasionally later – when the Popolo was challenging for authority and its councils came to share *de facto* in the commune's decision-making. Thus in a period of struggle (1256–57), one outcome of the Popolo's pressure was the consideration of a proposal for direct taxation by a joint meeting of the commune's Council (of the Bell) and the council of the Popolo.[59] When the Popolo was not combining with, or being devoured by, the commune, its council was of a considerable size. In 1258 its members numbered 150 (fifty per terzo), while in 1265 a few meetings of the Popolo alone – joint councils were the rule at this time – comprised 'the general council of the Popolo of the city of Siena with the addition of the lords of the gilds and companies (*societates*) and five hundred men per terzo'.[60] These were perhaps the largest conciliar meetings ever to be held in the city.

COMMITTEES AND THE 'ORDINI'

Examples serve better than lists of councils and officials to convey the way things were done. The *balia*, the *ad hoc* committee, is the most characteristic governmental institution of the Italian communes. In some ways it was also the most influential, since the long-lasting offices had themselves originated as *balie*. In any military or financial predicament – the second following the first 'as night the day' – the reaction of the Sienese was to appoint an advisory *balia*. In 1251 a Florentine

---

56   CG 31, ff. 35–6 (1286).
57   For the Popolo, see below pp. 101–4.
58   Above, p. 49.
59   CG 6 (for the joint meeting, f. 92).
60   CG 8, ff. 2 and v; 12, ff. 21, 23. For the *societates* see below, p. 102.

campaign threatened Montalcino; the Council's decision was to instruct the Podestà to act, 'and let him have four good men (*bonos homines*) known to him, those whom he considers most useful, from each *terzo*'.[61] In 1268 the bad news from the same direction was the Guelf capture of Montepulciano. On that occasion the advisers to the Council and Captain of the Popolo were the Twenty-four 'and twelve good men placed over the matters of the commune (*positorum super factis communis*) with the addition of eight wise good men from each terzo'.[62] The tendency was to accrete more 'wise' and 'good' men as the crisis developed. In 1270 Siena faced the consequences of the collapse of the Ghibelline cause in Tuscany. The Podestà consulted a 'secret' council of twelve throughout that summer which at times was reinforced by the rectors of the gilds. By October the twelve were meeting with 'other wise men' and in early December the arrangement was formalized as a gathering of the twelve and thirty others, ten per terzo. This element was expanded yet again on 16 December to twelve per terzo.[63]

The major offices which ranked with the signoria of the Nine (and their predecessors) to comprise the commune's 'orders' (*ordines*) were the four Provveditori of the Biccherna, the four consuls of the Merchant Gild (Mercanzia) and the three consuls of the knights (*milites*). The last of these presents problems of nomenclature in that it possessed an alternative title, the captains of the Guelf Party; even the statute collection of 1309–10 refers to 'the *capitani di parte* or *consoli dei cavalieri*'.[64] The principal *raison d'être* of this office was, or became, the management of the confiscated property of political exiles. In the 1270s this meant management by the Guelf party of Ghibelline property, hence from 1271 until 1279 or later the name of 'captains of the Guelf Party'. The change may well be connected with the terms of the abortive pacification of 1280 which decreed the abolition of the two parties. There may have been a period during which the office was in suspension; if so, it had reappeared by 1284 as *consules militum*, and it normally continued to be known as such thereafter.[65] The usual conciliar function of the *ordini* was to reinforce the permanent councils as representatives of financial interests and expertise. A characteristic role for the council of *ordini* (1279) was to meet at the request of the Podestà, with an additional twelve 'good men' per terzo, and the new body would decide, for example, 'concerning the matter of Torrita and about having a larger corps of soldiers (*masnata*) in the city of Siena'.[66]

61 CG 3, f. 65.
62 CG 12, f. 72.
63 CG 13, ff. 5v–77v.
64 *Cost. 1309–10*, 2, p. 524.
65 Bowsky, *Commune*, pp. 171–2; CG 14, ff. 11v ff. (1271); 23, f. 28 (1279); 29, f. 1(1284). For the 1280 pacification, below, pp. 120–2.
66 CG 23, f. 28.

OFFICE-HOLDERS

If the number of citizens involved in such councils is impressive, so is the number who actually held office. A volume of Biccherna expenditure for the first half of 1282 lists together conveniently the salaries paid to officials of the commune for that period.[67] 'Officials' in this context omits Siena's major office-holders (e.g. the Podestà) and all other external appointments such as judges. Omitted also are soldiers and the night watchmen. These middle ranks of the paid – mainly for tasks which were compatible with other employment – were engaged in a wide variety of duties. Some seventy of them had functions connected with the citizens' obligation to perform military service, the recruitment of mercenaries and other military matters. Rather over twenty had fiscal duties, in the widest sense, including concern with judicial fines and the laws against exporting foodstuffs, and several others performed secretarial or clerical functions. The duties of the remainder defy categorization: five men, at 5s. each for six months, were appointed 'to seek means by which the expenses of the commune may be diminished'; nine, at 10s., were to choose the syndics of the various *contrade*; three, at 5s., were charged with 'making ordinances against the butchers'. Others had to distribute office (*signoria*) in the contado, to make ordinances concerning the guarding of the city, to approve guarantors in the criminal courts. One recipient of a fee (perhaps he should not rank as an official) was paid 20s. because 'he showed an error of 400 l. concerning a condemnation which was to be cancelled, and this sum had been omitted; he wished his name not to be revealed'. In all 235 men were paid salaries (the 20s. reward has been excluded) and between them they received about 400 l. In the following six-month period 229 salaries were paid, or 246 if some border-line payments are included.[68]

The fact that over 200 men were thus involved by employment in middle-ranking jobs is an important feature of the commune. Undoubtedly this helped to tie them in to the system; they were part of the set-up. Yet the duties which appear in these lists are far from exhausting the full role of officials. Many very significant functions that are not included in this salary list were performed by Sienese, including the thirteen 'amenders' of the statutes and those all-purpose denouncers already mentioned who played such a characteristic role in delating on their fellow-citizens.[69] Two men were paid 25s. for six months service in investigating 'thieves and thefts, the cleaning of paved roads, and women spinning in the streets, girls wearing dresses with long trains, people throwing water and filth from balconies into the street, people mourning with loud

67 B 82, ff. 145–50v.
68 B 83, ff. 124–9v.
69 Above, p. 12.

lamentations and rending their clothing after funerals', and many other such tasks.[70] By 1302 no fewer than sixty men were receiving a retaining fee of 5s. as 'secret accusers of people who throw filth in public places and those who wear pearls and superfluous ornaments'.[71]

Valuers for purposes of direct taxation (*allibratores*) naturally required proper recompense both as a reward for expertise and as a precaution against corruption. Sixty *allibratores* for a dazio in 1282 received an interim payment of 225 l. for 2,350 days already worked, at 2s. a day each; further payments were made to them later and to their clerks and assistants (*famuli*).[72] Others had to place a valuation – in case payment of compensation became due – on cavalry horses and those used by the commune for other purposes.[73] The list of men on the commune's pay-roll could be greatly extended if it were to include the ambassadors (discussed later), and hordes of messengers, bailiffs, minor judicial officials, custodians of fountains, night watchmen, bell-ringers, and so on.

FINANCE

To the middle-ranking officials discussed above must be added those involved in the commune's financial and chancery business. The existence of a separate financial office, the Biccherna, has already been indicated, and its methods of work will be discussed later,[74] but its bureaucratic importance needs to be noted here. The principal officers of the Biccherna, the Chamberlain (*camerlengo*) and four *Provveditori* (provisors) were appointed for six-month periods. Under the 1262 statutes the Council appointed the Provveditori but by the early fourteenth century the choice was made by the Nine: all three terzi had to be represented contemporaneously, the fourth post rotating among them. The Chamberlain was chosen by the Provveditori and the Nine. The post was at one stage filled by a layman, but soon after 1282 it became normal for a monk, very frequently from the Cistercian house of San Galgano, to hold it.[75] The Biccherna had its own notary and as the account books were both maintained and copied in duplicate there must have been work for several others as well as minor employees such as messengers. Decentralization of fiscal matters had begun before the end of the thirteenth century with the hiving-off of the Gabella as a separate office, concerned with indirect and other farmed taxes, with its own chamberlain and minor officials.

70 *B.* 9, p. 143.
71 B 116, ff. 383–4.
72 B 83, f. 114 and v.
73 E.g. *B.* 17 (1257), pp. 109, 121, 175.
74 Below, pp. 181–3.
75 'Breve 1250', pp. 16–32; *Const. 1262*, p. 144; *Cost. 1309–10*, 1, pp. 75–7: see Bowsky, *Finance*, pp. 2–9.

Also involved with, but independent of, the Biccherna was the Mint (*Bolgano*), whose premises on the Campo were to form the nucleus of the great Palazzo. This was so clearly a separate entity that it could make loans to the Biccherna.[76] In 1262 there were three 'lords of the Mint', with two money-changers (*campsores*) appointed as technical advisers and a staff of moneyers (*intalliatores et inconiatores*), not to mention periodical *balie* appointed to consider such matters as the weight of the currency. Around the end of the century the three lords (*domini*) were reduced to one, and later control of the Mint seems to have passed to the consuls of the merchant gild, who appointed the *dominus* and *camerlengo*, each for a six-month tenure.[77]

CHANCERY

The letter-writing (chancery) aspect of the commune's work was less fully developed as a separate organization. The 1262 constitution stated that the commune should have a chancellor elected in the Council who was to be assisted by two notaries, each appointed for one year. The chancellor was to keep the commune's seal and to be responsible also for the preservation of its deeds and public records, including the cartulary in which its privileges were copied; this volume was to be kept up to date by appropriate additions. The commune's letters were sealed only on instructions from the Podestà, judges or Captain ('if there is a Captain in the city'). The chancellor held a supply of paper and sealing-wax, but the letters were written out (and promptly!) by the notaries. Responsibility for the wording of correspondence is not clearly assigned. Copies were to be kept of out-letters sent beyond Sienese territory, and a summary or calendar made of all other letters (but these have not survived for the period covered in this book). The chancellor was paid 1s. for each letter drawn up and these chancery fees were used to meet the salary of the chancellor and notaries. What remained after payment of salaries went to the Biccherna. The monthly salary of the chancellor was 8 l. in 1262; his was not considered an exalted post, for his notaries received slightly more (12 l. in 1250, when there had been only one, 10 l. in 1262). Expenses were also provided, but not for the purchase of parchment or paper, since the commune bought these separately. No fee was payable for making copies in the Caleffo, the cartulary of the commune's privileges.[78]

In the heyday of its activities the Popolo had a chancellor of its own, possessor of a seal to be used only when authorized by the Popolo's signet; both signet and seal bore a lion. Most of the archive recorded in the Popolo's inventory of the mid

76 Bowsky, *Finance*, p. 26.
77 'Breve 1250', pp. 78–83; *Const. 1262*, pp. 153–62; *Cost. 1309–10*, 1, p. 276; Bowsky, *Commune*, pp. 225–6.
78 'Breve 1250', pp. 54–7; *Const. 1262*, pp. 120–2.

1250s has vanished.[79] The loss may be due to the decline of the institution itself; but the analogy of the commune suggests that the notion of a chancery, with its own head official, became unpopular, possibly through fears that the chancellor might achieve some independence. Certainly the commune had a chancellor in the 1270s, but later references to a 'dictator of letters' or 'scribe' suggest that the office had withered away, probably in the time of Guelf control and before the regime of the Nine.[80]

The chancery was an archive as well as a letter-writing office. By the 1240s the chancellor had the duty of keeping the commune's archive, with the seal, in a chest in the sacristy of the Dominican church. All officials – there was particular insistence on the Biccherna – had to hand over their records to the chancellor on giving up office. The public deeds were supposed to be read aloud annually to the Podestà and various other officials, though the requirement sounds an unrealistic one even if only the new additions to the commune's book of privileges were meant. More chests were required by 1278, in which year Duccio di Buoninsegna was paid 2 l. for painting twelve chests 'in which are the commune's deeds' (*in quibus stant instrumenta communis*). However, in the year 1288 – which is a likely *terminus ad quem* for the chancery's downgrading – a statute provided for the division of the archive into two parts: the Caleffi (volumes of privileges) and older charters remained at S Domenico, but newly created papers were to go to the Biccherna and the Chamberlain inherited the task of registering the commune's rights and of storing the 'modern records' (as they would now be styled). Officials needing to consult the older records were allowed to withdraw for temporary use the deeds still stored in S Domenico, and occasional notes of such withdrawals have survived. Recourse to the records was a routine matter, as witness the Council's decision (1308) that a committee of six, appointed concerning a dispute with Chiusdino, 'should seek out the rights of the commune of Siena and look at the commune's cartulary and the rights and agreements (*pacta*) that the commune has with the commune and men of Chiusdino'.[81]

THE JUDICIARY

This search into the commune's rights (*iura*) leads on appropriately to consideration of Siena's judicial institutions. Though the topic is vast and cannot

---

79 CG 6, ff. 63v–6 (f. 64v for the chancellor), partly printed by L. Sbaragli in *BSSP*, 44 (1937), p. 48.

80 B 53, f. 6 (1273); CG 64, f. 115v ('scriptas et registratas pro communi Sen' manu ser Sozzi Bondonis dictatoris licterarum . . . communis Sen'': 1304); B 118, f. 308v ('Jacobus not' f. q. Ildibrandini vocatus Muccius olim scriba communis Sen' et . . . Cam' et iiii in Bich': 1306).

81 Good brief treatment in *Archivio di Stato di Siena: Guida-inventario*, 1 (Rome, 1951), pp. iii–viii; G. Cecchini, 'La legislazione archivistica del comune di Siena', *ASI*, a. CXIV (1956), pp. 224–57, prints relevant documents. The most important source is *Const. 1262*, pp. 118–25. See also CG 72, f. 48 (1308).

receive detailed treatment here, the commune's legal system is central to depiction of a culture where law provided the fundamental basis of men's outlook.

The second half of the thirteenth century was a period of rapid growth in the Sienese judicature. In 1250 the Podestà, himself a judge, was assisted by two other judges, one Sienese, the other a 'foreigner'. By 1262 there was no Sienese judge but there were then two 'external' judges, both chosen by three electors selected by lot from the general Council; their pay was 150 l. for one year's tenure, and they could not be from the same city or town as the Podestà. Each was mainly concerned with hearing criminal cases (*super maleficiis*), but a certain division of labour seems to have led to one being also the Podestà's assistant in Council while the other bore responsibility for the preservation of judicial records in the Biccherna. This task and that of receiving fees for exemption from the judicial 'ban' later devolved to a *dominus maleficiorum* who drew a mere 8 l. for his six months' office.[82]

Three judges – all Sienese – heard disputes connected with agricultural crops (*super intesinis*); their meagre earnings were derived from the fee (12d.) paid in respect of cases which came before them.[83] Another specialized court, with a very long history, was that of the Placitum (pleas), no doubt a very busy tribunal bearing in mind the frequency of early death and thus of orphanhood, since it was concerned with wardship: consuls of the Placitum swore that they would come to court 'to give validity to contracts involving minors, to appoint guardians and to do everything concerned with matters pertaining to minors'.[84] There were three of these consuls, one of whom had to be qualified as a judge, and one (a monk) had to act as the court's chamberlain. They had three subordinate judges (*iudices delegati*), each of whom took an oath to hear, settle and give sentence within two months in all cases referred to him by the consuls of the Placitum; they might keep only half of the 'tenth' paid in respect of such cases, the other half going to the commune. At some stage this rather complicated machinery was replaced. The appointment of paid advocates to represent orphans in the Captain's court (1290) suggests change, and by 1309–10 there was simply one judge for cases involving wards, and he was a non-Sienese.[85]

---

82 *Const. 1262*, pp. 89–94, 205–7; 'Breve 1250', pp. 12–16. This reconstruction is conjectural so far as the chronology of the period to 1262 is concerned, since the clauses on pp. 89–94 are undated. An invitation to a judge of Borgo S Sepolcro to serve as judge *super maleficiis* in 1256 is in ASS, Concistoro 1773, n. 17.

83 *Const. 1262*, p. 207.

84 *Il Constituto dei Consoli del Placito*, ed. L. Zdekauer, 1 (Siena, 1890), p. 16. For this institution see also Zdekauer's 'Dissertazione illustrativa' in *SS*, 9 (1892), pp. 35–75, particularly 70–3.

85 B 103, f. 77; *Cost. 1309–10*, 1, pp. 144–5; Bowsky, *Commune*, pp. 107–8.

The Captain of the Popolo, like the Podestà, was judge as well as executive officer. The struggle between the two offices certainly had a judicial aspect, particularly during the 1250s, but this has left few traces in the surviving records. In October 1256 the Council of the Popolo discussed the appointment of a *iudex foretaneus de populo* at a salary of 150 l., and no doubt some hoped that his jurisdiction would expand at the expense of that of the Podestà.[86] Presumably the office of *iudex populi* which makes a number of appearances in the 1262 statutes was the outcome of this debate, but it must have faded away a few years later with the Popolo's own increasing debility, and the successor was undoubtedly the *iudex foretaneus malefitiorum* chosen by the Thirty-six mentioned in the Guelf constitution of 1274.[87] The captaincy of the Popolo also disappeared, but was revived *c.* 1289, and for a time the Captain's court again became an important tribunal, with special competence in civil disturbances.[88] Though experimentation continued, the Podestà's 'foreign' judges remained the backbone of Siena's judicial system. Their quality was crucial, so much so that in 1302 200 l. was promised to the Podestà in addition to his salary of 3,200 l. 'in order that he should bring good judges with him' (*a cio che menasse buoni giudici*).[89] At the time of the 1309–10 constitution the judicial body numbered nine: two collateral judges, two judges for criminal cases, two civil judges and two assessors, and a judge for the Placitum (wardship).[90] Probably this was the result of recent adjustments, for fragmentary survivals of judicial records for a decade earlier suggest that each terzo then had its own judge *super maleficiis*.[91]

The commune was prepared to pay heavily to hire an external judiciary in order to avoid the perils of native judges subject to prejudices and pressure or suspicion thereof. Sienese lawyers must have been involved in pleading, but anti-magnate legislation made it illegal for *grandi* or members of *casato* families to act as advocates in the commune's court.[92] Justice provided much work for the city's notaries, though only a fraction now remains of the vast mass of *paperasserie* once generated. Five volumes survive of the records of the Podestà's court for the year 1298,[93] in which is recorded, with full judicial eloquence, every detail of the evidence given by each of the numerous witnesses in an imposing quantity of criminal cases, many of them minor ones.

86 CG 6, f. 51.
87 CG 10, f. 8v (1262); *Const. 1262*, pp. 60, 64, 72n, 90n, 93; *BSSP*, 46 (1939), pp. 24–5.
88 Bowsky, *Commune*, pp. 36–9. Surviving material for this period includes Capitano, nn. 3 (petitions, 1290) and 4 (fragment of proceedings, 1302).
89 B 116, f. 338v.
90 *Cost. 1309–10*, 1, pp. 142–6; 2, pp. 461–2; Bowsky, *Commune*, pp. 107–10.
91 Podestà 6, f. 1.
92 *Cost. 1309–10*, 2, p. 388; Bowsky, *Commune*, p. 110.
93 Podestà, 5–9.

Much legislation was devoted to the sittings of the courts. The presence of the Podestà and his *collaterali* was compulsory, as were daily sessions of the criminal courts. The main periods of vacation were determined by agricultural routine and ran from 24 June (Feast of St John the Baptist) to 1 August (for the grain harvest), and then from 14 September (Exaltation of the Holy Cross) to mid October (for the grape harvest), and the summer term itself was broken by a week's vacation in the period before the Feast of the Assumption (15 August).[94] A military campaign might also lead to a closure of the courts, as could a political crisis, each of which would demand the Podestà's attention. On 12 June 1304, for instance, the Council decided to begin the legal vacation sooner than normal because the situation in Tuscany was so serious that it would probably be necessary to suspend all hearing of civil cases until August.[95]

The courts gave rise to revenues apart from the fines levied and 'compositions' agreed. In certain civil cases, including appellate hearings and some wardship suits, a fee was payable based on the sums involved in the dispute, the full rate of payment being a tenth (*decima*).[96] In part the fines were funnelled off to provide the pay of minor court officials. In the period under consideration they were normally a useful rather than a major contribution to communal finances. At times, however, taking special measures, justice could be made an important source of revenue. The amnesties of 1302, 1303 and 1307 were attempts to regularize the position of large numbers of *banniti* (outlaws) by offering them *rebannimentum* at bargain prices; the proportion of the original fine for which pardons could be purchased was usually around 25 per cent but at times was as low as 10 per cent.[97] The 1302 amnesty was particularly productive and yielded more than 30,000 l. to the Biccherna. However, the frequency with which these offers were made inevitably led to diminishing returns, and must have diminished also the credibility of all fines at the time of their initial levy. There was also a tendency for the most productive fines to be dependent on political and social circumstances. In 1310 10,000 l. was extracted from the Tolomei and Salimbeni for 'illegal assembly',[98] but such levies amounted to a form of pressure on the wealthy which a regime could only maintain intermittently.

THE LAW

Turning from judges and courts to the laws they administered in these courts, the themes of this book will be most clearly illuminated by concentrating on attitudes

---

94 *Cost. 1309–10*, 1, p. 383.
95 CG 64, ff. 207–220v.
96 *Const. 1262*, pp. 256–7; v. Bowsky, *Finance*, p. 49.
97 Pazzaglini, pp. 87–90, 158–69; Bowsky, *Finance*, p. 52; B 117, ff. 53–389.
98 Bowsky, *Finance*, p. 50.

to crime and punishment and those problems with which the criminal law was principally concerned. Hence the criminal and penal code will be the main topics treated and little will be said at this point about commercial law, family law, sumptuary statutes or those parts of the code which dealt with the commune's institutions.

The fifth book, or Distinctio, of the Sienese statutes, the one concerned with the punishment of crime, deals first with the carrying of arms and will serve as an introduction to what follows. Bearing offensive weapons was punishable with a fine of 10 l. in 1262, which by 1309–10 had risen to 25 l. The equivalent fines for defensive weapons, i.e. armour, were 5 l. and 10 l. Various types of offensive weapon were specified, mainly forms of knife, sword and iron club, and a rather surprising example of versatility is suggested by the inclusion among them of *beccacenerem* (shovel for ashes). A suspicious but probably realistic provision made the penalty for having an empty quiver the same as that for a quiver containing a knife.[99]

The penalties for violent acts are perhaps best considered under five headings. First – to begin with the mildest – came various forms of threat not extending to actual physical violence, such as threatening with or without a metal weapon, chasing, insulting and holding by the garments; the fine for these varied between 10 l. and 25 l. in 1262, but by 1309–10 the penalties could be a great deal higher, the top end of the scale for giving chase, for example, having risen to 100 l. The next point in the scale covered such offences as pushing, tearing clothing or injuriously entering a house; for the first of these the minimum penalty in 1262 was 10 l. and the maximum 25 l. (rising later to 50 l. and 100 l. respectively), that for the second and third offences being 25 l. in 1262 (but not specified in 1309).[100] The third category includes various forms of 'striking' – 'with a knife or sword', 'with a stone', 'on the head', 'without spilling of blood' etc. In 1262 the penalties varied considerably, from 25 l. as a minimum for striking on the head to 200 l. as a maximum for assault with sword or knife. This maximum rose to 400 l. in 1297[101] and to 800 l. in 1309. The fourth degree, the infliction of grievous bodily harm – serious wounds such as blinding or severing a tongue, nose or limb – involved a fine of 400 l. in 1262 which rose to a minimum of 500 l. and maximum of 1,500 l. by 1309.

Homicide – the fifth category – was normally punishable with the death penalty. There were very few circumstances in which this was not automatic; they included accidental killing (during jousting, for example) and killing by a

---

99 This paragraph and the next three are based on *Const. 1262. Cont.*, *BSSP*, 1, pp. 141–2 and *Cost. 1309–10*, 2, pp. 332–44.
100 In 1262 (not specified in the 1309–10 code).
101 *BSSP*, 7 (1900), p. 245.

minor. By 1309–10 the list of exceptions had extended to include homicide committed in the course of a violent affray or riot (*meschia*), for which the penalty was a fine of 3,000 l. This change could be interpreted as a move towards milder treatment of those drawn by circumstances into unpremeditated homicide, but it may also indicate that the frequency of rioting had brought these judicially difficult cases to the attention of Siena's legislators.

Physical violence and the use of weapons were such normal eventualities that it seemed appropriate to begin this section with them, but the expression of hatred did not always take that form. Clause 203 of the fifth Distinctio in the 1262 code illustrates well some of the gentler modes: '*Item*, if a resident of Siena, or outsider, places or causes to be placed, or throws, before the door or house of any resident, by night, any of the following: bones, horns, animal flesh or anything else dirty, filthy or unpleasant, or any writing containing something dishonourable or insulting – let him be punished to the sum of 100 l.'[102] The reference to written insults is a tribute to the literacy of the thirteenth-century Sienese, whilst the entire clause also reflects the difficulty of enforcing the curfew (which should perhaps be bracketed with the prohibition of arms as the two major general measures against violence).

Such measures were precautions not merely against a normal and accepted violence of manners in people – particularly males – prone to lose their tempers rapidly and resort to physical expression. They were connected with an all-important social institution, the vendetta or family feud. It was laid down that anyone known to have 'capital enmities' might expect to be granted permission to carry defensive weapons, though they would have to obtain a licence for this from the Podestà and Captain.[103] A 'capital enmity' did not necessarily imply that the vendetta had already occasioned a murder; wounding would qualify in this context. But the vendetta was seen as a particular menace to the peace, a view reflected in an early statute (1238) which ordained perpetual banishment and the confiscation of all property as the punishment for those contravening the terms of a formal peace made in settlement of homicide or wounding. The judicial viewpoint on the vendetta is stated in a clause proclaiming that 'if any Sienese takes revenge (*fecerit vindictam*) on another Sienese for an offence committed by someone other than that person, he is to suffer punishment triple that laid down by statute for the offence'.[104]

The vendetta leads us into the territory of political violence. The law dealing with the difficult judicial borderline of homicide committed in the course of a riot

---

102 *Const. 1262. Cont.*, BSSP, 2 (1896), pp. 82–3.
103 Ibid., p. 81.
104 Ibid., pp. 89, 147; *Cost. 1309–10*, 2, pp. 253–4.

had political implications.[105] Clauses on 'bringing about a gathering' (*si quis concitaverit populum Senensem, vel fecerit aliquam coadunantiam populi*), or raising a riot (*chi concitasse el popolo a romore*) by shouting 'A l'arme a l'arme', which led in turn to others about joining in fighting and battles, were clearly dealing with political factionalism.[106] The section of the 1262 constitution concerned with acts of violence provides four different scales of penalty. The full fine is payable when the person attacked is a Sienese citizen residing in the city, but various combinations are set out which involve lower penalties. For instance, a half-rate applies when the victim, though a citizen, is not normally resident (even if the offender is a resident citizen) and a resident citizen who offends against an 'outsider' residing in the contado (*foretaneus de comitatu vel districtu*) pays only one quarter of the normal fine.[107] The status of the victim is not the sole criterion, however. These clauses would seem to imply that a citizen automatically ranked higher than a non-citizen in the eyes of the law, but in fact what is crucial to the underlying philosophy is the view that the commune was less menaced when violence did not involve people living close to each other within Siena. Such crimes were at least not episodes in a Sienese family vendetta. Hence offences involving non-residents were felt to require lesser punishment. The adoption of these criteria incidentally confirms the basic judicial treatment of violence in the statutes as a breach of the peace rather than an offence against a person.

Naturally theft plays a considerable part in the Sienese codes, even though its role may seem less prominent than that of violence. Certain clauses dealing with theft confirm the importance to the Sienese of horticulture and agriculture. Entering the vineyard, orchard, vegetable garden or irrigated plot of a citizen was punishable with a stiff fine of 3 l. 2s., one-third of which was retained by specially appointed guards whose sphere of duty extended to the area within two miles of the city. Inside the city each terzo had four 'spies against thieves', a 'neighbour-hood watch' with a vengeance, for these men received no pay other than a half share of the fines levied on the thieves whose capture they had ensured. Their responsibility extended to 'any damage to the plots, vineyards, orchards and other property' of the citizens. Stealing domestic doves and birds used in hunting (falcons etc.) was another crime (2 l.). By 1309–10 the scale of penalties for damage to vineyards and orchards had been fixed at 3 l. (entry), 10 l. (damage by day) and 25 l. (damage by night).[108]

The statutes do not themselves offer a full picture of the procedure followed in the Sienese courts, which in general terms was based on that of the Roman law.

105 Above, p. 66.
106 *Const. 1262, Cont., BSSP*, 1, p. 143; *Cost. 1309–10*, 2, pp. 237–8.
107 *Const. 1262, Cont., BSSP*, 3, pp. 84–5.
108 Ibid., 1, pp. 271–3; 3, p. 84; *Cost. 1309–10*, 2, pp. 345–6.

The judges *super maleficiis* were not judges in the full sense, since they did not pronounce verdicts but were, technically at least, advisers to the Podestà. Much of the hearings fell to them, but the verdict could only be formulated by the Podestà himself.[109] The administration of torture must have been common, but a formula was provided for the circumstances which justified it. Either the accused had to be 'of ill fame' or the case against him a strong one (*probabilis suspicionis*), or he had to be a 'public thief or forger', or the accusation had to be one involving false witness, the forgery of deeds, or treason. In the 1309–10 code it was laid down that torture might be applied in investigation of certain accusations, but only if there were at least five witnesses against the accused. An additional clause specified that the Podestà and judges should use moderation (*abiano temperanza*) in the use of torture.[110]

Although the gallows figure prominently in Lorenzetti's depiction of good government in the countryside, as well as in the statutes, the law of Siena did not readily condemn to death. Capital punishment was the normal penalty for murder (but not that of a *forestiere*), for certain forms of forgery and for arson. In these cases death was inflicted by burning. A woman found guilty of poisoning wells was flayed alive and then burnt. Mutilation also was inflicted, amputation of a hand or foot being a punishment for certain forms of civil warfare, and anyone who had undergone judicial mutilation was compelled to quit the city if he was not a citizen. A rash jester who made certain accusations (of parricide, for example) could lose his tongue, and a man's eye might be put out. Sodomy was punishable by a fine of 300 l., but if this was not paid within a month the offender was to be hung up 'by his masculine members' in the market-place. Banishment and confiscation of property have been mentioned above as penalties; a more surprising one was the subsidiary punishment inflicted on forgers – as well as being executed they were portrayed, by way of warning, in the Palazzo del Comune.[111]

Imprisonment had great disadvantages as a form of punishment; to keep people confined and fed was an expensive matter. Pardons to prisoners were a routine accompaniment of the religious festivals.[112] This was not exactly making a virtue of necessity, but there were occasions when starving prisoners had to be sent round the city to beg for food. Moreover those in gaol had to be housed in the

---

109 R. Celli, *Studi sui sistemi normativi delle democrazie comunali*, 1 (Florence, 1976), p. 313n. For these judges, see above, p. 63.
110 *Const. 1262, Cont., BSSP*, 1, p. 144; *Cost. 1309–10*, 2, pp. 276–7 (see also pp. 337, 403–4).
111 *Cost. 1309–10*, 2, pp. 271–2, 336–7, 354–5, 357. The death penalty could be applied for treason, but only in certain circumstances (2, p. 331): see also above, pp. 65–6. For the other punishments cited see B 35, f. 25 (1262).
112 E.g. CG 22, f. 64 (many other instances could be given): see also Pazzaglini, pp. 92–3.

style to which they were accustomed. No doubt conditions for the ordinary criminal were grim, but *grandi* and other 'good men' had a special place of detention so that they should not be compelled to mingle with 'thieves and those condemned for crime'. These privileged prisoners were permitted only one servant (for a group) and each of them was restricted to three guests for meals and overnight stays.[113] Since it was much more satisfactory to receive a fine than to receive a prisoner, the commune's preference was for the former, and imprisonment was not the punishment prescribed automatically for any type of offence, Prisoners, in the main, must have consisted of those who had been sentenced to pay fines but were unable to raise the money.

Those guilty of violence or theft, if they came to trial and were convicted, paid if they could and went to gaol if they could not, but there were many who fled rather than face a court. Contumacy (failure to appear at the trial) was treated as a confession of guilt and was punishable by outlawry, the *bannum*.[114] Although banishment could be applied in the case of a man who failed to pay his fine, its most normal use was as a response to contumacy. In these circumstances the *bannitus* was faced with a dilemma: his initial ban was a provisional one, and if he decided within a few days to come to trial, he was in time to escape the formal ban. If however he allowed the period proclaimed in his initial summons to pass and then let the provisional be followed by the formal ban (the interval between the two being eight days, till the late thirteenth century, and thereafter only three), he had opted for contumacy and flight.

The outlawry, which deprived the person condemned to a total loss of judicial rights and exposed him to the possibility of capture by all residents of Siena and its subject territory, comprised also a fine roughly equal to that which would have been imposed if he had gone to court and been found guilty. The proclamation of the ban by the commune's uniformed criers (*banditores*) from horseback was a common Sienese spectacle. An investigator has calculated that on average nearly 100 men were outlawed each month in the summer of 1256, over 100 in May 1258 and 180 in March 1259. These figures related to the initial, or provisional, ban, and in only about half these instances was this followed by the full formal ban; nevertheless the numbers are impressive. The ban was 'a guarantee of some form of punishment', even for the contumacious, but above all it was a means of driving those guilty of violence and theft from the city and its immediate environs. The law, it has been well said, 'did not worry about where the *bannitus* went; it concentrated more on getting him out of the community or forcing his return to court'. It must have served to reinforce many a robber band and

---

113 *Cost. 1309–10*, 1, pp. 92–3.
114 Pazzaglini; *Const. 1262, Cont., BSSP*, 1, p. 279.

mercenary company. If some outlaws frequented the more remote parts of Siena's own contado, others went further afield. In the 1290s four brothers, the sons of Cione Picchiati, fled and were placed under the ban after one of them had killed the murderer of his father. They settled some hundred kilometres to the south, in Viterbo, and rose to considerable prosperity as merchants.[115]

If banishment was a common institution, so too was purchase of the lifting of outlawry. Some 6,000 instances of *rebannimentum* are recorded for the years 1243–56 alone and this was a frequent and considerable source of revenue. Late payment of fines carried a fixed penalty of an additional one-third, but purchase of *rebannimentum* involved agreement on a sum as 'composition' for the condemnation 'in property and person'. Special offers of amnesty to *banniti* at reduced rates became common in the first decade of the fourteenth century. The terms offered (which in some cases were only available if the *bannitus* had reached a formal pacification with the injured party or his heirs) were composition payments of such amounts as 2,000 l. or 500 l. in the case of citizens, while contado inhabitants paid half these sums. In effect these were sales of pardons at anything from 25 per cent to 10 per cent of the original fine. They yielded very well, the amnesty of 1302, for example, bringing in more than 30,000 l.[116]

A renaissance in legal study and Roman-inspired law had been taking place in Italy since the beginning of the twelfth century. To what extent is this movement reflected in the outlook implicit in the Sienese constitutions? Certainly they embody many notions and practices surviving from the earlier medieval centuries. One instance is the role of the judicial duel. Two forms of duel were provided for, that between accuser and accused and that in which proof was sought by a duel between the accused and the commune's representative in combat, the champion. In the case of an accusation of dishonest use of a company's funds, settlement could be achieved by battle between accuser and accused or by champions on their behalf; victory by the former was treated as confession of guilt, by the latter as a decision for absolution. Some nocturnal offences such as murder of a Sienese citizen, or arson, could also involve proof by duel between the commune's champion and the accused ('and if he loses the duel, let him suffer punishment'). In certain other cases an individual on whom local repute laid blame could attempt disculpation by battle against the commune's champion. These eventualities were probably uncommon, but in 1248 the champion received payment for this service in a combat, and a few years later a judge sought

---

115 Pazzaglini, especially pp. 99–109; Waley, 'A blood-feud with a happy ending: Siena, 1285–1304' in T. Dean and C. Wickham (eds.), *City and Countryside in Late Medieval and Renaissance Italy* (London, 1990), pp. 45–53.
116 Pazzaglini, pp. 72–98; Bowsky, *Finance*, p. 52; B 117, ff. 53–289.

advice about his own presence at a judicial duel.[117] The institution of proof by ordeal had not totally disappeared from contemporary Tuscany but is not found in these Sienese codes.

More rational forms of investigating truth included the swearing of oaths and the provision of oath-helpers (*fideiussores*) and guarantors. The latter were so much a central feature of life that each terzo had to maintain a list of 500 men eligible to serve as legal guarantors.[118] The concept of reputation or 'good fame' also had a considerable part to play. The *famoso ladrone* (notorious thief) could not expect the same treatment as the man who enjoyed good fame, and many accusations – of 'secret' murder, for instance – called for investigation into reputation.[119] The guarantors of Sienese law may appear to be connected with the 'kin', but the distinction is an all-important one. Indeed, the role of kinship in the Sienese codes is a useful touchstone for the persistence of barbarian elements in the laws and the society for which they were designed; the statutes relating to the blood feud certainly show such a survival. Nevertheless, despite special provisions for the joint ownership implied by *consorzerie* and for such matters as paternal discipline,[120] the general emphasis of the Sienese laws is on the individual rather than the kin group.

The status of those involved – particularly the victim – as a determinant of the penalty is another indication of barbarian, as opposed to Roman, jurisprudence. The fine for using 'injurious words' depended on both the words and *la qualità de le persone*, while the different scales for violent crime have already been mentioned in connection with the commune's greater interest in the regular resident.[121] Yet the penalties for violent acts depended primarily on the severity of the injury inflicted or the degree of violence used; they were not linked with the social rank of the victim. The anti-magnate legislation in Siena, as elsewhere in Italy, provided for higher penalties against the socially prosperous, so the judicial scales were weighted against the mighty, not against those who offended them. By such tests the Sienese statutes emerge as fundamentally Romanist.

There is still an element of paradox in the situation of Siena's Podestà and judges, men trained in the Roman law, administering a code which made provision for the blood-feud and put some trust in trial by combat. In particular it seems ironical that a suit involving malversation of a bank's funds could be settled by a duel;[122] here one is at the point of intersection of two very contrasted worlds.

---

117 *Const. 1262*, pp. 227, 232, 234; *Cont., BSSP*, 1, p. 144 and 2, p. 322; *Cost. 1309–10*, 1, p. 443; 2, pp. 337, 552; *B*. 8, pp. 94–5; CG 6, f. 52.
118 *Cost. 1309–10*, 2, p. 457.
119 Above, p. 168; *Const. 1262, Cont., BSSP*, 1, pp. 144–5.
120 Ibid., *BSSP*, 3, p. 90 (= *Cost. 1309–10*, 2, p. 387).
121 *Cost. 1309–10*, 2, p. 350; above, p. 67.
122 Above, p. 70.

Proceedings in Sienese courts were naturally conducted in the vernacular, yet the voluminous paper-work involved, including the full recording of the evidence, was carried out in Latin.[123] Despite talk among legists of a 'common law', the fundamental feature of the situation was that each commune legislated indefatigably, seeking to provide itself all the answers for its own city.[124] Such independence was a natural expression of Siena's political status.

The main impression left by this review of the commune's institutions should surely be of the great volume of work transacted by Siena's citizens and the time dedicated by them to civic affairs of every variety. Their involvement in office and in conciliar meetings, great and small, offered them wide experience in many fields, financial, military, diplomatic and others, while they also received a training in the arts of verbal persuasion, the drafting of legislation and administration. Siena's policies were the outcome of their decisions and must have been the subject of their earnest thoughts and discussions outside the council-chamber as well as within it. Siena made them (as Dante said of one of the Tolomei) but they were conscious too that they made Siena.[125] With that in mind, it is worth turning briefly to the conditions governing citizenship and to the survival of the notion of the full gathering of citizens, the parliament.

EXCURSUS 1   CITIZENSHIP

The status of being a Sienese citizen has been mentioned more than once in the preceding pages. It might be expected that citizenship, with its implied civic rights and obligations, was of paramount importance to a resident. In reality, however, the question of citizenship arose quite rarely and its achievement was less significant than might be supposed. The topic is a complicated one and what follows is an attempt to treat it in brief outline.[126]

The payment made to become a citizen was itself too small to suggest a coveted and all-important change of status: it was 5s. until after the middle of the thirteenth century, then 20s., and from 1295 5 l. There were men who settled in the city and pursued their affairs in comfort without taking up citizenship. This was the experience of the Florentine Tano degli Infangati, a cloth merchant who lived at Siena and paid his taxes there for more than a decade before he decided to petition for citizenship, apparently because this was a necessity for joining the

---

123 Podestà 7 (1298), f. 1; Capitano 4 (1302).
124 Mondolfo, 'La legislazione statutaria senese dal 1262 al 1310', *SS*, 21 (1904), pp. 230–56; Celli, (n. 109 above), pp. 263–346.
125 *Purgatorio*, V, 134 ('Siena mi fe'').
126 The subject has been treated more fully in D. Bizzarri, 'Ricerche sul diritto di cittadinanza nella costituzione comunale', *SS*, 32 (1916), pp. 19–136 (a rather legalistic approach) and Bowsky, 'Medieval citizenship . . .', *Studies in Medieval and Renaissance History*, 4 (1967), pp. 195–243.

clothiers' gild. At some stage (the date is unclear) ten years residence in the city as a 'continual citizen' became a required qualification for membership of councils and tenure of office.[127]

The number of new citizens varied greatly from year to year. A document of the 1250s gives a list, which may not be complete, of about 150 men admitted as citizens in the years 1219–50. In the first half of 1251 more than 300 new citizens were created, but this was totally exceptional; quite often the number of new admissions in a half-year was below ten.[128]

Becoming a citizen was a different matter for one who was already a resident of the Sienese contado. These were a great majority among the new citizens and require treatment separately from the 'outsiders'. Clauses in the 1262 constitution made it clear that the commune's policy was to encourage *comitatenses* to immigrate to the city and become citizens, though there were safeguards for the interests of lords in the contado, many of whom were themselves citizens. Occasionally men were offered persuasion in the form of grants of fiscal exemption for a term of years, but it was normal for this privilege to be reserved for outsiders.[129] Indeed the payment of direct taxes to the commune was usually a *sine qua non* for the achievement of citizenship; it was vital to ensure that nobody escaped the tax-man by removing himself from rural fiscal lists without taking a place in urban ones.[130]

His oath bound a new citizen to a minimum of four months' residence in each year and he had to have a house in the city or *burgi*, though this might be rented. If a man paid his direct taxes and kept the terms of the oath he had the right to be 'defended as a citizen'. This status might assist him in his authority over his men (i.e. those of servile rank) if he was himself a lord in the contado and certainly aided him in securing repayment of debts.[131] But the gain was not absolutely clear-cut – citizenship was a recognition of standing and of duties performed rather than a promotion to privilege – as is revealed by a clause in the 1309–10 constitution which provided for the case of those whose fathers had been citizens and who themselves paid taxes yet alleged that they were not citizens.[132]

'Whoever comes to the city of Siena from beyond its contado and wishes to be a citizen and to live there continuously (*assiduamente*) like the other citizens, the

127 CG 68, ff. 156 and v; *Cost. 1309–10*, 1, p. 192.
128 Lira 1; *B*.11, pp. 4–27; 17, pp. 12–15, 29; 79, ff. 1–3v; 80, f. 29v.
129 *Const. 1262*, pp. 416–19; for fiscal exemption in 1260 see Lira 5, ff. 229, 230, 231v, 239, 263v (the names of the exempt do not suggest that they were all outsiders).
130 Bowsky, 'Medieval citizenship', pp. 210–12.
131 *Const. 1262*, pp. 409–10, 416–17; *Cost. 1309–10*, 2, pp. 169–70; *Il Constituto dei Consoli del Placito*, p. 37.
132 *Cost. 1309–10*, 1, pp. 393–4.

Podestà is to receive him as a citizen and defend him in his rights', proclaimed a law of 1292. Such migration was to be encouraged and the Sienese were forbidden to behave in an unfriendly manner towards the newcomer; he was not to be denied fire or water and the neighbours were not to greet him with silence.[133] This sort of citizen was making a more thorough change than the *comitatensis* and the accompaniments of his new status were different. The cases of two petitioners in 1292 illustrate the situation of a 'foreigner' seeking to achieve Sienese citizenship. Both had already served at Siena as judges. Conrad of Stradella was offered a ten-year tax exemption and eligibility for office as though he were one of the 'ancient and native-born citizens' (*antiqui et naturales cives*). Porrina, whose place of origin is not stated, explained that he intended 'to acquire most beautiful and agreeable (*pulcerimas et amenas*) possessions' in the city and contado and wished to spend large sums of money on their acquisition. The council voted in favour of his citizenship by 132 votes to 27, though three of the four speeches made opposed (unsuccessfully) the grant in his case of the full tax privileges received four months earlier by Conrad.[134] An earlier statute had granted such citizens exemption from direct taxation for a period as long as fifteen years, but specified that there could be no exemption from military service.[135] These outsiders had to acquire a house, but their fiscal advantages were such that they had undergone a very different sort of metamorphosis from the men moving in from the Sienese countryside.

EXCURSUS 2   PARLIAMENT

In the earliest stages of development of the Italian communes the 'parliament' or *arenga* of all the citizens had been the ultimate constitutional authority whenever a notional general consent was requisite. As councils took over its role this institution tended to wither away. However the word *parlamentum* was still used in Sienese documents of the second half of the thirteenth century and it is difficult to decide what sense it then bore and to what extent it continued to correspond to constitutional and institutional realities.

'Parliament' means, literally, 'talking', and its use was not necessarily a strictly technical one. It is to be found in the 1262 constitution in the general sense of 'a meeting', the usual context being a reference to a 'parliament or council' (*parlamentum vel consilium*).[136] The word was also connected with a more juridical

---

133 Ibid., 2, p. 177.
134 CG 43, ff. 77v–8; 44, ff. 148–9v.
135 *Const. 1262*, p. 423.
136 *Const. 1262*, pp. 28 ('cum fit contio sive parlamentum, gentes possint sedere et morari super ipsis gradibus'), 76 ('aliquod parlamentum seu contionem'), 77, 78, 91, 113, 118, 120, 141, 188; for similar use, CG 5, f. 96v (1255).

notion in that it could refer to an occasion on which formal publicity was given to an event or decision. In the first half of the thirteenth century it was commonly applied to occasions such as the choice of a Podestà or the reception of a new one, a proclamation of outlawry (*bannum*) or its revocation, the proclamation of a military campaign and the issue of banners and ordinances for the army, and the swearing of an important oath.[137]

The concept of a publicity-giving parliament survived, though the occasions themselves probably became rarer.[138] A characteristic use was to emphasize Sienese overlordship in the contado. Thus Count Guglielmo Aldobrandeschi took an oath to the commune in 1227 *in parlamento*, representatives of Montalcino and S Angelo in Colle were called *ad parlamentum* as were the Ardengheschi counts (1231), and knights were summoned from the contado in connection with the choice of a Podestà (*ad parlamentum fiendum pro potestate futura*).[139] The terms of the oath sworn by contado communes included the obligation of parliament (*facere parlamentum*, the equivalent of the feudal duty of giving counsel). Monte-pulciano's submission of 1261 incorporated a promise to send two representatives to Siena annually 'when the Sienese commune has a parliament' (*faciet parlamen-tum*), repeated in similar terms in the re-submission of 1294.[140]

References to 'the January parliament' in the 1262 code imply the continuation of a regular annual meeting, perhaps that at which the new Podestà formally took office. In 1273 a Council meeting agreed – noting that a two-thirds majority was needed for the decision – that a *parlamentum* should be called to give formal consent to Siena's acceptance of the pope's terms. Thus the interdict and excommunication came to an end and the commune returned to obedience in a public occasion of particular solemnity.[141] In the 1309–10 constitution the statute which forbade the Podestà to summon a parliament without the consent of a two-thirds majority in Council remained, as did a ruling that the statutes of Campagnatico could not be altered by any Sienese Council, 'nor even by the entire parliament (*tutto el parlamento*) of the city'.[142] By 1337, however, a *parlamentum* was merely a useful descriptive word for a forbidden gathering of armed men.[143]

137 B. 1, pp. 50, 58, 88, 89; 4, p. 122.
138 B. 15, p. 160 (outlawry, 1254); 28, f. 160 (new Podestà, 1258); 82, f. 148v (military ordinances, 1282), all in 'parliaments'.
139 B. 1, p. 40; 3, p. 341; 4, pp. 99, 150.
140 CV, 2, pp. 852–6 (n. 629); 3, p. 1388 (n. 992).
141 CG 17, f. 9v.
142 *Cost. 1309–10*, 1 pp. 172–3, 300–1. Elsewhere in this code (1, pp. 142, 151, 548; 2, pp. 325,361) this word is used as synonym for 'council'.
143 Rubric of clause in 1337 statutes (Statuti, n. 26) printed in Ciampoli, p. 65.

The Sienese parliament, then, was an occasion rather than an institution. It was not just another council meeting, the difference being most marked on those occasions when subjects and representatives of subject communities were present. It is not clear whether such gatherings ever involved the presence of non-conciliar elements from Siena itself in an approbatory role.

4 *Oligarchy*

Discussion of institutions on their own is somewhat barren and must be vitalized by consideration of those who exercised power through them. The question to be asked concerning a city-republic is not 'was it controlled by an oligarchy?' but 'what sort of oligarchy or oligarchies controlled it?'. Hence the need to investigate the social status of the principal office-holders and conciliar speakers and the degree of continuity: did political developments or the passage of time bring about significant changes in the personnel of the governing class, or did this class show strong powers of survival?

THE GREAT FAMILIES

The starting-point must be those dynasties of landowner-financiers characteristic of medieval Siena, for names such as Tolomei, Piccolomini, Salimbeni, Gallerani and Malavolti appear constantly as holders of prominent positions and conciliar orators. A tendency towards a more formal classification in the upper levels of Sienese society is implied by the increasing use of family names – the advent of the surname – after the middle of the thirteenth century; up to that time the use of a patronymic had normally sufficed. This development was almost certainly intensified by the 'anti-magnate' laws of 1277, in which fifty-three families were named as *casati*, whose members had to deposit a payment as pledge for good behaviour and were ineligible for the main office, then the Thirty-six.[1] Though the families declared magnates in 1277 are not identical with those which acquired surnames, it was uncommon for a dynasty not in the 1277 list to gain the additional 'de' with the plural (surname) form.

In the surviving list of 1260 tax payments[2] (which relate to the terzo of Camollia only) no payer is styled as 'de' in the surname form, but residents in the Malavolti *castellare* are styled 'de fundaco Malevoltorum' ('fundacus' or warehouse being another word for block or castle), so a collective word in the plural was already being applied to this family. A papal letter of 1263, probably based on the phrasing of a Sienese petition, applies a surname to one 'de Tholomeis'. The text of the 1280 collective peaces rarely employs surnames, but 'de Salvanis' and

---

1 For a fuller discussion below, pp. 102–3.
2 Lira 5 (there are of course instances of a territorial origin being indicated).

'de Ponzis' are to be found.[3] The record of 1285 tax payments strongly suggests that the use of surnames was on the increase in the years after the issue of a list of magnate families. In these records several men are styled 'de Talomeis', two are 'de Forteguerris', others 'de Galleranis', 'de Russis' and 'de Selviolensibus'.[4]

By the early fourteenth century the usage had become common. The minutes of the Consiglio Generale are preceded – at the start of each volume – by lists of councillors and those given permission to hold office, usually as Podestà, in other communes. Naturally these constitute lists of members of prominent families. By 1305–08[5] members of nineteen families figure in the dative plural (i.e. surname) form, fifteen of these being among the *casati* of 1277. There must be an arbitrary element in the notarial use of surnames as opposed to patronymics; it must, for example, be fortuitous that a Gallerani is 'de Galleranis' in 1285 whilst another is denied this form in 1305, as are some (but not all) Tolomei, Salimbeni, Piccolomini and Malavolti. All the same the half-century after 1260 shows a marked move in the direction of a clear-cut social differentiation in nomenclature.[6]

At this point it may be useful to list the nineteen families given surnames in the 1305–08 lists:

Table 5. *1305–08 family names*

Casati (in 1277 law)

de Accarisiis
de Bonsignoribus
de Forteguerris
de Maconibus
de Malavoltis
de Mingnanellis
de Piccolominis
de Ponzis
de Renaldinis
de Russis
de Salimbenis
de Saracenis
de Scottis
de Tolomeis
de Urogeriis

Non-magnate

de Balzis
de Mazzis
de Squarcialupis
de Ughettis

The fifteen families in the first of these lists may be described (with the addition of the Gallerani) as 'super-magnates', those who belong most clearly in this category being the greatest landowning bankers, Salimbeni, Tolomei, Piccolomini, Bonsignori, Gallerani, Malavolti. The political predominance of this very small group of wealthy families is indeed the special feature of Sienese oligarchy, though the Bonsignori, who were less numerous, provided fewer prominent figures in the thirteenth century than the Tolomei and Malavolti.

Each of these dynasties requires separate consideration. Of the Tolomei, those particularly conspicuous in the political arena were Scozia and Federigo di Rinaldo, Deo di Lotterengo and Tavena di Deo. Scozia was the most frequent speaker in Council meetings in 1270, very prominent in all discussions of both internal and external matters in the following years, in fact almost certainly the most influential individual in the city throughout this decade of plutocratic Guelf regime. His role as councillor, orator, ambassador, financial expert and office-holder perhaps diminished briefly around 1280, after he had acted as Siena's Podestà at Massa. This apparent eclipse may have been due to involvement in the family disputes which were the subject of formal pacification in 1280; Scozia was one of the sixty-two Tolomei concerned in the great 'peace' of that year. By the mid 1280s he had regained all his former prominence and he held office and spoke in Council frequently in the following years. He was entrusted with a lengthy embassy to various Tuscan cities in 1286. In 1295 he was still a frequent orator, but he probably died soon after that year. He had owed cavalry service of five horses (1263) and his tax assessment in 1285 also suggests very comfortable financial standing, though not necessarily extreme wealth.[7]

Federigo di Rinaldo Tolomei was a young brother (or, just possibly, cousin) of Scozia. He held important financial offices, as Camerlengo in 1271 and Provveditore on seven occasions between 1272 and 1288. The most active part of his political life was to come after his brother's disappearance from the scene and he may have been, in a sense, his political heir. From 1295 he was a very frequent speaker in Council meetings, and this was particularly true of the years 1301–04;

3 *CV*, 2, pp. 1114–230.
4 B 88, ff. 77–165v; 90, ff. 61–235. See P. Waley, 'Personal Names in Siena, 1285' in P. Denley and C. Elam (eds.), *Florence and Italy. Renaissance Studies in Honour of N. Rubinstein* (London, 1988), pp. 187–91.
5 CG 67, ff. 4–13v, 23–7; 68, ff. 26–8v; 69, ff. 26–9; 70, ff. 26–9; 71, ff. 15–20; 72, ff. 15–17v; 73, ff. 16–18.
6 This is a very summary treatment of a topic which merits fuller investigation.
7 CG 13–19, 21–3, 25, 29–31, 34–5, 37, 47: *CV*, 2, nn. 913, 922 (but some of the editorial identifications of Tolomei may be incorrect): B 37, f. 16v; 49, ff. 10, 11v (embassy); 56, f. 5v; 57, f. 1 (*camerlengo*, 1274); 90, f. 318v (*lira* payment, 31 l. 11s.); 92, f. 81 (embassy). On Scozia see also Bowsky, *Commune*, pp. 36, 145.

in 1303, for instance, his speeches in Council easily outnumbered those of all others.[8]

Another Tolomei who was extremely active in the commune's affairs was Deo di Lotterengo. He too came into prominence as councillor and emissary in the early 1270s. After some years of activity at the centre of the Guelf-Tolomei regime he died, probably quite young, in 1275.[9] Deo's son Tavena must have been a near-contemporary of his kinsman Federigo di Rinaldo. He was a member of an important embassy to the papal Curia in 1294 and in 1298 served prominently – perhaps as commander – with the Sienese contingent which participated in Boniface VIII's campaign against the Colonna. In the first years of the new century he was a frequent orator in Council and by 1304 a person of such weight that he was selected as Podestà by the city of Ferrara.[10]

Prosopographical information does not make exciting reading, at least for most readers. Yet it is not enough to convey general impressions; moving on from the Tolomei to the Malavolti, some more careers must be sketched. The Malavolti appear most prominently in the medieval history of Siena in connection with the bishopric and chapter,[11] but it was natural that such a family should also have deep roots in the city's secular affairs. A Malavolti had served as Podestà in the first years of the thirteenth century. At the beginning of the 1270s, when Siena turned her back on her pro-imperialist past, the two Malavolti most active in the commune were Filippo and Uguccione di Orlando. The latter was a very frequent speaker in Council throughout the first half of the 1270s and served three times (1246, 1255, 1273) in the principal financial office as chamberlain. He remained active in the following years and held office again, for the last time, in 1281.[12] Filippo di Braccio's period of distinction was brief (1270–74)[13] but his relative Mino 'Prete' di Guido enjoyed an exceptionally long career as councillor and office-holder, from 1274 or earlier until at least 1308. The sort of man who made an appropriate escort to royalty (to King Charles II, 1289) or a Podestà in a Tuscan town (Casole, 1308), his dazio payments in 1285 suggest the possession of very considerable wealth.[14] Filippo di Aldobrandino, another Malavolti, must have been about the same age. In 1278 he petitioned the commune of Siena on behalf

---

8 CG 47, 59, 63–4; B 67, f. 1; see Bowsky, *Commune*, pp. 113–14, 204 and English '5 Magnate Families', p. 511.
9 CG 13–16, 19; 20, f. 138v (death); B 49, f. 10v.
10 CG 59, 61, 63; 64, f. 17; 73, ff. 167–71v; B 110, f. 122; 114, f. 215; 121, ff. 293, 320v (embassy to Lucca, 1307).
11 See below, pp. 127–33.
12 CG 13–17, 19, 23, 25; B 56, f. 7; English, '5 Magnate Families', p. 468.
13 CG 13, 15–16, 18.
14 CG 18, 31, 34–5, 37, 47, 59, 63, 72–3 (v. 72, f. 17v); B 88, f. 163 and 90, f. 318v (two tax payments of 52 l.); 99, f. 109.

of the contado community of Torniella, which was being taxed by both Siena and the Aldobrandeschi counts, but this relationship turned sour and later (1308) the people of Torniella complained that Filippo was exploiting his lordship over them so vigorously that their only hope seemed to be to buy him out. Filippo may have been a turbulent character (in 1296 he was fined 25 l. 'on the petition of Pietro dei Forteguerri'), but he was an active participant in Council and was thought suitable for choice as an emissary to Florence (1288). His tax payments were about half those of Mino.[15] Another prominent Malavolti, roughly of the same generation as these and perhaps a brother of Mino, was Guccio di Guido, who figured as councillor and office-holder between 1285 and 1307. He was perhaps the 'Guicciolino' Malavolti chosen to command the Guelf cavalry force in Tuscany in 1278.[16]

The Piccolomini most conspicuous for his political role in these years was the classically named Enea (son of Rinaldo), born probably around 1230. His temperament may have been military and political rather than commercial, for he appears first as a borrower from the family bank rather than as banker, and in 1261, in the heyday of Siena's Ghibellinism, with six others he received spurs and a sword on their promotion to knighthood. He is recorded as a councillor and office-holder over the years 1270–95. He headed the commune's financial administration as Camerlengo in 1273 and in the following years very frequently undertook important embassies. He was one of the wealthiest of Sienese: in 1285 only three individuals made payments of direct tax larger than his.[17] Salamone di Guglielmo Piccolomini – as esoterically Hebrew by nomenclature as his kinsman was Latin – must have been of much the same age. He first appears in the Council in the same year and his energetic and eloquent activity as councillor and ambassador lasted rather longer; he was still orating as late as 1303. His tax assessments were much lower than those of Enea, nevertheless payments of over 30 l. towards the 1285 dazio place him among the richest men in the city.[18]

Approximately of the same generation of Piccolomini was Ranieri di Turchio, who was active as a banker from the 1250s. He was a considerable lender to the commune and helped at a difficult time by purchasing for 2,000 florins the communal lands at the Selva del Lago. Captured by German troops, he was forced to swear allegiance to Manfred (1263), yet by 1275 he was Captain of the Guelf party. Prominent in diplomatic negotiations, he was a tenacious holder of power

15 CG 22, Alleg. D; 29, 36; 73, ff. 151–62v; B 90, f. 346; 96, f. 69v; 113, f. 126v.
16 CG 22, f. 49v; 29, 34–5, 47, 59, 63, 70.
17 Prunai, p. 585n.; CG 14–19, 22–3, 29, 37; B 33, f. 64; 53; 90, f. 287 (86 l. 2s. paid, as also to dazio earlier in the same year; three joint payments were also for higher sums).
18 CG 13, 15, 18, 20, 22–3, 25, 28, 30–1, 34, 37, 47, 59, 63; B 90, f. 289v; see also Bowsky, *Commune*, pp. 103, 113–15.

throughout the storms of the 1250s, 1260s and 1270s – 'popolano' (yet at some stage knighted), Ghibelline (briefly) and Guelf in turn – and remained a leader in Sienese affairs as late as 1296.[19]

Perhaps the most active of Salimbeni in the commune at this time was Notto di Salimbene. He may have been more assiduous as a financier than those mentioned in the preceding paragraphs, for he figures in the list of exiled bankers to whom Urban IV granted exemption from his general condemnation of Sienese (1263) as Ghibellines. In the next decade he was pressing the commune to settle the large debt outstanding to his bank. He was closely linked with the Angevin cause and may have served (1265) as captain of the Guelf party. No doubt the pledges held by the Salimbeni strengthened their political position. Notto was very active in 1275 (only five men spoke more frequently in Council), but he probably died soon afterwards[20] and despite the family's wealth and standing no Salimbene was as prominent in the last two decades of the century.

The outstanding Gallerani of this period was Bonifacio di Giovanni. A frequent speaker in council from 1270 (in 1275 he was one of the five men who made more speeches than Notto di Salimbene), he remained prominent at least to the end of 1286. In the documentation of the 1280 family pacifications he is recorded as *miles*, so it seems that, like Enea dei Piccolomini, he had been dubbed a knight.[21]

These sketches of the careers of some Sienese magnates have contained references to landed estates and to heavy tax-assessments. The Salimbeni made much the largest payment of direct tax in 1285, the Gallerani the next. The extensive landed basis of Siena's great dynasties has already been emphasized, and the Malavolti lordship at Torniella is merely one instance of a general phenomenon.[22] The magnate families had territorial roots which were deep and enduring. They were linked with those landholding families which had not made the transfer into communal affairs, the lords of Prata, counts of Elci, Pannocchie-schi, even Aldobrandeschi, and they intermarried with them and also quarrelled with them, interminably, particularly over stolen sheep. In 1285 a campaign was launched against Poggio S Cecilia which typifies the set-up in the Sienese contado. The proposer of the campaign was Biagio dei Tolomei and the army's first objectives were to be the castle, which belonged to Enea dei Piccolomini, and certain properties of Biagio's own cousin Ranuccio di Baldistraccha Tolomei.[23]

---

19   *Reg. Urb. IV*, 2, n. 274; CG. 16–20 (especially 20, f. 36v), 29; B 33, f. 64; 53, f. 12v; 55, ff. 1v, 10v; 90, f. 287 (dazio payment of 23 l. 16s.); 104, f. 17; 113, f. 88. English, '5 Magnate Families', pp. 491–2.

20   *Reg. Urb. IV*, 2, n. 274; CG 13, 15 (especially f. 62), 16 (especially ff. 7v–8), 18–20.

21   CG 14, 16, 19, 29; 32, ff. 37v–8v; *CV*, 2, nn. 924, 927.

22   Above, pp. 80–1; *Repertorio*, p. 158.

23   CG 20, ff. 26–34 (where the Malavolti marriage link with the lords of Prata is also mentioned). For the probable relationship see Roon-Bassermann, genealogical table.

KNIGHTHOOD, CHIVALRY AND CAVALRY

Dubbing as a knight was the ceremony which marked the initiation into manhood of the authentic Sienese magnate. Like his contemporary counterpart in 'feudal' Europe, he was a warrior on horseback. Mounted warfare in itself did not serve to set him apart entirely from the professional sergeant or the *nouveau riche* compelled by the commune to owe the service of a warhorse, but there could be no mistaking the superior social standing of one who had 'received the belt of knighthood'. Possession of a charger and a squire was part of the joy and squires had to be forbidden to show off by galloping their steeds through the city without giving preliminary warning. The commune could authorize the conferment of knighthood, but the ceremony of dubbing, with its quasi-magical passing-on of powers, could only be performed by one who was already a knight. The celebrations lasted for two weeks (this was the maximum period) during which the new knight could 'hold court' with his friends in a wooden enclosure in the Campo, the palisade closing off an area for jousting. Sumptuary legislation against the wearing of new fur garments was suspended for the occasion, but not more than 2 l. might be expended on the pay of the cook, whose services could be retained for one week. The celebration was not held to justify gifts of gold, silver, money or cloth. The laws restricting the social aspects of these occasions were resented by those involved, who sometimes petitioned for their suspension so that friends and relatives might be suitably entertained. The commune however marked the occasion – which involved, at least notionally, an addition to its cavalry strength – by the gift of 5 l., to be spent on spurs and a sword.[24]

The emphasis on dubbing was no mere enthusiasm for dressing up, but a central and important part of the way of living and thinking of the urbanized noble. Chivalry is a basic theme in the literature of the time, not least in the poetry of Cecco Angiolieri and Folgore da San Gimignano, the former Sienese by birth, the latter probably by residence, at least for part of his life (he served briefly in the Sienese army, though not as a cavalryman). Cecco was of military age by 1281 and died shortly before 1313. His poems give an idea of the cynicism which doubtless characterized some members of Siena's clever young set. His mother was a Salimbeni, his father probably descended from a prominent banking family with papal connections.[25] Cecco felt or affected a disenchantment which is seen at its most striking in the poems deploring his father's survival. His speciality, in fact, was the literary genre of *vituperium* (blame, irony, censure). Certainly not an

---

24 *Const. 1262*, pp. 31, 291; *Cont., BSSP*, 2, p. 141; *Cost. 1309–10*, 2, pp. 311–13. For the petition referred to, which failed to secure the needed 2/3 majority, see CG 62 (1303), ff. 122v–4.

25 *DBI*, 3, pp. 280–3 (articles on Angioliero and Cecco) has incompatible versions of Cecco's paternity, the latter claiming that Cecco's father was banker to Gregory IX (1227–41) and died in 1296.

ivory-tower poet, he served in several campaigns and suffered fines for absence from others, broke the curfew, appeared in the courts on a charge of brawling and celebrated the pleasures of dicing. The literature of chivalry was the standard reading of his milieu and his sonnets contain Arthurian allusions, to Tristram and Merlin. Cecco engaged in a literary quarrel with his great contemporary Dante. He left at least six children and an estate so heavily mortgaged that the younger of them opted against accepting their inheritance.[26]

Folgore flourished in the first two decades of the fourteenth century (first mentioned 1305, died before 1332). His links were both with Siena and his native San Gimignano. His friends figure in his poems as Lancelot and other knights of Camelot or even as Trojans ('paiono figliuoli del re Priano'). He could hardly write a poem without mentioning horses, a reminder of Siena's long and still enduring relationship with the noble animal. His themes are tourneying ('breaking lances'), hunting and falconry. The sonnet introducing his sequence on the virtues of the true knight advocates mortgaging castles and estates so that the chivalrous hero can feed his numerous guests, possess fine rooms and have plenty of servants – and horses.[27]

It is not clear whether these two talented poets spoke for their generation. Their works were meant to give pleasure (and, in the case of Cecco, to shock), so one must assume that they were not totally unrepresentative. Cecco knew that he was not cut out for an economical way of life and recommended 'If you want to be healthy, do what you enjoy' ('S' tu voi star san, fa' ciò che ti diletta'). These poets bear witness to a younger element within the oligarchical milieu, benefiting from the labours of their ancestors in the bank and critical of the standards of their financier forebears. Their views and way of life must have dismayed the more conventional among their relatives whilst some will have regarded them with benevolent amazement.[28]

The many fines paid by members of the grander families for absence from Council-meetings show that some who would not feel the effect of a low routine fine preferred this to an hour of tedium in the committee chamber. Payers of such fines were often Salimbeni, Malavolti, Forteguerri and so on.[29] However most took up the patrician's burden, administrative and military, and lists of office-holders give the impression of an enduring oligarchy. In all councils and in the podestarie and rectorates of the contado, Salimbeni, Tolomei, Piccolomini,

26 A. F. Massèra, *Sonetti burleschi e realistici dei primi due secoli* (edn 2, Bari, 1940), pp. 63–173 (numerous other editions).

27 Ibid., p. 168. E. Fiumi (*Storia economica e sociale di S. Gimignano*, Florence, 1961, p. 229n) believes that Folgore was a person 'of little social standing', but the judgement seems to be based solely on the low fiscal assessment of his estate at S Gimignano in 1332.

28 Massèra, p. 107. There may be an analogy with the attitude of the generals and senior civil servants to their children who constituted the 'Bloomsbury' set of Stracheys, Grants and Bells.

29 Some examples from the year 1282: B 82, ff. 39–41v; 83, f. 13v.

Malavolti, Gallerani, Bonsignori, Forteguerri names continued to abound.[30] The four Provveditori for the first half of 1289 were Pietro di Ramella dei Forteguerri, Arrigo di Ranieri dei Piccolomini, Mochata di Bartolomeo dei Maconi, Federigo di Rinaldo dei Tolomei, all from major Sienese dynasties.[31]

The names of those entrusted with important diplomatic missions are perhaps the best clues to those who were at the centre of power. In the autumn of 1278 an embassy was despatched to the papal court to negotiate with Nicholas III. The mission involved eight names, all from the very heart of the oligarchy, four of them judges (Bandino, Gregorio, Gratia, Griffolo), one a notary (Giacomo 'Sardus'), a banker (Ciampolo di Albizzo), another oligarch, Ugolino di Rustico, whose family name remains untraced, and Enea di Rinaldo dei Piccolomini.[32] In 1289, while the Provveditori named above were in office, Minione dei Tolomei was commanding a force of mercenaries on behalf of the commune, Biagio dei Tolomei was emissary to the Guelf parliament at Empoli, Salomone dei Piccolomini was ambassador to the Aldobrandeschi countess Margherita, Simone dei Tolomei, Sozzo dei Salimbeni, Ciampolo dei Gallerani and Mino dei Malavolti were ambassadors and escorts to King Charles II of Sicily.[33] The tendency to send lawyers to negotiate, nobles to accompany royalty, was a natural one.

These oligarchs certainly did not shirk military responsibilities – one speaks of responsibilities rather than dangers, for casualties on most campaigns were low – in favour of administrative ones. Giacomo di Rinaldo 'Gilii', probably a Tolomei, commanded the city's mercenary cavalry at Grosseto in 1295 – just as a Tolomei had led in 1289 – and clearly found this compatible with his role at the centre of the commune's business as a councillor and ambassador.[34] In 1302 the commanders of Siena's five cavalry corps, all Sienese aristocrats, were Vintotto dei Renaldini, Goffano and Ghino dei Forteguerri, Mino and Tavena dei Tolomei.[35] The summer campaigning season was perhaps an enjoyable change, a semi-holiday with a purpose or 'theme'; some young men have enjoyed the annual territorial camp in more recent times. In Folgore's sonnets of the months, August is spent in a mountain valley with thirty castles:

> e palafreni da montare'n sella,
> e cavalcar la sera e la mattina[36]
> (And saddled palfreys to mount
> To ride evening and morning.)

---

30 An example: lists of councillors and office-holders in 1288 (CG 35, ff. 116–118v, 128 and v).
31 B 99, f. 40. For the last of these, see above pp. 79–80.
32 CG 22, ff. 42v–3v; for Enea, above, p. 81, for Bandino, Griffolo and Giacomo Sardus below, pp. 87–90.
33 B 99, ff. 60v, 77, 92v, 109. For Salamone and Mino, above, pp. 80–1.
34 B 112, f. 100 (probably identical with the subject of English, '5 Magnate Families', p. 512).
35 B 116, ff. 272, 288, 306, 356v, 357v.
36 Massèra, p. 161.

To pass the summer in the open in Tuscany on horseback must have been a pleasurable experience. Often the purpose was hunting, but cavalry service was at times so frequent as to become almost an annual routine.

In the summer of 1307 the commune called those owing cavalry service, in all three terzi, for a period of just over three months (6 June to 8 September). Not all the 285 men summoned served for the entire duration of the levy, indeed some came for two weeks only, but the average time served was about two and a half months. The campaign, fought in alliance with the Florentines, was against Arezzo, and therefore conducted in most agreeable countryside, not at all distant from Siena. Seventeen villages were sacked, among them Ambra, later a favourite resort of Lorenzo de' Medici. Cignano, Oliveto and Gargonza were burnt and almost entirely destroyed. Sixty workmen were brought from Siena to demolish the walls of Cignano and Gargonza and thus employment was given as well as pleasure. No casualties are reported among the Sienese contingent and it may be supposed that a good time was had by all except the population of the places ravaged. Among the cavalrymen serving for long periods in the campaign were at least seven Salimbeni, three Gallerani, three Malavolti, two Tolomei, Piccolomini, and indeed representatives of all Siena's magnate families.[37] To see these men in all their dimensions they must be envisaged on horseback, hunting or on military or diplomatic duty, in the fields and granaries of their estates, as well as in the council-chambers of the Sienese commune.

LAWYERS

Categorizing men according to their social origins and affiliations must be undertaken warily. In some instances the family connections and occupation of men prominent in the commune's affairs remain mysterious. Those who resist categorization must be taken into account, particularly in view of the danger of oversimplifying the structure of Siena's oligarchy by arguing from too few examples. However one stratum of politically active Sienese below the magnate class can be clearly identified in the form of lawyers, i.e. judges and notaries. The high standing of the judges shows in the lists of 1285 tax payments, in which they ranked above all other occupations disclosed by taxpayers, whilst their average contribution was more than twice that of a notary.[38]

The minutes of the General Council being extant from 1249 – though there are serious gaps – the identification of politically prominent Sienese becomes easier from that date. Some legal men were at the head of the commune's affairs at that time, whereas many of the magnates mentioned above only became intensely

---

37 B 121, ff. 312–18 (the cost of this cavalry levy amounted to 3,541 l.); *RIS, CS*, pp. 296–7.
38 See above, tables 1 and 2.

active from about 1270, after the city's abandonment of a Ghibelline foreign policy. Guiduccino, a notary, ranked second in the number of speeches delivered in council during 1251. He came first in this respect in 1255, was again the second most frequent speaker in the first half of 1260 and in 1266–67 much the most frequent of all. He served as a member of the governing Twenty-four (1258) and in 1261 had the agreeable task of drawing up the terms of the treaty with Florence which followed the victory of Montaperti.[39] Guiduccino had disappeared from the political stage by the 1270s, possibly through the revolution in foreign policy but more probably on account of age or death. Another very active councillor of the period, figuring in many discussions during the years 1251–62, was the judge Graziano; he leaves the scene sooner and may have been older.[40] In a slightly later generation a very prominent man was the notary Cacciaconte, who was a councillor by 1258 and a very frequent speaker and occasional office-holder in the period 1270–79.[41]

Guiduccino and Cacciaconte, as notaries, had received a much less considerable legal training than the judges, though their gild insisted on two years as the minimum for a notarial education. After Graziano several judges came to the fore in the affairs of the commune, the earliest being Griffolo and Recupero. Almost certainly Griffolo descended from a family of magnatial standing, though his descent cannot be traced within any of the families designated as magnates in the Sienese legislation of 1277. He owed cavalry service and his five sons were participants in the private treaties which sought to pacify feuding dynasties (1280). Griffolo was a councillor by 1260 and in the next year a member of a crucial mission to the papal court. He became a practised emissary and acted at least twice as Provveditore. There was a period in the mid 1270s when he was so much at the heart of Siena's regime that it was normally he who proposed those measures which were discussed and agreed to in council. 1278 found him again at the papal Curia, this time on a three-week mission connected with negotiations for a Guelf-Ghibelline pacification. By 1281 he was a rather infrequent speaker in council, but he was still active in politics in the following year, after which he disappears from the conciliar scene, perhaps at a fairly advanced age.[42]

A near-contemporary of Griffolo, probably less powerful but destined for an even longer period of distinction, was another judge, Recupero (or 'Ricovero'). He

39 CG 3, ff. 60–1, 62v, 65, 68, 90, 91v, 93r and v, 98v; 5–11; B 32, f. 25v. On Guiduccino's career see U. Morandi, 'Il notaio all'origine del comune medievale senese' in Il notariato nella civiltà toscana (Rome, 1985), pp. 311–36 (ad 325–6).

40 CG 3, 5–6, 8–10.

41 CG 8, f. 2; 13, 16–19, 22–3.

42 CV, 2, dd. 929, 933; CG 9 (f. 82), 10, 14–16, 18 (especially f. 146v)–23, 25, 26 (especially 10r and v): B 33, ff. 74–5; 49, f. 1; 65, f. 41; 71, f. 1; 73, f. 44v; 82, ff. 145–50: Bowsky, Commune, pp. 72–3. For notarial education, Statuti . . . giudici e notai, p. 67.

first figures as a leading councillor in 1271 and continues in that role with increasing prominence until 1288. He may possibly be identical with the Ricovero di Tebaldo di Rinaldo who was Provveditore in 1262 but, if he was, he did not yet rank as a judge. In 1287 he was one of Siena's representatives – another being Enea dei Piccolomini – at the parliament of Tuscan Guelf powers held at Castelfiorentino. His tax assessment suggests that he was by no means wealthy; in 1285 he and his brothers made a dazio payment of 2 l. 7s.[43]

Another legal man at the centre of affairs was the judge Giacomo di Guiduccino, who was probably a son of the Guiduccino (the name is uncommon) mentioned above as a notary very prominent in the period 1251–67. Giacomo's energetic career falls within the years 1273–86. He served as a Provveditore in 1274. In 1275 he was one of the most frequent of conciliar orators, in 1285 he was the most loquacious of them all. When Siena found itself temporarily without a Podestà (1281) it was Giacomo who put forward the proposal which solved this dilemma; Giacomo de Gandinis of Crema, who held a judicial appointment at the time, was promoted to fill the vacancy, without increase of pay.[44]

Bandino was a judge who enjoyed a much longer period of authority. He lived in the most prosperous part of the terzo of S Martino, his neighbours on either side being two of the most prominent Piccolomini, Enea and Ranieri di Turchio; this topographical proximity may well be evidence of a socio-political affinity. Bandino's years of eminence extend from 1272 to 1303. He was a big lender to the commune in 1272–73 and in 1285 made a considerable tax payment (with his brothers) of 17 l. 9 s. He was Provveditore in 1274 (in the half-year previous to Giacomo di Guiduccino) and again in 1277. His diplomatic missions included a three-week embassy to the pope in 1288.[45]

Lawyers were more prominent as speakers in council than as ambassadors or financial officials; it was not uncommon for several speeches to be made on a topic, each of them by a lawyer. On 13 January 1283 two routine clauses came up for discussion: 'What action should be taken concerning men from the Aldobrandeschine or Pannocchieschi lands and those of the bishop of Volterra who owe money to Sienese citizens?' and 'What action should be taken concerning Sienese held as prisoners in Tuscany?' Five speeches were made in that session, four of them by judges, one by a notary.[46] Was there a judicial attitude towards policy which characterized the viewpoint of Siena's lawyers? If there was one, it is not

---

43 CG 13–14, 16, 18, 20, 25, 28–32, 34–5; B 35, f. 1; 90, f. 254v; 95, f. 101v.

44 Above, p. 87; CG 18, 20, 22–3, 25 (especially ff. 34v–5v); B 57, f. 1.

45 CG 20, 22, 29, 32, 34, 47; B 51, f. 23v; 53, f. 12; 56, f. 1; 65, f. 41; 67, f. 1; 90, f. 287v; 97, f. 74.
    For the location of Bandino's residence see the will of Ranieri di Turchio's widow Contessa, Dipl.,
    Spedale, 11.10.1299 (text in English, '5 Magnate Families', pp. 310–17).

46 CG 27, ff. 17v–18.

easy to detect. Many of the questions discussed were fundamentally legal ones or had legal implications. Whether Griffolo was giving his opinion on Siena's arbitration between Grosseto and Count Aldobrandino, or Guiduccino his on such matters as a dispute with the community of Monticchiello, or on taxing the contado, or the bishop's peace-making mission to the papal court or how many cavalry Siena should provide for the Ghibelline army, almost all of these – the military contribution is only a partial exception – had legal aspects. Not only was a legal training appropriate for oratory and decision-making, but the lawyers were the educated element within the city; with the exception of the theologians, they were the only people who had received higher education. Evidence on the point is meagre, but some of the lawyers owned books; Bonagiunta di Pepone, a notary, had a library of fourteen volumes, including the corpus of civil (Roman) and canon law.[47]

OTHER OLIGARCHS

It would be misleading to imply that authority rested permanently with a narrow and unchanging oligarchy. Office-holders with 'new' names did make their appearance from time to time.[48] Also there were oligarchs who cannot be assigned to the categories of 'magnate' or 'lawyer' (or, like Griffolo, both), either because they belong to neither class or through lack of information about their social attachments.

Aldobrandino del Mancino is one who seems to belong with the magnate–oligarchs, but he is not identifiable as a member of any family named in the 1277 anti-magnate legislation. He was a financier on quite a large scale, as a lender to the commune and within Siena. His relatives were involved in the 1280 family pacifications – a sure indication of social grandeur – and he or his dynasty gave their name to one of the fiscal regions (*libre*) in the terzo of Città. The years of his political prominence were from 1275 to 1295.[49] Ciampolo di Albizzo appears to come into this category also. He may possibly have been a member of the 'Albizi de Platea' family listed in the 1277 legislation. He was prominent in the Ghibelline period, at least between 1255 and 1260, but he figures in the list of bankers pardoned by the pope in 1263. He was among the most frequent of orators in the

---

47 Morandi, 'Il notaio' (cited above n. 39), pp. 333–4.
48 Several new names occur, for example among the incoming Fifteen in November 1285 (CG 30, f. 34v).
49 See below, pp. 120–1. *CV*, 2, nn. 914, 930, 934: CG 20, 22–3, 29, 31-2, 35: B 87, f. 46; 93, f. 1v; 95, f. 9v; 103, ff. 54–7v; 106, f. 30; 109, f. 78v. He was probably an early member of the Nine (O. Malavolti, *Dell'Historia di Siena*, Venice, 1599, 2, p. 53v). Lack of information about the personnel of the Nine makes it difficult to use this as an indication of prominence (see Bowsky, 'The Buon Governo', *Speculum*, 37 (1962), p. 371n).

Council-meetings of the years 1270–88; in 1270–72 he made more speeches than any other councillor and in 1275 lost this supremacy to Griffolo by the margin of one speech only. He served frequently as a diplomatic emissary. His social standing seems confirmed by his participation in the peace-making of 1280.[50] Guglielmo 'Benachi' also figures in the 1263 list of bankers. Like Ciampolo, he was wealthy; he and his brothers possessed an important palazzo and he and other kinsmen owed cavalry service of two horses. He figures much in Council-meetings between 1270 and 1274, then disappears, presumably through his death. His daughter held land at Mensano (1290) and was accounted of magnatial descent ('de magnatibus et maioribus civitatis').[51]

Another wealthy oligarch whose social links are hard to locate is Giacomo 'Sardus'. His name indicates a Sardinian derivation, but he was as politically active as any other Sienese citizen over the quarter-century 1270–95, as councillor and ambassador. On some occasions he is described as a notary, so possibly he should appear among the lawyers, yet the appellation was not normally applied to him. Perhaps he sought to shed it and his tax assessment certainly suggests a social level a good deal higher than that of even the grander notaries; paying 11 l. 3s. in response to one 1285 dazio, he ranked below Bandino, the wealthy judge, but close to some members of aristocratic houses, Forteguerri and Tolomei.[52] He may have seen some of his work on behalf of the commune as a necessary financial perquisite, to judge from the salary he drew as scribe to the Consuls of *milites* in 1292 (2 l. per month) at a time when he was absent on an embassy to Florence.

A good deal below 'the Sardinian' in the fiscal scale (at 3 l. 11 s.) was Giacomo di Bencivenne. He came to prominence by 1274 and was still a very frequent orator in 1301, ranking only after Federigo dei Tolomei in the number of speeches made in that year, and he served in the responsible and sensitive office of Rector of the Hospital of S Maria della Scala. His father had been a butcher: in general tradesmen are notably lacking among Sienese political leaders, but the exceptional case of Giacomo di Bencivenne shows that such a descent was not a barrier to the next generation.[53]

CONTINUITY

Oligarchs deserve consideration as individuals no less than as constituents of classes and families. It will have been noticed that several of those mentioned

---

50 CG 13, 15–16, 18–23, 29, 32, 34–5; B 69, f. 25; 73, f. 44v; 92, f. 81; 96, f. 81.
51 CG 13–14, 16–18 (especially 18, f. 145); B 79, ff. 29, 31; Capitano 3, f. 48v.
52 CG 13, 15, 20–2, 29–32, 34–5, 37, 47; B 49, ff. 10v, 16; 73, f. 44v; 95, ff. 102v, 105v; 96, f. 42; 104, f. 81v; 107, ff. 144v, 148v; 109, f. 120v; 111, f. 127v. See also Bowsky, *Commune*, p. 225.
53 CG 19–20, 29, 34, 37, 59; B 107, f. 172; 109, ff. 119v, 123; 110, ff. 137v, 144v, 147: Redon, 'Autour de l'Hôpital S. Maria della Scala à Sienne au XIIIe siècle' *Ricerche Storiche*, 15 (1985), p. 20: Bowsky, *Commune*, p. 211

above were prominent over a long period. Nine of them – the selection being more or less arbitrary, there is no doubt that the length of their careers is typical – held positions of power for at least a quarter of a century. This was true of Scozia and Federigo dei Tolomei, Mino and Filippo dei Malavolti, Enea, Salamone and Ranieri di Turchio dei Piccolomini among the magnates, Bandino the judge, and Giacomo 'Sardus' among the uncategorized.[54] The duration of these careers suggests strongly that individuals tended to remain in positions of authority after policies with which they had been associated were abandoned and even reversed. The extent to which this was the case is now to be discussed.

First it is necessary to establish 'turning-points', after which it should not be difficult to establish whether there were indeed many individuals whose leading roles survived these chronological breaks and whether survival was the norm or was subject to many exceptions. At this juncture it may be noted that one agile survivor has already been identified in the person of Ranieri di Turchio Piccolomini.[55]

The Ghibelline allegiance which had characterized the commune's foreign policy for nearly two decades was totally abandoned in August 1270, following the collapse of the pro-Hohenstaufen cause in Tuscany. The Guelf regime which ensued was diluted to an important extent by the participation of 'popular' elements and the issue of legislation to check the activities and authority of magnate families; the year 1276 was an important watershed in these developments. A third landmark, even less precisely locatable in time, can be placed around 1286–87, when the institution of the Nine, destined to last seventy years, was established with the declared aim of consolidating the role of prosperous mercantile elements.

Diagrammatic presentation should make consideration of this point less conducive to the tedium which always threatens prosopographical analysis. For this purpose the four chronological periods adumbrated in the previous paragraph (1250–70: 1270–76: 1276–86: 1286–*c*. 1308) will be styled (a), (b), (c) and (d), so that the careers of selected oligarchs may be set out and ascribed to their respective periods. The table which follows (table 6) depicts the duration in positions of power (and hence the 'turning-points' survived) of twenty oligarchs. The selection has been made to include lengthy careers – since the question at issue is that of 'survival' – but cases of possible homonymity have been strictly excluded; also some of the careers listed could have been extended had strong but not conclusive indications of political activity been admitted. The names selected include a number of those discussed in the earlier parts of this chapter.

54 Above, pp. 79–90.
55 Above, pp. 81–2.

Table 6. *Continuity in office-holding*

	(a)	(b)	(c)	(d)
Alfonso di Pelacane (Tolomei?)[56]	x	x	—	—
Griffolo (judge)	x	x	x	—
Giacomo dei Pagliaresi	x	x	x	—
Ranieri dei Pagliaresi[57]	x	x	x	—
Uguccione di Orlando dei Malavolti[58]	x	x	x	—
Ciampolo di Albizzo	x	x	x	x
Ranieri di Turchio Piccolomini	x	x	x	x
Enea dei Piccolomini	x	x	x	x
Scozia dei Tolomei	—	x	x	x
Recupero (judge)	—	x	x	x
Giacomo 'Sardus' (notary)	—	x	x	x
Giacomo di Bencivenne	—	x	x	x
Bandino (judge)	—	x	x	x
Ramella dei Forteguerri	—	x	x	x
Mino Prete dei Malavolti	—	x	x	x
Salamone dei Piccolomini	—	x	x	x
Giacomo di Guiduccino	—	x	x	—
Bonifazio dei Gallerani	—	x	x	—
Guccio di Guido dei Malavolti	—	—	x	x
Filippo di Aldobrandino dei Malavolti	—	—	x	x

Key: a=1250–70,   b=1270–76,   c=1276–86,   d=1286–1308

Continuity within an oligarchy needs to be considered in terms of successive generations as well as single careers, but examples of such succession in the major Sienese dynasties are so numerous and predictable that it is unnecessary to list and discuss them. The case of Guiduccino and his son (in high probability) the judge Giacomo di Guiduccino has been mentioned. Another is that of Rinaldo 'Gilii' (Tolomei), extremely prominent in 1255–60, and his son Giacomo, very active in council and on missions between 1273 and 1295.[59]

Does the degree of continuity suggested by table 6 imply the assumption that a change in measures need never mean a change in men? Did a total break or reversal in policy, internal or external, never involve the disappearance from the political scene of a figure committed to a superseded view? Clearly continuity in authority was normal and expected. Several men in table 6 (and others not listed

56 CG 6–21 (references are given here only for 'oligarchs' not dealt with earlier in this chapter).
57 CG 6–22. The Pagliaresi were among the *casato* families (1277).
58 English, '5 Magnate Families', p. 468.
59 Above, pp. 87–8. CG 4–9, 18–47.

there, such as Orlando Bonsignori) had come to the fore by the 1250s and remained at the centre of things in the Guelf 1270s. If men did sometimes relinquish power, by force or on principle, because they were associated with a policy which had been abandoned, cases of this cannot be adduced from the surviving evidence. Guiduccino, outstandingly prominent in the two decades of Ghibellinism, disappears from sight after 1270, but the reason for this may have been old age or death. Storms and the need for tacking were predictable and were not reasons for risking a new hand on the tiller of the ship of state, particularly in view of the tenacity of older hands.

There might have been a test case for the possibility of political survival after total commitment to a cause which suffered defeat and abandonment. Provenzano Salvani came from a family which was named among the *casati* and prominence in Sienese affairs was his birthright. From 1247 or earlier he assumed that position and in the critical years of the Ghibelline regime (1257–62) his authority was such 'A recar Siena tutta alle sue mani' (*Purgatorio*, XI, 123). Provenzano was put to death after his capture at the battle of Colle (11 June 1269) and the Sienese destroyed his palazzo. The importance of the Salvani family outlived the collapse of Ghibellinism, but it will never be known whether Provenzano himself, had he survived, might have assisted the Guelf regime in the 1270s, perhaps assuming office as Captain of the Guelf Party.[60] The Sienese themselves would have found it understandable had he abandoned Ghibellinism after the collapse of Hohenstaufen power in Italy. Even Dante, hardly a 'realist' in politics, turned seriously to Ghibellinism only when imperial authority was resurrected by Henry VII.

The diplomatic revolution of 1270 was the deviation most obviously forced upon the Sienese by external circumstances. In the 'popular' (or anti-magnate) developments of 1274–78 and the institutional changes of 1287–92 there was a much stronger element of volition and choice. The former were perhaps the outcome of local pressure on a narrow Guelf regime, whilst the latter involved a programme proclaiming the aim of a more formalized oligarchy and thus possibly the reinstallation of a narrower one. It is time to turn to this last development and to consider the city's ruling class in the last decade of the thirteenth century and the first of the fourteenth.

THE NINE

The establishment of the regime of the Nine may be dated to February 1287, though in the next few years there was some not very significant experimentation in the numbers of office-holders. It has been usual to consider this institutional

---

60 On Salvani see F. Tempesti, 'Provenzano Salvani', *BSSP*, n.s. 7 (1936), pp. 3–56.

change as marking the advent of a 'new' oligarchy consisting of a merchant class which excluded the magnate families.[61] However it is by no means clear that the *casati* were driven from power or elbowed out of it – or even that their wings were clipped. Professor Bowsky sees this as a period of compromise. The Noveschi (i.e. the stratum whence the Nine were drawn) 'tried to maintain a monopoly over the most sensitive organ of government, while powerful magnates also enjoyed sufficient power to satisfy them with the regime's continued existence'. The *casati* only accepted exclusion from the Nine, he suggests, 'because they could share in the formulation of all important government decisions and policies'.[62] But can one speak of the regime of the Nine 'merchants of the middle people' as a governing oligarchy if it could only govern when it possessed the goodwill of the socially and financially powerful magnate families? These years from the 1270s onwards should surely be seen as a period during which authority was shared between the old magnate group and elements which ranked only just below them in the social scale.

If the Nine's first leaders saw themselves as superseding the 'old' families they were to encounter disillusionment. This appears clearly enough from Bowsky's own treatment of the Nine. 'Exclusion of magnates', even from the sole office for which they were notionally ineligible, that of the Nine, 'was not absolute' and some citizens who held office frequently as members of the Nine 'were no less noble than the excluded *casati*'. Prominent among the Nine were two sons of Griffolo, the judge who had been at the heart of Sienese affairs since the 1260s and whose family ranked among the feuding parties involved in the private peace settlements of 1280.[63] Dr Edward English has realistically described Siena's 'anti-magnate' measures as 'symbolic rather than really harmful'.[64] If the Nine were recruited from the very men whose violent and quarrelsome way of life the 'anti-magnate' legislation of 1277 was in part intended to check, the case for the Nine as representing a dominant and distinct stratum situated socially *below* the magnates becomes very difficult to sustain.

From the start the magnates were immensely prominent in the discussions, administration and diplomatic activity of the Nine. In the first six months of 1288, near the beginning of the Nine's regime (to accept temporarily the reality of this label), the most active councillors include Gallerani, Tolomei, Piccolomini, Salimbeni, Malavolti, Bonsignori, Forteguerri, Selvolesi. There was certainly no question of these dynasties weakening in their hold over the city's contado. In the same period Tolomei were chosen to be Podestà in such important subject

---

61 E. g. Marrara, p. 247.
62 Bowsky, *Commune*, pp. 80, 83, 64.
63 Ibid., pp. 72–3: above, pp. 87–8.
64 '5 Magnate Families', p. 143.

communes as Massa (twice) and Chiusdino, whilst a Salimbeni held that office at Ischia and a Forteguerri at Montauto (near Monteriggioni).[65] In the next year the four Provveditori were (as already mentioned) magnates to a man. At this time the commune sent four 'ambassadors' to act as escorts to King Charles of Sicily; all of these also were magnates. Meanwhile other Piccolomini undertook major diplomatic missions and other Tolomei represented Siena at Tuscan parliaments and accepted military command.[66] A strange form of exclusion, this, from the city's governing oligarchy!

In 1290 there was a brief experiment, numerical rather than constitutional. The Nine were replaced by the Eighteen, then very briefly by the Six, till in the summer of 1292 it was decided that after all Nine was the most convenient number for the highest magistracy. The Eighteen consisted of six *gubernatores et difensores communis Senarum* (this was the usual formal title of the Nine), together with twelve *domini nobiles regentes civitatem*. The twelve *nobiles regentes* were, literally, nobles, not men styled 'noble' by courtesy. It would seem, in fact, that the regime of the Eighteen (1290–91) represented an *entente* between the 'good and lawful merchants' and the *casati*. This compromise was perhaps an *ad hoc* arrangement connected with the readmission of exiled Ghibellines (1290), but whatever its origins it confirms that the time of the Nine was one of authority shared between magnates and *mezza gente* rather than of control by a non-magnate oligarchy.[67]

The active role of the magnates continued to characterize the regime in the last years of the thirteenth century and the first decade of the fourteenth.[68] The most prominent Sienese of this time, most of whom have been mentioned above, were four Tolomei (Federigo, Tavena, Deo and Giacomo di Rinaldo), a Piccolomini (Salamone) and two Malavolti (Guccio and Mino).[69] The regime of the Nine was not one with which the magnate dynasties felt unhappy. They continued to have a say in fiscal matters, perhaps the most crucial aspect of internal policy. The *casati* were prepared to settle for a political structure within which they were quite heavily taxed but in return had a large share in the government of the city.

Assessment for the direct tax was just one of the matters on which the Nine could not act independently, but required the consent of other major officials, the *ordini*, comprising the Provveditori, the Consuls of the Mercanzia gild and the Consuls of the Knights or Captains of the Guelf Party. The Mercanzia was perhaps

---

65 CG 35, especially ff. 116–20v, 128r and v.
66 B 99, ff. 40, 109, 42, 60v, 77, 92v.
67 B 107, f. 12v. See also a reference (CG 39, f. 13) to *domini viiii qui pro tempore fuerint in officio pro parte rebellium et extitiorum communis Sen'*. See Bowsky, *Commune*, p. 59.
68 For some other examples, Marrara, pp. 257n–8n.
69 See above, pp. 79–82.

the institution (though little is known of its workings) best adapted to assist the continuation of magnatial control.[70] Elections to the General Council and the choice of officials in the contado communities were other matters requiring the agreement of the *ordini*. Altogether it is not surprising that the magnates did not press for constitutional change. At some period shortly before May 1310 all *casato* families had even been given the opportunity to shed this status and therefore become eligible for election to the Nine, though the offer was then withdrawn in respect of some of the greatest dynasties. A good deal later (1347) a constitutional change intended to promote their interests was put forward, but the motion was opposed by Pietro the son of Salamone Piccolomini and failed to gain the required two-thirds majority.[71]

Hypotheses of this type are not susceptible of proof, but the evidence available suggests that the years 1290–1310, the last third of the period covered in this book, saw an increase, rather than a diminution, in the domination of the great dynasties of banker–landowners. Leading elements of the Nine are described by Bowsky as having 'intimate social and business ties with the magnates' and he has noted no fewer than forty-seven 'excluded nobles' as intermarried with families represented on the Nine. The fiscal arrangements of the period bear the mark of a regime dominated by bankers and concerned to further their interests.[72] To sum up, the magnates' alliance with certain families of the 'middle people' was not such as to attenuate their enduring social and political control.

70 This is the suggestion of English, '5 Magnate Families', p. 146.
71 Malavolti, *Dell'Historia di Siena*, 2, pp. 64v–5; Bowsky, *Commune*, p. 61 (for Pietro's position see index entries, p. 323).
72 Bowsky, *Commune*, pp. 73–4; see also below, pp. 175–8.

5 Problems

It is time to turn to the problems which presented most difficulty to the commune whose institutions and personnel have been discussed. They will be considered under three headings, first those relating to public order within the city itself, secondly those concerned with the maintenance of control over the contado, and thirdly those connected with external policy and the structure of alliances in the Italian peninsula as a whole.

INTERNAL DISORDER

The maintenance of order within the city presented difficulties to all the medieval communes. The laws against carrying arms show what sort of trouble was feared. Shooting with a bow or crossbow was forbidden on pain of a 200 l. fine and if this was not paid within a month the guilty person was to have his hand amputated. Throwing stones, particularly from a tower, was a serious offence, as was 'starting a battle in the city'. Men tended to be on a short fuse, easily took offence and gave expression to their anger in physical violence, hence the laws referring to *rixe* and *meschie* (quarrels and fights, mêlées). Mercenaries, for example, were forbidden to enter the house of any magnate at a time when there was a *rumore* or *meschia* and there was a heavy penalty for summoning aid from outside the city at such a time.[1]

'Defensive arms', i.e. armour, were permitted only to those holding special permits and the sole *prima facie* case for receiving such a permit was that the applicant had *inimicitias capitales*, 'capital enmities'.[2] A total of 131 payments were made in respect of such licences (at 36s. each) in the early months of 1291; the holders were mainly from prominent families, though fifteen of them were servants or retainers (*famuli*).[3] No doubt aristocrats were particularly attached to the institution of the vendetta and most liable to have recourse to arms when they thought their honour impugned. What started as a fight could easily end as a murder. In 1273 nine men were condemned for 'having been present at a mêlée (*meschia*) and homicide' but were sentenced *in absentia* because all had managed to get away to Petriolo in the contado. One of these received the heaviest fine

---

1 *Const. 1262, Cont., BSSP*, p. 143; *Cost. 1309–10*, 2, p. 239.
2 *Const. 1262, Cont., BSSP*, 1, p. 141; 3, p. 81.
3 B 104, ff. 4–6v, 12, 13r and v, 15, 16r and v, 18, 19–21v, 23, 26v, 29v, 30v, 32v–3v, 35.

because he had mutilated the body of the victim. All were sentenced to fines only, possibly because their crime was one of revenge, having a political rather than a personal motive.[4]

Penalties for fights which had no fatal consequences tended to be light. In 1289 Pela di Ranieri Baldinotti paid fines of 200 l. on behalf of his two sons 'for a *meschia* they had with Berto Piccolomini', whilst Duccio 'de Lacontessa' paid 90 l. (60 l. plus a miscalculated one-third extra for late payment) for a fight with Bindo di Aldobrandino.[5] A few years later (1296) a number of unpaid fines for fighting were settled by payments of an agreed percentage of the original sentence. Among these was one of 300 l. paid on behalf of a Piccolomini (Enea) by his son Naddo, who intended to secure reimbursement from his father, and a rare fine for fighting levied on a woman, the widow Diamante.[6]

When political issues arose, violence could easily involve street fighting and attacks on the commune's officials. A revolt against Provenzano Salvani broke out on 30 April 1262 and an urgent council meeting had to consider 'the many serious crimes committed today, the blows and wounds inflicted and the armed people going around by day and night'. An official of the Capitano had been hurt when his men attempted to deal with fighting in the Campo.[7]

A decade later a special Council had to be called (October 1272) when Ciampolo Salimbeni, a prominent citizen and councillor, led his household retainers and other 'followers' in an assault on the city's own guard. Ciampolo's punishment for this offence was a fine of 1,000 l., but the strength of the Salimbeni family's position shows in the provision that only half of the fine had to be paid in cash, the remainder being deductible from money owed to Ciampolo by the Biccherna. That episode led to a law providing that henceforth the punishment for wounding a member of the commune's household or guard was always to be 1,000 l. and for killing one 1,500 l.[8] The penalties seem decidedly light and they were not always adhered to. In 1288 a man 'was found armed by night and he wounded one of the Podestà's guard'. The fine levied for this and other offences was 800 l., which was paid on his behalf by his guarantor, again a Salimbeni. In the intervening period (1276), shortly before all magnates were required to take oaths of obedience and pay surety, a serious dispute between the Salimbeni and the Podestà led to an appeal to San Gimignano for arbitration; that

---

4 CG 17, ff. 94–100; the murder was connected with one committed by a member of the Salimbeni family in 1262 (see Tempesti in *BSSP*, 43 (1936), p. 26).
5 B 99, ff. 14–15.
6 B 113, ff. 15v, 16, 25, 26, 30, 50, 58, 60v.
7 CG 10, ff. 29–30v (partly printed in *BSSP*, 43, pp. 50–1). For this period see below, p. 117.
8 CG 15, f. 94v.

commune sent two emissaries to negotiate concerning 'the good and pacific state of the commune of Siena'.[9]

Hot-blooded behaviour was expected of the young and felt to be more excusable in their case. In 1304 the Podestà and his officials investigated a report about threats made against Neri dei Pagliaresi and various others. After the imposition of the ban against those suspected, a council meeting decided that fines would be sufficient punishment in this instance. All that had happened was that 'on account of the good news of victory over the Ghibellines, they had shouted "To arms, to arms" or "Death to the Ghibellines". No death followed, thanks be to God, or destruction of any house or robbery or fire.' Moreover 'those who are said to be guilty . . . are young and not yet weighty in their understanding' (gravis sensus).[10] Such references to 'the young' are reminders of the milieu of the poets Cecco and Folgore.[11] However youth was not always accepted as an excuse. One of the Podestà's duties was to see that no unauthorized company should be formed among the young (non lassare che si faccia alcuna compagna o vero compagnia di giovani).[12]

Formalized fighting in the Campo, in theory a sporting contest between the terzi, verged on violence and public disturbance. Twentieth-century readers do not need to be told that sporting events can easily become violent occasions. Judicial immunity, granted in connection with accidents in horse races, also applied to wounds inflicted 'in the usual game and battle' (pro ludo et in bataglia) in the Campo. Participants wore a helmet and other protective clothing and carried a shield. Their main weapons were clubs, but throwing stones was a recognized gambit. Casualties, including fatal ones, were common. In 1291 events got so out of hand that at least ten players were killed, and thereafter an attempt was made to confine the Campo fights to fisticuffs, though it did not meet with much success.[13]

MAGNATES

The threat to internal peace came most of all from the great families, principally because their wealth gave them the means, such as household retainers, of overawing other elements in the population. Legislation designed to prevent the building up of family connections forbade close relations to hold certain offices contemporaneously or consecutively. In defining a 'family' it seems to have been

9 B 97, f. 43v: Davidsohn, Forschungen, 2, p. 204 (apparently the only source for the 1276 episode).

10 CG 65, ff. 64–8v.

11 See above, pp. 83–4.

12 Cost. 1309–10, 2, p. 238.

13 See W. Heywood, Palio and Ponte. An account of the Sports of Central Italy from the Age of Dante to the 20th century (London, 1904), especially pp. 174–96; for a chronicler's account, RIS, CS, p. 76.

found adequate to talk of members of the same house (*domus* or *casamentus*), 'as this is commonly understood'.[14]

Those who framed the laws knew a family when they saw one, as it were, and they also knew a magnate. Possibly the first use of that word in an official Sienese context occurred in January 1272 when a 'secret' council was summoned, its members being the Captains of the Guelf party, the court (Curia, the Podestà's officials) and 'many magnates of the city' (*plurium magnatorum civitatis*).[15] The word and concept fulfilled a need and had come to stay, at Siena as elsewhere. Soon after this there would be councils including sixty *boni homines de magnatibus civitatis* or 'a great number of magnates and rich men of the city'. Although the word 'grandi' continued to be employed in vernacular legislation, *magnates* remained the normal word in the 'popular' laws designed to limit the powers of the wealthy, as it had been for some decades at Padua and Bologna.[16]

Some of the magnate families came to have many branches and fissility could be a danger as well as solidarity. The numbers were often large. The consequences of this for the dispersed pattern of landholding in the contado have already been noted, as have the twenty-four part-owners of the Tolomei palace (1254). In 1310 sixty Tolomei involved in pacificatory proceedings met at the palazzo and claimed that they constituted at least two-thirds of all the male lay members of this *domus*, *progenies* and *casatus* then in Tuscany.[17] In 1292 officials were given power to send into forced residence the factions which were at enmity; the scandal and danger to the city's peace had come about 'on account of the discord and dissension between noble men of the house of Piccolomini'.[18]

But quarrels within a family were the exception. The typical magnatial dispute was one between families and factionalism of this sort – polarised at times by the external forces of Guelfism and Ghibellinism – was what the pacificatory moves of 1280 (treated later in this chapter, pp. 120–2) aimed to eradicate: the pacification was thus concerned with problems arising both from internal and external sources of discord. Characteristic affrays were those which resulted in Piccolomini being fined for involvement in brawling with others and Gallerani for inflicting wounds in similar circumstances (1302).[19] A serious quarrel could easily escalate into a private war: 'a hatred had grown up between the Tolomei and Malavolti', explains a chronicler (1306), 'there seemed no way of getting rid of it, and daily

---

14 'Breve 1250', §53.
15 CG 15, f. 36v.
16 CG 17, ff. 5, 8, 31v; 18, ff. 55–6: *Cost. 1309–10*, 2, p. 239. For *magnates* see G. Salvemini, *Magnati e popolani in Firenze dal 1280 al 1295* (Turin, 1960), p. 33n; G. Fasoli in *RSDI*, 6 (1933), pp. 351 ff; N. Rubinstein, *La lotta contro i magnati a Firenze, 2: Le origini della legge sul sodamento* (Florence, 1939).
17 Above, pp. 7, 37. Dipl., Tolomei, 3.6.1310 (text in English, '5 Magnate Families', pp. 343–7).
18 CG 43, ff. 70v–1.
19 B 113, f. 15v (one of many such fines in the second half of 1296); 116, f. 164v.

they put Siena in an uproar' (*a romore*). This enmity was characterized as 'a menace to the peace of all Tuscany' and the Nine were granted special powers to deal with the dispute, which led to the formation of a force of 3,000 armed men to deal with such quarrels. The chronicler has it that 'Siena's delinquents and those who did not wish to live reasonably' were chastened by this move[20] but family disputes continued; they were after all not merely a symptom of magnate-ship but a spectacular symbol of that status.

THE POPOLO

The expression of the magnates' overbearing social power, whether concentrated by political allegiance or lacking it, was the greatest threat to the city's peace. As early as 1229 those who felt excluded from the governing oligarchy and menaced by the ways in which its strength was expressed had developed an organization to counter this situation.[21] By the late 1230s the Twenty-four, an office of 'popular' origin, were the commune's main officials. Siena's Popolo was regional in its organization, being based on the terzi. Around 1253 its officials, the priors, were reinforced by the appointment of a non-Sienese Captain of the Popolo. The Popolo gained a share of political authority in a constitutional struggle waged mainly over fiscal and institutional issues. A counterweight to the monopoly of earlier oligarchy, it was also the creator of new problems for the internal peace of the city. The Popolo must be seen as an anti-oligarchical, not a democratic, body, as is made clear by a contemporary (1257) definition of the electors to its captaincy as 'noble and great (*magni*) citizens'.[22]

A characteristic decision of the council of the Popolo (1257) related to direct taxation. The body of assessors for the new *libra* (direct tax) was to have a majority of *populares*, i.e. members of the Popolo. Hitherto (the council decided) the 'rich and powerful' had not been assessed, as *populares* had, in accordance with their property. Now 'it was up to these *populares* to levy the tax'. The assessors were to levy it 'well and legally so that all those who have rich purses are assessed in full'. One speaker in the debate hoped that the Captain of the Popolo would warn the assessors 'that they should aim to the best of their ability at equality for all' (*ad egualgliantiam communem*).[23]

The main constitutional struggle was fought around the years 1255–57.[24] The Popolo asserted its right to a share in the work of legislation, in policy within the contado and in justice, and to defend the gilds against action by the Podestà. The

20 *RIS*, *CS*, pp. 86, 294–5; CG 68, ff. 113–16v.
21 For this paragraph see Mondolfo, *Populus*, chapter 2.
22 'Breve 1250', docs. (*ASI* (1866), 4), p. 54.
23 CG 6, ff. 124–5.
24 CG 6; excellent analysis in Mondolfo, chapter 2.

Popolo hammered away, seeking to strengthen its own organization and demanding innovations such as joint meetings between its council and the commune's. It put forward a programme of claims concerning office-holding: at least half the members of the General Council should be *populares* and the same should apply to smaller councils other than those concerned with diplomatic negotiations. This rule should hold also for the Emenders of the statutes and the electors of the Podestà. At least one of the three Provveditori should be 'of the Popolo'. The contestants reached formal constitutional agreements from time to time[25] and by 1262 all the Popolo's aims relating to office had been achieved.

An important gain by the same year was legal immunity for acts of revenge carried out by members of the Popolo 'at the wish and order of the Captain or the Twenty-four and their priors' and measures were passed dealing with armed gatherings, street-fighting and offences committed during Council-meetings.[26] Thus the Popolo both acted to check the social violence of the mighty and itself threatened violence. The wariness prevailing is confirmed by the formation of regional armed companies. On 4 May 1262 the Popolo decreed that 'there should be companies of those subordinate to the Popolo and its sworn members; all those who belong should be compelled to join'.[27] Some of these bodies had topographical titles, others received names such as 'Star' and 'Sailors'. Anti-popular companies also existed: a certain Ricovaro refused to be a councillor of the Popolo on the grounds that he had belonged to such a body, the 'King's men' (*societas realium*), though he denied actually bearing arms against the Twenty-four or the Popolo.[28]

Between 1262 and 1277 the Popolo lost much ground. The office of Captain disappeared in 1271 or soon after and although it was revived briefly in 1278–79 and more lastingly in 1289 it never regained its former authority.[29] Suspicion of the great families certainly survived. A very important measure of about 1271 prohibited the election of any member of a magnate family (*de casato seu de casatis*) and anyone 'who had received the honour of knighthood' to the senior office (now numbering Thirty-six).[30] That law, which seems the very essence of a popular programme, was incorporated in statutes issued in 1274, yet those statutes make no mention at all of the Popolo as still possessing its own council. Unfortunately these are very ill-documented years, so that nothing is known of

25 *Const. 1262*, p. 79.
26 CG 6, ff. 76–8.
27 CG 10, f. 32.
28 *Const. 1262*, Introduction, pp. lxiv, lxxv; CG 6, f. 185.
29 Ciampoli, pp. 25–9.
30 G. Francini, 'Appunti sulla costituzione guelfa del comune di Siena secondo il Costituto del 1274', *BSSP*, 46 (1939), pp. 11–28; Marrara, especially pp. 244–5; Mondolfo, *Le cause e le vicende della politica del comune di Siena nel sec. XIII* (Siena, 1904), pp. 35–7.

the process whereby the Popolo was virtually disbanded at a time when what it stood for seemed to have been achieved.

The measures against magnates were reasserted in May 1277 and given a precision which was likely to make them more effective. The authority of the Podestà and Thirty-six was reaffirmed and the former ordered to punish the guilty, be they 'great or small'. The Thirty-six were to be 'good, law-abiding merchants and lovers of the Guelf party'. Members of the *casati* were ineligible, and 'since doubt arises concerning the *casati*', a list of these was now issued, comprising the names of fifty-three families. They included: Piccolomini, Tolomei, Bonsignori, Gallerani, Salimbeni, Malavolti, Ugurgieri, Forteguerri, Sansedoni, Rinaldini, Pagliaresi, Selvolesi, Provenzani and Salvani – all the most famous names in Sienese banking and the conduct of the commune's affairs.[31] Members of these families were now banned from membership of the Thirty-six, but they were not to suffer the other legal disadvantages which characterized the 'anti-magnate' legislation of many of the Italian communes.[32] The law was a reaction to the great strength of Siena's leading families, but it was not drafted as part of the programme of a self-proclaimed anti-aristocratic organization (a 'Popolo'), nor was it aimed to deal specifically with the disturbances for which the magnates were notorious. In any case, 'magnate' and feuding families were not synonymous. Nearly two-thirds of the families branded as *casati* in 1277 were not involved in the major pacification of 1280 between leading Guelfs and Ghibellines, whilst several families in the 1280 lists were non-magnates.[33] The families which were listed as magnates in Florence in 1286 had to provide financial guarantees for their future good behaviour and the Sienese laws of 1277 contain the same provisions, yet they should be seen as an assertion of unwillingness to accept political domination by the great families rather than measures designed to check violence as part of the magnates' way of life. They express opposition to oligarchical monopoly of power, but one of the principal themes of this book is the ineffectiveness of that opposition. Their very limited efficacy is illustrated by the prominent role in the conciliar meetings of 1277–78 of members of such families as the Salimbeni, Piccolomini, Tolomei, Malavolti, Forteguerri and Pagliaresi.[34]

31 The text is printed by P. Luigi Sbaragli in *BSSP*, 44 (1937), pp. 59–62.
32 See G. Fasoli, 'Ricerche sulla legislazione antimagnatizia nei comuni dell'alta e media Italia', *RSDI*, 12 (1939), pp. 86–133, 240–309.
33 Below, pp. 120–2.
34 See P. Cammarosano, *Tradizione documentaria e storia cittadina. Introduzione al Caleffo Vecchio del comune di Siena* (Siena, 1988), p. 73 and n. I agree completely with the opinion of A. K. Isaacs (*I ceti dirigenti nella Toscana tardo comunale* (Florence, 1983) p. 86) that 'i casati nobili . . . restano forza portante del comune' throughout the period of the Nine.

The Sienese Popolo shrivelled away at the very stage at which it might have been expected to exert most influence. What had happened was that the well-to-do Guelf traders had overcome their 'left-wing' rivals, the *populares*, through a tacit alliance with their 'right-wing' rivals, the magnates. In 1289 the captaincy of the Popolo made a brief reappearance in an emasculated form and at that time the citizens were ordered – many of them in vain – to take an oath of obedience to the Popolo and its Captain. Soon afterwards the captaincy came to be nothing more than a judicial post ranking below the podesteria.[35] No effective check had been placed on the tendencies which made for internal violence.

THE CONTADO

The problem faced by Siena's authorities in the city's subject territory were more time-consuming and scarcely less crucial than those involving the peace of the city itself. Few Council-meetings passed without some discussion of difficulties encountered by the commune in its considerable territorial empire.

By the middle of the thirteenth century this zone of influence extended approximately to the boundaries it was to maintain for the remaining three centuries of the city's independence. To the north, where Siena's neighbour was the most powerful of the Tuscan cities, the frontier with Florence ran a mere fifteen kilometres from Siena; the territory in the Val d'Elsa and Chianti constituted a very meagre buffer indeed. The siting of the city within its own dominions was absurd, for its southern sphere of influence, in contrast, stretched far across the Maremma uplands to Grosseto, more than sixty kilometres to the south-west, and thence via the Aldobrandeschine county (where Siena claimed overlordship) to Montalcino, Montepulciano and the west side of the Chiana valley, where the neighbouring contado was that of Arezzo. To use a national analogy, this was a little as though the capital of Italy had remained at Turin. There was a contrast also between the fertility of Siena's miniature northern sphere of influence and the wide but often barren spaces of the south.

The process whereby Siena, in common with the other medieval Italian communes, was drawn into the acquisition of subject territories, requires little explanation; the city which remained a mere 'legal island' is a more puzzling phenomenon. Proximity drew the communes into a nexus of authorities, and as cities embarked on the process of achieving dominion they were sucked into the game in defensive reaction to the gains of their neighbours. As frontiers, based on dioceses, were claimed, prestige became involved in this interplay of power. During the high tide of Frederick II's sway Siena lost much of its rural authority, but in 1251, soon after his death, officials were appointed with the task of

35 Ciampoli, pp. 25–30.

N

Staggia

Castiglion Ghinibaldi
Abbadia a Isola
Strove
Montauto
Monteriggioni

Selvole
Quercegrossa
Cerreto
Castelnuovo Berardenga

Casole d'Elsa

Siena
Montaperti
Castiglioni

Mensano

Petriccio
Torre a Castello
Poggio S. Cecilia

Montaguidi
Sovicille
Rapolano
Rigomagno

Selva
Ampugnano
Serre di Rapolano
Farnetella

Radicondoli
Monteroni d'Arbia
Asciano
S. Gemignanello

Lucignano d'Arbia
Castelnuovo Grilli
Ripa
Sinalunga

Campriano
Trequanda
Guardavalle

Crevole
Murlo
S. Giovanni d'Asso
Ciliano
Torrita
di Siena

Chiusdino
S. Lorenzo a Merse
Percenna
Montisi

Gerfalco
Monticiano
Macereto
Resi
Buonconvento
Montefollonico

Montieri
Castel di Tocchi
Vallerano
Cosona
Montepulciano

Rochette dei
Pannocchieschi
Campriano
Petriolo
Montepertuso
Castiglione
del Bosco
Torrenieri
Corsignano (Pienza)
Fabbrica
Monticchiello

Boccheggiano
Pari
Montalcino
S. Quirico d'Orcia
Chianciano

Massa Marittima
Torniella
Montacuto di Pari
Vignoni
Palazzo di Gete

Sassoforte
Casenovole
Camigliano
Rocca d'Orcia
Castiglioncello
del Trinoro

Roccatederighi
Roccastrada
Monte
Antico
Sant'Angelo
in Colle
Castelnuovo
dell'Abate
Castiglione
d'Orcia

Castello del
Vescovo
Montemassi
Civitella Marittima
Perignano

Gavorrano
Sticciano
Paganico
Monteverdi
Montenero
Potentino
Seggiano
Campiglia d'Orcia

Scarlino
Giuncarico
Montorsaio
Sasso d'Ombrone
Porrona
Montegiovi
Radicofani

Campagnatico
Cinigiano
Castel del Piano
Abbadia
S. Salvatore

Montelaterone
Arcidosso

Stribugliano
Piancastagnaio

Santa Fiora

Cana
Roccalbegna

Castiglione della Pescaia
Grosseto
Castell'Azzara

Semproniano

Scansiano
Sorano

Pitigliano

0   10   20 km
0   5   10 miles

3 THE CONTADO.

proposing 'how the contado of Siena may be brought back into the city's possession'.[36] Later it became a duty of the city's officials 'to augment the city and jurisdiction of Siena in the Maremma, the "mountains" (west of Siena) and elsewhere, by the purchase and acquisition of castles, entire or in part, and the acquisition of rights wherever possible'.[37] A committee of *savi* had the function of making recommendations to extend the 'arm and power' of Siena in the Maremma. Action along these lines was frequent and could be very expensive; to give a single instance, in 1298 it was resolved to buy Cerreto, a castle in the southern Chianti, for 36,000 l., though in the event the negotiations were only partially successful.[38]

Economic motives were involved in the extension of the contado, above all that of supplying the urban nucleus with bread. The grain of the subject territory was reserved for Siena and fixed quantities had to be provided; at times, frontier patrols were organized to prevent its export.[39] Less crucial, but important because local supplies were inadequate, was fish. The commune attempted to improve the supply by constructing fishponds in various suitable areas.[40] Lordship applied also to materials other than foodstuffs; any part of the territory could be ordered to send stone for the fabric of the cathedral.[41]

The military motives are no less clear. The boundary with Florence, not well defined by geographical features, constituted a 'frontier system' and one bastion of this, Monteriggioni, is a spectacular survival. To the south Siena's territory was dotted with castles whose small garrisons could serve to hold down local dissidence or, at other times, to check invasion.[42] The commune lacked the means to retain standing garrisons of any size. A typical conciliar debate (1289) concerned Trequanda, Sinalunga and Fabbrica, all in the south-eastern contado: the question was which of these three fortresses should be held, and the alternative to garrisoning was destruction.[43] In the southern Maremma there was no powerful bulwark at all but from the 1290s onwards costly attempts were made to found and populate two defensive sites, at Roccalbegna and Castelfranco Paganico.[44] The contado was above all a buffer for defence in depth against a

36 *B.* 11, p. 96.
37 *Cost. 1309–10*, 2, p. 503.
38 CG 53, ff. 70–2; 54, ff. 25v–7. On Cerreto, *Repertorio*, pp. 40–1.
39 CG 61, ff. 49v–50v (1302).
40 CG 5, f. 19 (1255); *B.* 26, p. 208 (1257).
41 *Cost. 1309–10*, 1, pp. 64–8.
42 Redon, chapter 1.
43 CG 38, f. 13.
44 Bowsky, *Commune*, pp. 194–5; P. Angelucci, 'Genesi di un borgo franco nel senese: Paganico' in *Università e tutela dei beni culturali: il contributo degli studi medievali e umanistici. Atti del convegno . . . 21–23 genn. 1977* (Florence), pp. 95–135.

raiding enemy – the methods of warfare made it the main victim of campaigning – as well as being a recruiting ground. As a condition of their subjection rural subjects provided cavalry, infantry and in particular the necessary corps of pioneers and sappers. The function of the contado was negative too, in that the commune endeavoured to deny its territory as recruiting land to the neighbouring cities of Florence (above all) and at times Arezzo and Orvieto.[45]

The commune's attitude towards its subject territory was harsh. The population was regarded as rootless – one should perhaps say, more literally, foundationless. The Sienese (not at all exceptionally, for it was known that villagers could carry their humble homes with them to another site) saw dwellers in wooden-hutted villages as creatures who might be moved around in accordance with military necessity. Hence, for example, those who cultivated the low-lying land round Abbadia a Isola were constantly ordered to reside in the nearby defended hill-site of Monteriggioni. Further east along the same frontier attempts were made to populate Quercegrossa at the expense of places on the Florentine side of the border.[46] In the Ardenga territory to the south-east similar efforts were made to shift population, despite the protests of the abbot.[47] In 1291 the decision was made to rebuild Rigomagno on a new site[48] and many other examples could be given of such policies. The measures were often the consequence of military needs. At one time residence in the town of Asciano was forbidden, though probably this order was ineffectual.[49] The *burgum* of Montepulciano was destroyed in 1281, the *rocca* of Roccastrada in 1302.[50] At Montalcino two men earned 18 l. 5s. by their good work in supervising the demolition of the town's churches (*pro salario quando steterunt ad faciendum destrui et dissipari ecclesias de Montalcino*). A clause in the 1262 constitution decreed the total destruction of all buildings and even flora on the hill where Montalcino stood, 'so that the hill itself should become a wild place, uninhabited in perpetuity'. The expressions 'discastellare' (to disfortify) and 'reincastellare' (to refortify) were found most useful by legislators.[51] It was indeed an obligation on the Podestà to destroy and 'keep destroyed in perpetuity' any place rebelling against Siena. Imperialism had economic as well as military aspects; thus an attempt was made to forbid money-lenders from operating at Montepulciano 'lest scandal should arise between us and the Montepulcianesi' (i.e., presumably, lest there be competition

45 *B.* 4, p. 86.
46 *Const. 1262*, pp. 376–9; CG 4, f. 16v; 35, f. 19; *B.* 28, p. 152.
47 CG 3, f. 64v.
48 CG 42, f. 46.
49 *Const. 1262*, p. 375.
50 B 80, f. 115; 117, f. 316.
51 B 35, f. 23; *Const. 1262*, pp. 385, 497 (index).

against Siena's own bankers).[52] Not everything that was decreed occurred, but much anxiety and misery were caused. The subject population and its humble residences were, in the eyes of their Sienese overlords, totally mobile.

So many things could go wrong in the contado that it is no surprise that difficulties occurred constantly. The territory was anything but a bloc, rather it was a fragmented, haphazard collection of lordships and townships, having almost nothing in common except its fragile subordination to Siena. To the south castles perched on isolated hill sites overlooked much parched upland, there was much pastoral land and cattle-stealing was a way of life. The seignorial norm was lay and monastic lordship. Around Siena itself more typically Tuscan agriculture tended to prevail, of mixed cultivation dominated by grain and the vine. Land tenure there was characterized by the stronger influence of the city, at the expense of seignorial families. A large proportion of the contado peasants must have lived little above the level of subsistence. The population was a mobile one for economic reasons as well as for Siena's strategic ones, hence deserted sites abounded.

Perhaps the greatest difficulty was the very nature of Sienese suzerainty, which everywhere involved compromise with other lordships. A person or community subject to the commune of Siena was commonly described as subject to its jurisdiction ('de iurisdictione'), but in reality the city's jurisdiction had to share with that of lords and other communes. Siena recognized that its judicial rights 'should not be to the prejudice of the true lords of places (*terrarum*), holding jurisdiction in whole or part'. The same principle applied to office-holding in the communities of the contado; when these had their own lord, 'possessing jurisdiction', he it was who appointed the local rector or official. Rights of private lordship over individual villeins were similarly guarded by Sienese law. The situation in the lands sold to the Salimbeni in 1275 was typical. There the Sienese courts had the right to hear suits involving murder and, in the case of strangers, wounding; theft and violence would go to those courts only if a delay of a month had passed without action in the local court.[53]

The conciliar discussions of the first six months of 1255 will serve to exemplify the sort of problems which arose in the contado.[54] Purchase of rights at various places was considered and negotiations over a purchase actually took place with the abbot of S Antimo. The Count of Elci's rights at Monte Ciriota and the obligations of the Montepulcianesi to pay tolls were debated. The taxation of villeins of Sienese citizens was a favourite theme, and factional struggles and a political murder at Torrita an anxiety. Questions arose over the garrisons at

52 *Const, 1262*, p. 381.
53 Redon, pp. 196–7.
54 CG 4.

Montorsaio and Campagnatico, fortifications were rebuilt at Montefollonico, new fortifications in the Val di Strove and Val d'Elsa were mooted. Serious robberies occurred on the Petriolo road and near Torrita. Raiding by Aldobrandeschi forces towards Grosseto was reported which raised questions about Sienese relations with the lords of Sassoforte, but this was the only major military incursion and indeed it was quite rare throughout the period covered by this volume for external enemies to campaign in Sienese territory.

Problems concerning food supply often involved other difficulties, for instance troops were needed for patrols to prevent the export of grain from the contado but these men could only be paid if taxation and fines were levied in the contado. It was a vicious circle: domination required money for soldiers, but the money could only be raised if the subject territory was already being taxed.[55] At their worst, the afflictions of the contado poor were appalling. The year 1295 was one of starvation and sickness in the countryside; the rural communities had defaulted in their tax payments, hence their residents were forbidden to travel, even to see the doctor. The city eventually relented to the extent of voting 1,000 florins as alms for the sick in the contado 'to the honour of God and the Blessed Virgin Mary and in order that the Omnipotent and His Mother may keep the city of Siena in peace and tranquillity'. The following year the poor of all those communities in the contado which were 'broken and dissolved' (i.e. bankrupt) submitted a petition claiming that only a few residents remained in each of these places and it was impossible for this handful to face the fiscal burdens still placed on them.[56] In 1297 the poor of the city and contado received a joint gift of 4,000 l.; but charity on that scale (denoting a period of bad harvests and exceptional suffering) was quite abnormal.[57]

With three tiers of authority in much of the contado – commune of Siena, lord, local commune – the questions that arose were dilemmas affecting the city's fundamental policies. Above all, should Siena settle for 'indirect rule', leaving government and administration to a local seignorial or communal authority? If so, what should it do when things went wrong, as frequently happened? One is inclined to feel that the Sienese should have opted more firmly for the colonial principle of indirect rule, yet this decision on its own would not have solved fiscal problems or those of public order. In March 1255 the council discussed the re-fortification of Montefollonico and 'the well in that place which has been petitioned for';[58] one could give numberless examples of this sort showing how the city was drawn into matters of local detail.

---

55 E.g. CG 41, ff. 44–68, 123v–4 (1291).
56 CG 48, ff. 50–5v; 49, ff. 79r and v; 50, f. 37; B 112, f. 116.
57 CG 51, ff. 103v–8v.
58 CG 4, f. 45

The Ardengheschi counts were overlords of the communities of Pari, Civitella, Montacuto and Fornoli, and Siena had to decide its position on the jurisdiction of these various authorities. A decision (1257) recognized the superior position of the counts, but it was not an easy one since the counts were normally regarded as a focus of resistance and lawlessness.[59] Where there was no intermediate lord the existence of communal organization was more obviously in Siena's interest, hence the decision (1283) that the inhabitants of places in the contado not possessing a commune should be compelled to have one.[60] It was a welcome development when the population of Buonconvento offered to reform their commune, which had suffered fiscal bankruptcy and fallen under the suzerainty of Percenna, a neighbour; they offered to 'bear the same burden as other *comitatenses* and pay the same dues'.[61] One difficulty of direct rule was the expense of appointing a full-time Sienese rector, another the problem of finding an able man who would face exile in a small place. A common compromise was to appoint a man whose obligation to reside locally was limited to four days in each month (as at Selva, from 1250).[62]

In a conciliar debate (1255) a speaker suggested that 'no noble holding rights of toll from time immemorial (*ab antiquo*) should be dispossessed of them'.[63] This may already have sounded an old-fashioned view. Earlier the commune had been confronted in the contado by lords most of whom held rights *ab antiquo*, but by the mid thirteenth century the situation had become much more complicated. It was difficult to reconcile the city's interests with both those of the subject communities and those of its citizens who might themselves be lords (or merely landholders or cultivators) in the countryside.[64] Legislation became necessary to deal with 'citizens possessing jurisdiction in any castle', citizens subject to the lordship of other citizens, villeins refusing rent in kind to lords who were citizens, and the local tax obligations of sharecroppers and others who quitted their native localities to move into Siena.[65] The taxation of villeins whose lords were Sienese citizens was a particularly difficult matter – the lord resented taxation by the city so heavy that too little remained for him – and sometimes the Sienese council heard petitions from sufferers who endured double taxation, by Siena and another lord.[66]

59 P. Angelucci, 'Gli Ardengheschi nella dinamica dei rapporti con il comune di Siena' in *I ceti dirigenti dell'età comunale nei sec. XII e XIII* (Pisa, 1982), pp. 119–56, especially 137–45. See also Redon, pp. 182–3 and *CV*, 4, pp. 1560–6.
60 CG 27, ff. 37–8.
61 CG 46, ff. 46–7v.
62 *CV*, 2, pp. 667–9 (for Selva, *Repertorio*, p. 32).
63 CG 4, f. 56.
64 See Cammarosano, especially pp. 191–2.
65 *Cost. 1309–10*, 1, pp. 313–14; 2, pp. 160–2.
66 CG 7, ff. 12v–i3v and Alleg. A (1256); 22, Alleg. D (men of Torniella taxed by Count Aldobrandino and by Siena, 1278).

While it was accepted by the Sienese authorities that in the contado the commune was one lord among many, the military strength of its seignorial rivals was a matter for anxiety. Hence, for example, the large fine (500 l.) threatened for any *signore* or *nobile* of the contado sending armed men into the city to participate in a civil disturbance.[67] Moreover lordship was never a static institution. The abbot of S Salvatore (Monte Amiata) was losing ground to the abbey's local communities and the Ardengheschi losing authority to the Malavolti and Incontri families and the Sienese commune itself.[68] By the fourteenth century the most formidable forces in the contado were no longer the older 'contado nobles' but rather 'Sieneses families, both magnate ones and those of other social groups'.[69]

Statutes proclaimed the intention that the commune 'should extend its arm and power in the Maremma', but this was the area least under control. Siena derived little financial advantage from the territory and complained that its population was 'oppressed by the communities and nobles' of the region, both by tolls and direct taxation. The Podestà was ordered to send letters forbidding such taxation to 'the Aldobrandeschi counts and all the other barons and nobles and *lambardi* (military tenants) and the cities and communities of the Maremma' and many similar resolutions and threats are recorded. The Sienese themselves were forbidden by their commune to swear fealty to any 'lord or baron' of the Maremma (1284) and they were supposed to apply for permission before acquiring any form of fief there, including castles, jurisdiction or lordship.[70] The belief that problems arising from fundamental weaknesses in finance and communications could be solved by legislation seems unrealistic. A law was also passed (1302) whereby any Sienese citizen marrying a count, lord or baron of the Maremma was to suffer loss of citizenship, outlawry and a fine of 3,000 l., but a proposal that receipt of a fief or knighthood from any of these nobles should be forbidden failed to win acceptance.[71] The weakness of Siena's position was emphasized when the Aldobrandeschi recruited men within this region of Sienese suzerainty (1291) to fight against the commune of Siena.[72]

The Aldobrandeschi counts were supposed (and had been since 1221 or earlier) to pay Siena an annual *census* of 25 silver marks. Promises were occasionally made to fulfil this obligation but they never seem to have been effective, a sad indication of the inutility of 'rights' unsupported by power.[73] A fine of 1,500 l. levied by the

---

67 *Cost. 1309–10*, 2, p. 240.
68 Angelucci, in n. 59 above; Redon, chapter 1.
69 Isaacs, in n. 34, pp. 81–2.
70 *Cost. 1309–10*, 2, pp. 186, 503; CG 28, f. 28r and v.
71 CG 61, ff. 112v–14v, 122v–6v.
72 CG 42, f. 28v.
73 Ciacci, 2, pp. 111, 142–4, 167, 222; *Const. 1262*, p. 96n.

commune on Count Umberto, son of Count Aldobrandino of Santa Fiora, probably for involvement in a murder, was taken more seriously and eventually (1278) paid.[74]

BANDITRY

The problems of the contado were seen at their most extreme in the phenomenon of banditry. A common sequence of events was this. A man or men committed a violent crime. Unwilling to appear in court, they fled to the contado or beyond and meanwhile were condemned *in absentia*, put under ban (*bannitus*), i.e. outlawed. They then set up in the contado – not too close to Siena – with banditry (the word 'bandit' of course derives from *bannitus* = Italian *bandito*) as their way of life and means of subsistence.[75] Contado communities were threatened with heavy penalties for harbouring outlaws and the Podestà was supposed to send out anti-bandit patrols at least once a month, but neither of these measures achieved much.[76] The consequences are vividly portrayed in Lorenzetti's depiction of a highway robbery in the Palazzo Pubblico (in the rarely reproduced scene of the rural consequences of bad government). In the scene of 'good government in the countryside' Security, bearing a gallows in her hand, proclaims optimistically that 'so long as this lady (Justice) is in power', 'all men may freely travel without fear and all may sow and till the soil'.[77]

The most famous of Siena's bandits, Ghino di Tacco, won mention in the *Divina Commedia* and is the hero of a tale in the *Decameron*.[78] Ghino entered folk legend as a sort of Robin Hood figure, but Boccaccio did not misrepresent his occupation; he was indeed a highway robber (*rubatore delle strade*) whose band (*masnadieri*) robbed all who travelled in those parts (*chiunque per le circustanti parti passava*). Ghino descended from the Cacciaconti, a seignorial family whose homeland was in the Valdichiana where Sienese dominion had a frontier with Arezzo. He and his brother were outlawed by Siena (the reasons are unknown) around 1276. The main centres of their operations were Torrita and Rigomagno, north of Montepulciano. War between Siena and Arezzo gained Ghino support from the rival city and a nominal cause (Ghibellinism or, more accurately, anti-Florentinism). The Sienese condemned him for robbery on the Via Francigena near San Quirico (1288) and near Montepulciano (1291); on the latter occasion his victims were Florentine merchants. A few years later he moved his sphere of operations further

---

74 Ciacci, 1, pp. 230–1 and 2, pp. 251–2; B 73, f. 2.
75 Pazzaglini, pp. 103–8. See above, pp. 69–70.
76 *Const. 1262*, p. 221; *Cost. 1309–10*, 1, pp. 68–70.
77 The message on the scroll runs: 'Senza paura ognuom franco camini/E lavorando semini ciascuno/Mentre che tal comuno/Manterra questa donna in signoria/Che alevata arei ogni balia.'
78 On Ghino, see G. Cecchini, 'Ghino di Tacco', *ASI*, 115 (1957), pp. 263–98.

south, to the papal border (Radicofani), but in 1297 alarm was caused in Siena by the news that he was building a fortress – perhaps on the model of Siena's strategic foundations? – back in his home territory, between Sinalunga and Guardavalle.[79] After that he disappears from the list of Siena's anxieties and the date of his death is not known.

Ghino di Tacco was the archetypal bandit, but many other groups operated more briefly and on a smaller scale. Often their deeds caused sufficient disquiet for them to secure discussion in the General Council. The Brescian Bertolino who was Podestà of Siena in 1286 was in such fear when he set out for home at the end of his period of office that he called for military protection on the road.[80] A few years later Nuccio of Corsignano and his band achieved a spectacular coup at nearby Petroio, burning houses and stealing cattle and other property. He was caught and sentenced to death, yet the council eventually decided by a majority of 207 votes to 38 to pardon and release him.[81]

When a band disintegrated, its members, a floating brigand population, set the same problems as unemployed soldiery.[82] It is difficult to guess the average size of such bands. One which operated round Montepulciano (1303–07) had twenty-six members. They originated from various nearby places and not all came from impoverished backgrounds; several were described as sons of *domini* and others of *magistri*.[83] Not all Sienese groups of robbers operated in Sienese territory. In 1271 a company of Sienese 'Ghibellines' (the label probably had no serious political connotation) stole cloth from Florentine merchants in the district of Perugia. This was not an instance of successfully exporting one's problems, for the Perugians reacted to the theft by confiscating Sienese (Tolomei) cloth as a reprisal.[84]

THE CONTADO: CONCLUSIONS

The sources of trouble in the subject territory mentioned hitherto by no means exhaust the subject. Another was office-holding. There was often bitter contention for podesterie and rectorial posts. Whatever the precautions, it was difficult to persuade all that justice was being done in the allocation of these posts.[85] There was a belief that plenty of money could be made from such appointments and that those who made it were contriving to pay suspiciously low taxes.[86] The very number of the posts reveals why the subject took up so much time, particularly in

79 CG 52, ff. 107v–10 (printed in *ASI*, 115, pp. 296–8).
80 CG 32, ff. 33r and v.
81 CG 41, ff. 74–6v.
82 E.g. CG 49, ff. 39v–40, 51v; 50, f. 82r and v (1296).
83 B 121, f. 217v (1307: condemned in 1303).
84 CG 14, ff. 55r and v, 62.
85 CG 7, ff. 5v–6 (1256).
86 CG 42, ff. 21v–2, 36v–7, 47v, 50v–1v (1291).

view of disputes about which of them involved appointment by the Sienese authorities.[87] In the 1260s about 280 communities in the contado were organized as communes. Professor Redon (from whose map these figures are calculated) has well defined the status of these communities by styling them 'subjects rather than *fideles*'.[88]

Other territorial preoccupations existed in plenty. An ambitious programme of founding watering-places was the subject of much legislation. The resorts were thought to have fiscal possibilities and the revenues from them were farmed out.[89] The city's water supply was another matter involving negotiation with rural areas. A constantly open question was that of an outlet on the seacoast. This was an obvious objective in connection with the encouragement of maritime trade, hence the laborious but rather unsuccessful attempts to establish a port on the Tyrrhenian at Talamone.[90]

Historians have not hesitated to attempt a sort of 'credit and debit account' for Siena in respect of its subject territory, particularly in the financial sense. Above all the question is asked: was the contado 'exploited' by the city? The means of calculating the total revenue drawn from the contado – mainly through indirect taxation – simply do not exist. The same applies to the calculation of indirect military advantages and to expenditure on all sorts of matters involving the contado. The profits of justice were not considerable. They consisted for the most part in the very irregular payment of 'compositions' of overdue fines, amounting perhaps to one tenth of certain fines notionally due. In 1293 (to give one example) thirteen localities in the contado paid such compositions and these rendered the not very impressive – but still useful – total of about 2,500 l.[91] The contado was taxed, rendered a lot and cost a lot. Questions about the total balance and the fairness of contado taxation are unanswerable, certainly by this author at this juncture.

GHIBELLINISM

Another category of problem was that deriving from the commune's relationship with the power systems and alliances of Tuscany, which in turn were connected with those of the peninsula as a whole. These blocs, linked respectively with Hohenstaufen and papal-Angevin leadership, were coming to be described by the mid century as 'Ghibelline' and 'Guelf'. References to Ghibelline bands operating in the contado (for instance) show that this categorization, by implying a

---

87 E.g. CG 7, f. 22v.
88 Redon, p. 221 and map: and see particularly chapters 1, 4 and 5.
89 D. Barduzzi, *Provvedimenti per le stazioni termali senesi nei sec XIII e XIV* (Siena, 1899).
90 *Cost. 1309–10*, 1, pp. 342–3; Bowsky, *Commune*, especially pp. 175–6.
91 B 109.

distinction between social and political causation, does violence to the intricacies of the past; but lines have to be drawn.

The commune's external relations show Siena as a proud but not particularly powerful vessel tossed in the high seas of a stormy epoch. Throughout the 1240s the authority of Frederick II had predominated in Tuscany, his representatives (vicars general) being first Pandulf of Fasanella, then his own bastard son Frederick of Antioch. An imperial official held sway in the Sienese contado and at times Siena's Podestà was nominated by the Emperor. It seems likely that those who did not sympathize with the commune's pro-Hohenstaufen alignment were driven into exile in 1248 or about that time,[92] but Frederick's death in December 1250 totally altered the situation. Hohenstaufen authority in Tuscany rapidly dissolved and the major communes set about the restoration of their dominion in the countryside. Florence soon proved the greatest beneficiary and the Sienese found their ambitions, even in the south, blocked by their formidably assertive neighbour.

Only when another of Frederick's illegitimate sons, Manfred, began from 1257 to build up alliances in central and northern Italy, did Siena again become committed to the Ghibelline side. The following ten years saw the heyday of the city as the nucleus of Tuscan Ghibellinism, and also the apex of Siena's standing within Tuscany. The fateful decision to support Manfred, though in a sense it was the continuation of the commune's alignment through the 1240s, was in part a reaction to the pro-papal rapprochement of the Florentines, the most powerful claimants to hegemony in Tuscany and thus Siena's principal rivals.

Siena's Ghibelline decade is closely connected with the career of Provenzano Salvani, who had held office in the Biccherna in 1247 and 1254–55 and already in Frederick II's time featured in council meetings as a protagonist of the Hohenstaufen cause. In 1251 he was involved in negotiations with Florentine and Perugian Ghibellines. Although Provenzano was very prominent in promoting the 'popular' constitutional changes of 1256, the development which brought him to a position of near-dictatorship was Manfred's diplomatic campaign from 1257 to set up an anti-Guelf shield in Tuscany, a defence against the papacy and whatever candidate the pope might recruit as Manfred's opponent.[93]

In the summer of 1259 Siena became totally committed to Manfred's cause, the commune's officials swearing an oath of fealty to him in return for the promise of protection. This was a turbulent period, with much opposition to Provenzano's policy, but in a crucial conciliar meeting (August) he secured a majority of

92 Davidsohn, 2, pp. 347, 363n, 390n, 434; CG 1, ff. 57, 60v, 68v, etc. (1249); *B.* 9, pp. 71–4, 83–6, etc.
93 See F. Tempesti, 'Provenzano Salvani', *BSSP*, 43 (1936), pp. 3–56 (pp. 42–56 are docs). See also above, pp. 101–2.

fifty-seven votes to eight for resolutions that Manfred should have a say in the choice of Siena's next Podestà and that 'any man speaking words against the honour of King Manfred and his cavalry (*milites*) should be punished by the Captain of the Popolo, in his person and in his possessions'.[94]

The first large force of German cavalry reached Siena towards the end of 1259 and by the beginning of 1260 the leading officials held office 'by the grace of God and of the lord King of Sicily'.[95] A brief spring campaign brought the Florentines to the gates of Siena and in the summer a much larger force was collected, with elements from a number of Guelf cities. This swept through the countryside, then settled in camp some five miles east of Siena, at Montaperti. There on 4 September it suffered total defeat in one of the most famous of all medieval battles.

The outcome of the campaign appeared decisive. Provenzano Salvani, it seemed, had backed the right side and the Florentine decision to oppose Manfred had been a disastrous error. Manfred's relative Count Giordano of S Severino ruled Tuscany as his vicar and was installed as nominal Podestà at Siena, though he appointed successive representatives in that post.[96] The triumph over Florence was glorious, yet Siena's situation could not be without anxiety. Diplomatic relations, for a power dealing with stronger neighbours, are bound to be costly if humiliation is to be avoided. This was Siena's situation *vis-à-vis* Florence and, in a sense, *vis-à-vis* the Hohenstaufen succession state also. The commune's relationship with Ghibellinism in the 1260s fully justifies the inclusion of foreign policy in a chapter on 'problems'.

The German cavalry were very good soldiers, as they had proved, but also very expensive ones. By March 1261 Siena's financial situation was serious. Money was needed at once for one hundred cavalry and even an embassy to King Manfred, a showy affair requiring an enormous number of horses, was so costly that the commune could not meet the bill. Moreover an awkward difference of opinion had arisen with the royal representative about the border fortress of Staggia. To the Sienese the capture of this strategic point was one of the many happy consequences of Montaperti, yet the royal vicar claimed the place together with the nearby castle of Poggibonsi. It was humiliating that Provenzano had to give way, with the not very impressive proviso that if the vicar ever yielded up Staggia to any commune it should be to Siena.[97] The 'Sicilian' (royal) authorities pressed for more and more money, while the Sienese eyed nervously the

94 CG 8, ff. 40, 46v, 52, 57r and v (partly printed, with inaccuracies, by Tempesti, pp. 47–8): Davidsohn, 2, p. 645.
95 CG 9, f. 3v.
96 Concistoro 1773, nn. 43–4.
97 CG 10, ff. 18v, 20–1, 25.

ambitions of these allies in the Maremma as well as on the Florentine frontier. A fifty-day embassy to Manfred is an indication of hard-fought negotiation, while contemporaneous missions to the papal court show the realization that other options had to be kept open.[98]

The Manfredian alliance meant retaining a considerable cavalry force in the field. The 'league' (*societas Tuscie*) required a minimum standing force of 500 and there was even talk of 1,000. For several years the Sienese *tallia* (share) remained at around 100 to 120 horsemen and the city continued in a state of financial crisis, probably because the cost of the critical year 1260–61 was a liability which had not yet been liquidated.[99] Montaperti had been an expensive triumph and Manfred was, to most, a not altogether attractive ally. When the disturbed state of the peninsula brought large armed blocs into being the expense seemed appalling to a commune such as Siena which still thought of warfare in terms of small scattered garrisons and raids by citizen militias.

The Sienese banking houses which gave aid to Manfred's cause were punished by a papal condemnation (1262) the terms of which forbade the repayment of debts to them. A large-scale political exodus from the city followed the pope's action; many financiers, by no means all of them from the leading banking families, had decided that the Manfredian alliance was the less satisfactory alternative. It is understandable that few banks should have had sufficient capital to withstand a situation in which their debtors had orders from the highest religious authority to make no payments to them. Their landed wealth probably made the position of the greatest firms less vulnerable, but the papacy was itself an extremely important client and whoever was launched by the pope as a rival claimant to Manfred's kingdom was likely to be one also. Over one hundred Sienese bankers, including eight Tolomei, five or more Salimbeni, and three Piccolomini took the decision to seek exile, at Chiusi and Radicofani, and there (March 1263) formally reverted to obedience to the Church.[100]

Many other Sienese Guelfs followed what was virtually the only way of life open to parties in exile; they 'made a company together', says a chronicler, 'and went robbing, now in one place, now in another'.[101] Some met defeat at the hands of the Florentines (by then a Ghibelline power) in the Val di Greve, others were captured in a raid against Radicofani by German cavalry. However there were bankers among Siena's Guelfs able to make considerable loans to Count Charles of Anjou, the papal candidate for the Sicilian kingdom, and by the time of

---

98 Ibid., ff. 46v, 57v, 63v, 88–9.
99 Ibid., ff. 66, 67v, 78v–9; 11, ff. 27, 34v–5, 67v, etc. For the tallia see below, p. 201.
100 *Reg. Urb. IV*, 2, n. 274: Davidsohn, 2, pp. 745–7.
101 *RIS, CS*, pp. 63, 222.

Charles' arrival at Rome (June 1265) the situation within Siena itself had begun to look extremely insecure.

Manfred's defeat and death at Benevento (February 1266) at the hands of Charles of Anjou ushered in a time of stress and dilemma for Sienese Ghibellinism, but there was still a formidable German cavalry force in Tuscany and Siena's Ghibellines proved tenacious. To the pope (Urban IV) it must have seemed clear that all was ready for the negotiation of the city's abandonment of a lost cause and the mission of his representative Bernard de Languissel (May-?September 1266) began encouragingly. Provisional terms were reached between Siena's two parties, and the papal interdict on the city was lifted.[102] Yet somewhere things went wrong and no final agreement was reached. When a Guelf regime took over in Florence (April 1267), Siena and Pisa were left as the isolated protagonists of Tuscan Ghibellinism. The pope then tried again; in May seven representatives of the Sienese regime were at the papal court, as was a proctor of the exiled Guelfs. Negotiations proceeded for a compromise whereby power was to be shared between Guelfs and a Popolo, but terms could not be reached with the stubborn Ghibellines.[103]

Angevin forces continued to apply pressure in Tuscany, but the spring of 1268 saw the advent of Frederick II's grandson Conradin, the last possible saviour of Ghibellinism. Again external military connections proved an expensive commodity; the cost of the link with Conradin was tremendous. Siena paid 33,520 l. 13s. 11d. to Conradin in the spring of 1268 and over 7,500 l. (via the Bonsignori bank) to his ally Henry of Castile, the Roman senator. Later in the year the bill for German cavalry and the expenses of Conradin's Sienese sojourn (24 June-mid July), including presents for his entourage, totalled about 34,000 l. By then the commune's German liaison was costing it about five times the normal annual expenditure of the 1240s. And by the time the 1268 Biccherna accounts which record these expenses had been totalled up, Conradin in turn had met defeat (Tagliacozzo, 23 August) and death (29 October).

The last act of Sienese Ghibellinism proved to be as prolonged as the earlier ones. Salvani's semi-lordship ended in his death in an engagement fought outside Colle Val d'Elsa in June 1269 and the following April Florence and the Angevins won a further victory at Montevarchi. When Pisa withdrew from the alliance, Siena's Ghibellines at last reached terms with the city's Guelfs. The headquarters of the long-exiled Guelfs was close to the city, at Lucignano d'Arbia, and there Siena formally submitted to the Angevin King Charles (4 August 1270). The

---

102 *Archivio del Consiglio Generale . . . Siena* (Rome, 1952), p. 135; CG 12, ff. 25v–7v, 40v–1; Davidsohn, 2, pp. 813–14, 823n, 842–3.
103 *Registres de Clément IV*, ed. E. Jordan (Paris, 1893 ff), n. 472; Davidsohn, 2, pp. 847–60; 3, pp. 3–6.

survivors among the prisoners taken ten years before at Montaperti were freed. A new Podestà 'by the grace of God and King Charles' took office, a 'gift' of 3,200 florins was made to the King's vicar in Tuscany and the Sienese carroccio was repainted with a decoration of Guelf lilies.[104]

GUELFISM

Now it was the Ghibellines' turn to seek exile. They scattered, to Poggibonsi, Pisa, Cortona, Arezzo. The commune's authorities placed them under a ban, pronounced capital sentences on them and set about estimating the value of their property, which was confiscated in its entirety.[105] Should one speak of this development, as Bowsky does, as the fall of 'the Ghibelline regime'?[106] It might be more accurate to write of 'the Provenzano Salvani regime'. Those in control had persisted in backing the German rather than the French alliance and found a reversal a very difficult process. Loyalty to the Hohenstaufen was not a quintessential characteristic of the 'popular', predominantly merchant, regime, merely a policy favoured by it. Ghibelline or imperialist principles and attachment to the Hohenstaufen tradition do not seem to have been deeply felt by a large number of Sienese. Perseverance in a losing alliance was in part due to the belief that Florence's side could not possibly be Siena's, in part to a stubborn reluctance to compromise in diplomatic negotiation. It must have been hard indeed to accept that the triumph of Sienese and German arms on 4 September 1260 would be a unique occasion. Also Siena was to find participation in the pro-Angevin bloc no inexpensive option and this must have been predicted by the upholders of Ghibellinism. It was an ominous start for Sienese Guelfism that the city remained for three years (i.e. until June 1273) under papal condemnation.

In exile Siena's Guelfs had assumed the institutions of a legal corporation.[107] A conciliar gathering of their Party and *universitas* (corporation), then headed by two Captains, Pietro dei Tolomei and Notto dei Salimbeni, is recorded at Città della Pieve, near the borders of the Sienese, Perugian and Orvietan spheres of influence. This institutional persistence simplified the situation when the Guelfs returned to Siena.

The formalization of political exile applied also to the preservation of Ghibelline continuity. In February 1271 the Sienese Ghibellines met at Cortona to elect their officials, who included a Captain and 'the Twenty-four of the Popolo and city of

---

104 B 42, f. 105; 43, ff. 108, 111. Davidsohn, *Forschungen*, 2, pp. 161–3, 169.
105 Davidsohn, 3, pp. 83–6.
106 Bowsky, *Commune*, p. 258.
107 G. Francini, 'Appunti sulla costituzione guelfa del comune di Siena secondo il Costituto del 1274', *BSSP*, 46 (1939) pp. 11–28. The date given by Francini to the Città della Pieve document (1255) must be incorrect.

Siena'.[108] The Twenty-four had their own priors and there was an 'inner council'. They had a representative, a member of the Salvani family, within Sienese territory at Fornoli. They were busy diplomatically, and attempted to purchase the friendship of one of Arezzo's officials with a gift of 5,000 l. and (so it was said) the promise of Siena's contado when the city was regained. Banned from holding office and with their palazzi destroyed and their property confiscated, the leading Ghibellines had little to lose by opting for exile.

Many must none the less have chosen to remain, since as early as 1272 they were made responsible for raising fifty or sixty out of a total force of 200 cavalry. The allocation was not a summons for personal service, but a heavy financial imposition; those on whom the levy fell had to provide suitable armed riders or, if they could not, make a money payment in lieu.[109] By 1275 the Ghibelline share had risen to 100 out of a force of 300, with no alternative to a straight payment of 230 l. for each horse; in other words this was a tax on the wealthier Ghibellines designed to raise 23,000 l.[110] Confiscated Ghibelline property was offered on lease by the commune, without any tax advantage. The profit or interest on these leases was at one period earmarked for the Guelf Party, which received small gifts from the commune and loans totalling 2,000 l. (1273), but never became a powerful entrenched interest in its own right, as did Florence's Parte Guelfa.[111]

The history of Siena's Guelf Party after its victory is peculiarly ill-documented and elusive, perhaps through the destruction of its archive in accordance with the terms of the 'pacification' of 1280.[112] The regime proclaimed itself Guelf with an articulacy lacking in its Ghibelline predecessor, and its programme determined the commune's external policy into the fourteenth century. The Party's Captains were leading officials of the city and helped to elect the ruling Thirty-six, who had to be zealous supporters (*zelatores*) of the Guelf cause, and the Party also had its own conciliar structure. A new constitution was dedicated 'to the reverence and honour of the Holy Roman Church and its pastor' and 'the honour and exaltation of our lord King Charles of Sicily' and ordered the 'perpetual and firm maintenance of fealty to his serene Highness'. Yet somehow the Sienese Guelf Party lost its standing as an institution in the course of the 1270s, for reasons which are not clear but must include division within the city's leading groups at this time.

---

108 G. Giannelli, 'Un Governo di fuorusciti senesi nel 1271–72', *BSSP*, n.s. 8 (1949), pp. 80–92.
109 CG 15, f. 27. See below, p. 180.
110 CG 20, ff. 35–6.
111 CG 14, f. 11v (small donation from the commune to the Guelf party, 1271); 15, f. 50v; 17, f. 2v; *Cost. 1309–10*, 1, p. 320; Mondolfo, *Cause e vicende . . .*, pp. 50–1.
112 Francini. The poor surviving documentation of the parties in the 1270s may possibly be due to obedience to a clause in the 1280 pacification agreement under which the parties were to yield up their archives (see below, p. 121).

The notion of parties, both Guelf and Ghibelline, survived in Siena through the 1270s. This is evident from the development of a pacificatory movement towards the end of the decade, one aspect of which was the proclamation that both parties were to be 'broken and destroyed' (*rupte et casse*) and their very names and memory to be abolished. The background to this ambitious attempt to blot out the factional history of thirty years is the Tuscan mission of Nicholas III's legate Cardinal Latino Malabranca.[113] The Cardinal's base (1279–80) was Florence, the most important target for his enterprise, but his task extended to the 'pacification' of all Tuscany and Romagna. The supersession of the Thirty-six at Siena at some time before 12 September 1280 by Fifteen *gubernatores et difensores populi et communis* should probably be connected with the legate's scheme for a Tuscan general peace between the two factions.[114] The reappearance of the word 'Popolo' in the nomenclature of the governing Fifteen, after its absence from Siena for more than a decade, suggests the extent to which the city's older families were linked with the two parties. A movement to abolish them would naturally adopt the 'popular' label.

The process of formal pacification involved securing the agreement of numerous members of many families, some of them within the city, others still in exile a decade after the great Ghibelline exodus. The terms proposed by the Podestà and Fifteen provided for the return of the exiles, the restoration of their confiscated property and payment of compensation for the destruction of their homes. Certain families were to deposit financial pledges for their future good behaviour and families between which a particular enmity had arisen were to be linked by marriage. In specified cases dowries were to be provided to encourage such matches. To ensure the total abolition of both parties, these were to appoint no officials, hold no council meetings and hand over all their written records including statutes. More than 400 individuals were named in the main document warning members of both parties to abide by the terms of the arbitration. Another document names more than 150 Ghibellines in exile (excluding those Salvani who were in France or on financial business 'overseas'), revealing that a considerable nucleus of irreconcilable Ghibellines were still exiles after ten years.[115]

The immense labour of this work for peace seems to have been almost entirely

113 Papal interest in Siena is clear from the mission of Sienese representatives to Nicholas III's court in the autumn of 1278 (CG 22, ff. 42v–3v).
114 The earliest reference to the Fifteen as holding office appears to be *CV*, 3, n. 901 (pp. 1114–16): the CG minutes for this period have not survived.
115 For the pacification see *CV*, 2, pp. 1114–230 (nn. 901–39). For later payments of dowries see (e.g.) B 85, ff. 45v, 52, 54v.

ineffectual. If there was a Ghibelline return to the city it was a brief one indeed.[116] Siena renewed its participation in the Guelf League, a papal relative took over as Podestà and the scheme for abolishing the parties was totally forgotten. The following summer (1281) the Ghibellines, under Niccolo Bonsignori, launched an attempt at a *coup d'état* with assistance from Aldobrandeschi troops (he had married a daughter of one of the Counts). The raiding force of 200 cavalry reached the Campo and was only driven out after a sharp clash. Campaigning in the contado continued but there was no further endeavour by the exiles to take over control at Siena.[117]

From 1270 the Sienese answer to the commune's external problems – Siena's 'foreign policy' – was Guelfism. In Tuscany this meant membership of an alliance in which the chief regional power was Florence, even though Bolognese, Roman and, above all, Sicilian (i.e. Angevin) involvement was essential to the power bloc and Sicilian grain was the crucial element in its economic interdependence. The fundamental feature of the bloc was its continuing military league or 'tallia' (share).[118] The terms on which the Guelf Tuscan alliance was renewed in 1281 will serve to illustrate the nature of this league. The contracting powers included Florence, Siena, Lucca and Pistoia, as well as a number of minor communes (Volterra, Prato, San Gimignano, Colle, Poggibonsi). The renewal was for ten years, though the initial arrangements concerning the cavalry element were for one year only. The members of the league were to hold parliamentary gatherings ('colloquia') every three months. The Captains (military commanders) were to be chosen, for a six-month period, in such gatherings and each member commune was to appoint its own adviser to the Captain. The cavalry component was to consist of two thousand men from the contracting communes together with 500 French horsemen. Thus the foreign cavalry element numbered the same as in the 1260s, when the horsemen had been Germans; *plus ça change . . .*! The contribution of the various powers to the pay of the 500 was laid down, the major shares being those of Florence (166), Lucca (118), Siena (103) and Pistoia (47). The very lengthy terms of the alliance included much detail about military obligations.[119]

Throughout the 1270s and for the remainder of the century membership of this

---

116 There are difficulties about the chronology of the Ghibelline return in August 1281 alleged by the chroniclers (*RIS, CS*, p. 225) which seems incompatible with the attempted coup of July 1281. There are no extant CG records for 1280 (and gaps June 1277–June 1278, January–June 1279, June 1283–June 1284).

117 *RIS, CS*, pp. 225–6; Davidsohn, 3. pp. 235, 271–4.

118 On the tallia see L. Naldini, 'La "tallia militum societatis tallie Tuscie" nella seconda metà del sec. XIII', *ASI*, 78 (1920), 2, pp. 75–113 and Bowsky, 'Italian Diplomatic History: a Case for the Smaller Commune' in *Order and Innovation in the Middle Ages: Essays in Honor of J. R. Strayer* ed. W. C. Jordan, B. McNab, T. F. Ruiz (Princeton, 1976), pp. 55–74, 437–43.

119 *CV*, 3, n. 955 (pp. 1290–301).

league and its financial implications dominated Siena's perspective. Meetings of the Guelf parliaments were usually preceded by discussion in the Sienese council of the line to be taken by the commune's representatives. In 1275 this was concerned with the danger that the league might embark on an aggressive and hence expensive policy. The Sienese preferred a pacific attitude and urged opposition to plans for a campaign against Volterra.[120] On that occasion, as on others, the Florentines had informed the Sienese in advance of what their representatives would be proposing. The normal meeting-place for the League's parliaments was Empoli, a conveniently central town which had once been the meeting-place of Ghibelline gatherings and had now become a common residence for the Angevin vicars in Tuscany. The discussions were predominantly military, but more general diplomatic questions could arise, such as the attitude to be taken by the communes to the imperial claim of Rudolf of Hapsburg.[121]

The sharing of the financial burden, the provision of troops, military strategy and the salary of the Captain were the main business.[122] Siena's share in the French or foreign cavalry element (*de lingua seu gente francigena seu ultramontana*, by the 1281 terms) varied greatly; the 103 men of 1281 were exceptional, at other times Siena's contribution towards a much smaller corps was forty (December 1270) or even as few as ten (December 1273).[123] Plans for big armies were found daunting by the Sienese. A cavalry force of 500 mercenaries might imply wages for 125 as the Sienese share, a force of 1,000 the immense burden of a contribution of 250. The fact that Lucca's contribution in 1281, as well as Florence's, was much larger than that of Siena is a reminder of the commune's difficulties in asserting its role as a great Tuscan power.

The number of men due to be provided by the commune itself varied greatly also but could be very high; in 1292, a critical time on account of the Pisan war, Siena had to send 380 horsemen towards a total cavalry force of 1,500.[124] It was inevitable that the commune should frequently fall behind in its payments. The Captain's salary was itself a considerable item. The 1281 terms put his pay at 2,000 l. for a six-months term of office, but by 1307 it had risen to 1,000 florins, the equivalent, in terms of the weakening Sienese currency, to a rise of more than 30 per cent.[125]

Bowsky has styled Siena at this time, perhaps rather ruefully, a 'second rate' political power.[126] It rated, with Lucca, Pisa and Arezzo, appreciably below

120 CG 20, f. 98r and v.
121 Davidsohn, 3, p. 156.
122 CG 37, ff. 88v–9.
123 CG 13, ff. 85–7; 18, ff. 81–2.
124 CG 43, f. 42.
125 *CV*, 3, pp. 1296–300: B 118, f. 270v (1308).
126 Bowsky, *Commune*, p. 73.

Florence, and the terms of the league emphasized that in a way which perhaps diminished the city's prestige yet more. But Siena could not expect to stand on its own amid the turbulence, and Guelfism must be seen as a sort of military insurance policy with a high premium, a conscious investment.

The network was a very extensive one and this fact itself was surely a disadvantage to the Sienese. When King Charles was attacked by the Aragonese and became involved in a long war in defence of his Sicilian kingdom (the Sicilian Vespers, 1282–1302) he turned to the Tuscan cities for aid. A Sienese corps despatched to serve in the Regno cost some 4,000 l. over a four-month period in 1284 and was one of many such commitments.[127] When Count Guy de Montfort was the Vicar-general in Tuscany it was natural that he should require a *douceur* of 1,000 florins, but it could hardly have been foreseen that almost twenty years later he would be begging for 2,000 florins towards his ransom after capture by the Aragonese in a naval battle. The council was favourable to this petition, but the negotiations failed and in 1291 he died in captivity.[128] Another distant and complicated Guelf entanglement concerned the Colonna family. Pope Boniface VIII's quarrel and eventual war with the Colonna (1297) involved Siena in sending a contingent to Latium. This was not the end of the matter because the campaign was so effective that it was followed many years later by an appeal from the Colonna; they asked the Sienese to contribute to the cost of the fortresses and houses destroyed at Palestrina and elsewhere. A motion that the city should donate 500 l. was lost by a very narrow margin (118–114).[129]

The Guelf link with the papacy also had more direct consequences. The pope might become the city's (titular) Podestà and in all circumstances numerous diplomatic missions to the Curia were found necessary, some of them very prolonged. In 1292 four Sienese representatives were absent for twenty-seven days on such a mission and two for fifteen; embassies of this type required plenty of horses and involved a heavy bill for salaries and expenses.[130] Missions to the Angevin court were no briefer; in 1277 two envoys were away for 106 days (drawing a salary of 55 s. a day each) on an embassy there.[131] Papal legates as well as the popes themselves expected to receive presents, as witness the gift of a gold cup costing 200 florins to Cardinal Pietro of Piperno, Boniface's legate in Tuscany (1296).[132] As well as being expensive, pressures from powerful allies could be embarrassing or even humiliating. It cannot have been pleasant for the Sienese

---

127 B 85, ff. 37, 45v.
128 B 46, f. 28 (1270): CG 36, ff. 28v–9, 31: see also Davidsohn, *Forschungen*, 4, pp. 208–10.
129 CG 52, ff. 62 ff; B 114, f. 215; CG 69, ff. 127–8v.
130 B 96, f. 86; 107, ff. 146–7, 153, 168, 247; 114, ff. 219 etc.
131 B 69, f. 25.
132 B 113, f. 150v.

authorities to learn (1272) from the Angevin Vicar that he sought a special suspension of the sumptuary laws forbidding women to wear more than five pearl buttons in favour of Alessandro Salimbeni's daughter-in-law and certain other (no doubt zealously Guelf) ladies and maidens.[133]

Presents of money and valuables were a continuing drain on the commune's means. The commanders of the Guelf *tallia*, who were usually Tuscan baronial personalities, had to receive the occasional purse or belt or gold cup.[134] These were small items compared with the gifts required for the Angevin royal family and their officials and retainers. In 1271 2,000 florins and 1,000 ounces of gold were needed for the King, in 1273 1,200 florins for him and 600 for the Queen, 200 for royal 'barons and councillors', together with numerous minor gifts of jewelry and goblets for archbishops, marshals and judges, as well as a visiting cardinal.[135] At the same time another 1,000 florins were called for to aid a Guelf campaign against Genoa.[136] The fiscal grievances underlying the Sicilian anti-Angevin revolt of 1282 come to mind.

Royal visits were particularly expensive occasions. When the second Angevin ruler, Charles II, came to Siena in 1289 he received 1,000 florins and a valuable silver cup.[137] The next member of the French royal house to visit Tuscany was another Guelf leader, Charles of Valois. During the Count's stay in Siena (November 1301) his wife gave birth to a daughter and the infant received a present of 500 florins. The following spring the Count mentioned that further financial aid would be acceptable. Varying opinions about the amount to be offered were expressed in a council meeting. Finally a proposal for a sum of 2,000 florins scraped home by 155–77, just one vote more than the two-thirds majority required.[138]

CONCLUSION

The commune was thus much at the mercy of prevailing winds. To quote the contemporary poet, it was 'in gran tempesta'.[139] Problems of internal lawlessness were the most crucial of all, whilst those involving the contado perhaps gave rise to most discussion in the councils, but the very scale of the diplomatic and military involvements caused endless anxiety and brought home constantly the superior strength of Florence, the great rival. The disputes over diplomatic

133 CG 15, f. 43v.
134 B 80, f. 94v; 85, f. 23.
135 CG 14, ff. 39v–40, 98, etc.; 17, ff. 16v–23v, 26v, 31v, 82.
136 B 55, ff. 21–2.
137 B 65, f. 39v; 99, f. 100v.
138 CG 60, ff. 68v–9v, 82v–3v; 61, ff. 78–9.
139 *Purgatorio*, VI, 77.

alignment also drove many Sienese into the discomfort and deprivation of exile.

The diplomatic revolution of 1270, the belated abandonment of the Hohenstaufen connection in favour of the Angevin one, left a curious legacy in the form of personal names. Some parents rashly called their infants by names which denoted their own loyalties. One may be sure that any Sienese 'Manfredo' was born before 1266, that any 'Carlo' was born after 1270. No doubt there were plenty of Sienese sceptics concerning Ghibelline and Guelf 'principles', but the 150 or more Ghibelline exiles of the 1270s and 1280s should be borne in mind. Clearly many felt a loyalty so strong that they could not stomach residence in a Guelf Siena, while some may have regarded themselves as too committed to withdraw from their position. Loyalty to party, as well as loyalty to family, was capable of competing with Sienese civic patriotism.

Altogether the men who advised on and administered the commune's policies bore no light burden. Internal turbulence, an unruly territorial dominion, the anxieties of a foreign policy dependent on stronger powers, made this a testing time indeed. Also it was humiliating, after the 1260s, to have to face existence as a junior partner of a once defeated foe. The relationship with Florence was a special one, in that it was one of a particularly bitter nature for the Sienese.

6 Religion

The medieval Sienese would certainly not have accepted that part of their notions and activities could be contained within a discrete category bearing the label 'religion' and in that sense the title of this chapter is an anachronism. Yet ecclesiastical institutions, at least, are distinguishable from secular ones. The Christian activities and spiritual outlook and feelings of the Sienese is a vast field but, oddly enough, little has been published on the medieval Church and religion of Siena.[1] What follows is a survey based on some of the primary sources.

BISHOP AND COMMUNE

The theme of the interdependence of commune and Church may be best approached through the bishopric and a discussion in the General Council on 7 July 1307[2] will illustrate the importance of the bishop to the city authorities. The news had spread that Rinaldo Malavolti, bishop since 1282, was dying and that the canons were nervous about danger to episcopal property and pressure being applied to them over the election of Rinaldo's successor. The councillors debated the possibility of the cathedral chapter being overawed in the matter of the election and consequent threats to the peace of the city; 'the magnates and other men might easily turn to rioting and fighting' (*rixas et arma*), thought one speaker. It is not clear what lay behind these rather generic formulae, but one possibility must have been a challenge by another Sienese dynasty to the well entrenched ecclesiastical authority of the Malavolti. Each of the three men who spoke at the meeting accepted that it would be proper for the commune's officers to become involved in the situation, for example by the Nine having talks with the chapter. The eventual decision was that the Nine should co-opt a number of wise men (either six, nine or twelve), 'lovers of the commune', to join them in deciding how the emergency should be handled.

No evidence has survived to show whether pressure was in fact applied to the canons in 1307. The Malavolti were strongly established in the chapter, but Rinaldo's successor was not a member of that family nor a native of Siena. However the choice had not fallen on an outsider; the Dominican Ruggiero of

---

1 See Bowsky's survey, for the period 1287–1355, in *Commune*, pp. 261–76.
2 CG 71, ff. 56v–57v (discussion with partial translation of the source, in Bowsky, *Commune*, pp. 271–2).

Casole d'Elsa was a familiar figure who had been lector in philosophy and theology at the Sienese Dominican house and served as vicar to Rinaldo. Casole was situated in the diocese of Volterra but lay within the zone of Sienese influence.[3] In the event Ruggiero's tenure proved to be no more than a brief break in the tradition of Malavolti rule, for after him three members of that family in succession occupied the see between 1317 and 1370.

Ruggiero was an untypical bishop of Siena in that he was not a Malavolti, but his religious affiliation was typical; one of his predecessors, Tommaso Fusconi (1253–73) had been a Dominican, and the fact that two of the five bishops in the period 1253–1316 were members of that order bears witness to its powerful influence in the city. The choice of Ruggiero was confirmed by the papal legate in Tuscany, Cardinal Napoleone Orsini, who often intervened at Siena in this period in such matters as disputed benefices and men held prisoner by the commune.[4] Whatever the role of the commune and papacy (then based beyond the Alps), it is likely that the Malavolti had a dominant voice in the election of 1307. At least eight Malavolti canons are recorded between the late thirteenth century and the middle of the fourteenth, among them the three members of the family who were elected to the see.[5]

In many cities the juridical standing of the bishop had led to early 'submissions' of lords and communities being made to him rather than to the nascent commune. This does not seem to have been the case at Siena, nevertheless the link between commune and diocese was a close one. It was in the cathedral, for example, that the citizens had gathered to grant powers for the conclusion of peace after their long war with Florence (1235).[6]

This interdependence is emphasized in the constitution of 1262. The terms of the Podestà's oath bound him 'to protect the bishopric and chapter of Siena with their property and all their possessions, wherever these may be'.[7] It was also his duty when the bishop died – the clause is of course relevant to the fears felt in 1307 – 'to hold the castles and the property of the bishopric . . . on behalf of the commune and for the use of the bishopric, and to cause the entire income of the bishopric to be protected or spent to the advantage of the bishopric'. 'If anyone

---

3 Pecci, pp. 251–2. For Ruggiero's arbitration, at Clement V's request, in a dispute between mendicants and secular clergy, see Davidsohn, 4, p. 548. The bishop of Siena appointed a vicar each year.

4 CG 72, ff. 76–8v, 112–16v, 138–40v; 73, ff. 72–3v. Other cardinals who fished in Sienese waters were Napoleone's relative Matteo Rosso (CG 18, ff. 12, 19) and the Sienese Riccardo Petroni (CG 63, ff. 15–17, 129–36). The bishop 'Tommaso Balzetti' alleged by Gams and Pecci is a 'ghost': see C. Eubel, *Hierarchia catholica*, 1 (Munster, 1913), p. 446.

5 Zdekauer in *BSSP*, 7 (1900), pp. 231–40; Bowsky, *Commune*, pp. 268–9.

6 *CV*, 2, n. 277.

7 *Const. 1262*, pp. 25–7.

attempt violence (against this property), I shall compel them to desist and, if they have taken anything, to restore it.' These obligations extended also to the protection of the property of the cathedral chapter.

The bishop's position as referee in the event of disputes over the interpretation of the commune's constitution is clear evidence of his erstwhile authority within the city. A clause in the 1262 constitution laid down that in the event of doubt over any article a ruling was to be given 'by the lord bishop or the chapter'.[8] There is no evidence that such an arbitration was ever called for and the 1309–10 constitution omits the clause. But there were other circumstances in which co-operation between commune and bishop was prescribed; this applied to agreement about the number of churches needed in the city, and mutual financial arrangements included a routine meeting at which the bishop was asked to authorize clerical contributions towards expenditure on fortifications, in return for which he could hope for assistance in his own building projects.[9]

In practice the bishop was much more likely to be drawn into the work of internal pacification or negotiation between Siena and the pope than into constitutional matters. A number of instances are known, though such activities must often have gone unrecorded. In 1256 a body of gild representatives was added to the Twenty-four to 'settle all affairs relating to the peaceful state of the city . . . with the lord bishop'.[10] The bishop's involvement in the commune's often difficult diplomatic dealings with the popes was crucial. In November 1262, Siena's Ghibelline commitment having led to a complete rupture with the papacy, the Twenty-four decided that their next move would be easier if they knew the terms of a recent letter from the pope to the bishop about the commune's misdemeanours, so they appointed representatives to 'go to the lord bishop and speak and treat with him and bring it about by handsome words (*pulcra verba*) that they secure the letter said to have come from the court of the lord pope'.[11] Some years later (1267), when the need to reach terms with the pope had become even more pressing, Bishop Fusconi himself agreed to go to the Curia on behalf of the commune to 'excuse' and 'defend' it and to help in negotiating an agreement between the city and its Guelf exiles.[12] Cardinal Latino's attempted general pacification in Tuscany (1278–81) naturally involved the bishop of that time, Fusconi's successor Bernardo di Ghezzolino Gallerani.[13]

8 Ibid., p. 80 (not in the 1309–10 constitution).
9 Ibid., pp. 48, 79.
10 CG 6, ff. 29v–30.
11 CG 10, f. 89.
12 CG 11, f. 23.
13 For a papal approach to the bishop about this pacification, CG 22, ff. 38v–9. Bishop Bernardo's identification as a Gallerani is a strong probability, not a certainty.

THE BISHOP'S LORDSHIP AND JURISDICTION

The extent of the Sienese diocese was not considerable. Apart from a very small enclave further north, it was hemmed in by the neighbouring dioceses of Grosseto, Arezzo, Fiesole and Volterra, the last of which included territory quite close to Siena and normally subject to the commune's influence.[14] The bishop's own lands were more essential to his standing than was the size of his diocese and they had the considerable advantage of compactness, without being particularly extensive or profitable. Most of them lay to the south of the city, within some ten miles of it, grouped around the castle of Murlo and the neighbouring places, Resi, Casciano, Vallerano, Montepertuso, Lupompesi and Crevole.[15] Here were the estates that the Podestà's oath obliged him to maintain and protect, just as he had also to compel men of the lordship to 'render taxes, rents, services and other dues' to the bishop.[16]

The bishop's strength lay in this lordship rather than in the city, and he sought tenaciously to retain his authority there, at times in opposition to the commune. The bishop's men had the possibility of playing off their two masters against each other, hence presumably the decision of the people of Murlo (1256) to defy the bishop by declaring their subordination to the commune.[17] The status of the bishop's men was the subject of many disputes. In the main the commune accepted that jurisdiction lay in the first place with the bishop, while asserting a right of appeal to the commune's courts. The bishop claimed for his men exemption from the city's taxation, sometimes ineffectively, though at other times the commune did not press its fiscality on this not particularly prosperous region. On one occasion (April 1274) it was agreed that a *dazio* should be levied there by the commune but that what was received should be applied solely to the advantage of the bishopric. At the same time obligations to the commune connected with military service and the upkeep of roads were reaffirmed, and the bishop's men were to be answerable to the commune's court in civil and criminal cases. One characteristic seignorial claim by the bishop demanded that his men should not be accepted by Siena as citizens.[18]

To the commune controversy over the bishop's lordship was less important than questions regarding the jurisdictional and fiscal status of the clergy, for here the bishop asserted claims which implied serious inroads into its own authority.

---

14 See map in *Rationes Decimarum Italiae nei sec. XIII e XIV. Tuscia*, 1 (Studi e Testi, 58: Città del Vaticano, 1932).
15 See N. Mengozzi, *Il Feudo del Vescovado di Siena* (Siena, 1911: previously in *BSSP*, 16–18), not a reliable work.
16 *Const. 1262*, p. 410.
17 Mengozzi, pp. 23–4.
18 Mengozzi, pp. 29–30; Pecci, pp. 233–4; *CV*, 3, pp. 1038–40.

The main zone of contention was jurisdiction over clergy in criminal cases, but a number of other issues arose, such as the appellate powers of the bishop's court and matters where ecclesiastical jurisdiction over laymen might be asserted (including usury). The bishop's occasional protest that certain statutes were 'against ecclesiastical liberty'[19] is so generic that it is sometimes difficult to know what was at stake. At times, however, the issue was clear enough. In March 1260 Brother Aldobrandino OP petitioned the commune on the bishop's behalf, asking that one Venta, held for murder, 'should be released from prison and restored to the lord bishop of Siena since he alleges and states that the man is an ecclesiastical person, who has been absolved from the ban and condemnation pronounced against him by the commune's court'. This petition was eventually successful.[20]

A serious dispute developed in 1288–89 concerning both the jurisdiction of ecclesiastical courts over the laity and the more usual issue of lay authority over clerics. The quarrel seems to have originated in a claim by the bishop's vicar-general to jurisdiction in a criminal case involving a layman. This was followed by the condemnation for murder in the Podestà's court of a certain Vanne, allegedly a priest and a man of noble descent into the bargain. The bishop was unable to prevent a capital sentence being carried out and he proceeded to excommunicate the Podestà and judges. The matter was then referred to the papal court which summoned the Podestà and a representative of the commune, while the bishop put pressure on the commune to dismiss the former. The Podestà claimed compensation for wrongful removal from office and loss of salary and it was not till 1293 that the affair was settled.[21]

A few years later an attempt was made to provide a lasting solution to the disputed issues. The Nine and the bishop came to an agreement whereby the commune would withdraw certain specified laws 'against the liberty of the Church' including one concerning usury cases and another dealing with the obligation of clergy to pay towards the upkeep of roads, while the bishop's concessions were to forbid the wearing of clerical dress by unauthorized persons and to issue constitutions making clerics liable to the same penalties as laymen. The sole exception to this was the substitution of life imprisonment in cases where capital punishment would have been inflicted. The bishop's elaborate code contained fifty-five clauses specifying the penalties to which clerical offenders were henceforth subject. Agreement was also reached about usury cases first heard in the commune's courts; if these were not settled within two months, jurisdiction was to pass to the ecclesiastical court. Finally, the bishop's powers in

19 E.g. CG 4, ff. 66 and v (1255).
20 CG 9, ff. 88 and ff.
21 This complicated affair is elucidated in Bowsky, *Commune*, pp. 32–3.

cases involving wills, presentations to benefices and pledges were reaffirmed. The acceptance of sentencing for the clergy as for laymen and indeed the entire compromise represents a triumph for the good sense of Bishop Rinaldo Malavolti, an able administrator whom Boniface VIII employed for a year (1298–99) as provincial rector of the Patrimony in Tuscany. A rather later measure went even further in the same direction in providing that the bishop's vicar would accept advice from a communal judge concerning cases which involved criminous clerks, the proceeds of fines levied in such cases being applied to the building operations of the bishop.[22]

Inevitably these solutions did not instal total and lasting peace in this difficult territory. Controversy continued about the bishop's own prison (objected to by the commune) and about his reception of men who were under the ban of the commune. Clauses in the 1309–10 constitution show that appeals to the bishop's court in cases concerning debt also continued to be a grievance with the commune.[23]

Clerical taxation seems to have been a less important issue, presumably because it was periodically the subject of realistic compromise. A clause in the statutes forbidding fictitious gifts to ecclesiastical corporations for purposes of tax evasion suggests that these were normally exempt, but the Biccherna accounts contain entries which show that direct taxes were sometimes levied on the Church. In 1252 a notary spent a week in the contado 'summoning clergy to pay money for an aid to the commune' (*pro adiutorio faciendo*) and in the succeeding years taxes were levied on churches and clergy 'in the contado of Siena but not in the diocese'. Clerics naturally paid taxes on their own personal property. A direct tax levied on the clergy only (*datium clericorum*) in 1270 seems to have brought in the disappointing return of 355 l.[24]

THE SIENESE AND THEIR BISHOP

Was the bishop perhaps a shade peripheral to the religious interests of most Sienese? He was an imposing figure with an impressive household of men who wore his livery and could have weapons and armour.[25] The vast cathedral and the processions which culminated there meant that he can never have been far from people's minds. However, wills tend to show much more concern for mendicant and monastic orders, hermits and local churches, than for the city's bishop. Some

22 Zdekauer, 'Statuti criminali del foro ecclesiastico di Siena (sec. XIII–XIV)', *BSSP*, 7 (1900), pp. 231–64: for Malavolti's rectorate in the Papal State see Waley, *The Papal State in the thirteenth century* (London, 1961), pp. 113, 252–3, 311.

23 Zdekauer; *Cost. 1309–10*, 1, p. 312 (and see Bowsky, *Commune*, pp. 115–16).

24 *Const. 1262*, pp. 132, 134n; Bowsky, *Finance*, pp. 219–20 (citing Statuti 26); B. 13, pp. 134, 141; 14, pp. 26–8, 60, 64, etc.; 44, f. 5v. The virtually forced loans from the Church cited by Bowsky are from a later period.

25 Zdekauer in *BSSP*, 7, pp. 256–9.

asked to be buried in the cathedral yet made no special provision for it in their wills, others made bequests much inferior to those in favour of the friars.[26] The will of a clothier (1274) typically assigns 125 l. to various ecclesiastical bodies, but of this only 10 l. was for the fabric of the cathedral, 5 l. for the canons and 3 l. for the bishop. A testatrix who named the bishop as one of her executors could only spare him 2 l. (to be spent on the adornment of S Giacomo) and the chapter 5 l., as against 25 l. allocated for crusading purposes.[27] But these wills seem generous in comparison with that of a Piccolomini widow (1299) who left legacies to a score of religious bodies, the beneficiary who received least – a paltry 5s. – being the bishop, and a Gallerani widow who died as a Franciscan tertiary could spare 5 l. for the Dominicans but could only manage 5s. for the bishop.[28] The cathedral fabric was a little more popular as a recipient of legacies. The bequests to the bishop sometimes appear to be mere gestures, perhaps the outcome of a reminder from the notary drawing up the will. It seems most unlikely that these meagre offerings were intended as insults; possibly the feeling was that the bishop had sufficient wealth already.

Certainly the bishops themselves were not mere landed prelates, Malavolti who had opted for clerical advancement in preference to the career in banking which was normal among their relatives. The founder of the hospital of Santa Croce, the notary Taurello, involved Bishop Rinaldo Malavolti in every stage of his project.[29] The foundation deed (1294) was drawn up in the bishop's chapel and its terms were ratified by him before he proceeded to choose the founder as the first rector and to invest him with that office. Future elections would also require episcopal confirmation. A few years later Bishop Rinaldo received a palazzo as a gift from his brother Niccolò for another hospital, to be reserved for the sick poor.[30] Nor was this the only hospital to be set up by Niccolò Malavolti. The warden of the hospital to which Niccolò presented a building was to be chosen by the Dominicans and it is clear that the Malavolti as the chapter's dominant family collaborated with Siena's flourishing Dominican house in promoting works of charity in the city. Far from being isolated figures, the bishops were closely associated with the mendicants, the most vital religious movement of their day.

PARISHES

How many parishes were there within the walls and in the neighbouring Masse? The question is a difficult one to answer, partly because Sienese ecclesiastical

---

26 Dipl., AGC, 13.11.1291, 16.5.1299; ASS, Ms B 73, ff. 212v–213, 256–8v.
27 Dipl., AGC, 28.2.1274, 17.2.1277.
28 Ibid., 17.10.1300.
29 Ibid., 28.9.1294.
30 Pecci, p. 249.

institutions still await full investigation, partly because the process whereby the areas of baptismal churches (*pievi*) were divided into parishes was still incomplete. In 1275–77 twenty churches which appear to be parochial were listed as owing papal tenths, and the comparable list for 1302–03 contains twenty-five. The titles of fiscal *libre* and *popoli* provide twenty-four parish names in 1285–86 and twenty nine in 1318–20, confirming a rather approximate answer to the question asked above. There were roughly the same number of parishes in the Masse, a fact which attests the city's rapid extension. The 1302–03 list names twenty-eight, though not all were in the suburbs, some of them (Salteano, Isola, Lucano, Arbiola, Cuna) being as far as seven kilometres from the city's centre.[31]

It is even more difficult to assess how much these churches meant to their parishioners. Wills of the time contain rather few references to parish churches, in contrast with the almost universal legacies to mendicant orders, monastic houses and anchorites. There is certainly some plausibility in the suggestion that in the thirteenth century the new orders were 'the true religion of the city or rather of the city-state',[32] but not all the testamentary evidence points in this direction. One testator left the considerable sum of 10 l. for the purchase of a chalice for his parish church of S Vincenzo, another asked to be buried in S Andrea, his parish church, to which he bequeathed 3 l. *pro anima mea*, his only other religious legacy being a request to his brothers to set aside 25 l. more 'for my soul', to be assigned generically for the funeral expenses and 'religious places and the poor'. A clothier, who like so many could spare much more for friars and nuns than for the cathedral, remembered also the priest (*plebanus*) of Lucignano d'Arbia (whence he himself probably came) and made a legacy of 5 l. to the baptismal church of S Giovanni Battista, where he wished to be buried. A stonemason who wished to be buried at S Domenico did not forget his parish church (S Antonio) and its priest, while there was a man who remembered the Dominicans but opted for burial in the church of S Giorgio. Other examples could be cited, including those who expressed loyalties to the collegiate church of S Martino.[33]

If enthusiasm tended to be channelled into the mendicant orders, did this mean that the parish clergy had deservedly forfeited their claims on it? Little evidence bears on this point, though a conclusion along these lines seems inescapable. The

---

31 *Rationes Decimarum Italiae. Tuscia*, 1, pp. 105–18; 2 (Studi e Testi, 98), pp. 142–4; Balestracci Piccinni, Carta n. 1. The estimate of Bortolotti, pp. 54–5 (about 35) includes several monastic institutions and is clearly too high. Knowledge of the subject will be enormously increased by the publication of *Die Kirchen von Siena*, a German project of which one volume only (1985, eds. P. A. Riedl and M. Siedel) has appeared at the time of writing.

32 G. G. Merlo in *Piemonte medievale* (Turin, 1985), p. 224.

33 Dipl., AGC, 7.5.1276, 10.8.1281, 23.6.1288, 27.9.1288 (10 l. to S Andrea, one half towards bells, the rest divided between the rector and the purchase of candles), 25.8.1306, 23.8.1307.

constitutions issued by Bishop Buonfiglio in 1232[34] indicate the difficulty of enforcing discipline among the secular clergy in the very years of maximum impact of the Franciscan and Dominican movements. 'No cleric is to wear a garment of green or red cloth.' 'No cleric is to gamble or dice in the *piazza* or street.' 'No cleric is to enter a tavern or any place which may reasonably be held dangerous to clerical honesty.' Confessions by women must always be heard in a public place in church. *Jongleurs* must not be allowed to eat at table with clerics nor to perform in church during the service.

MONASTICISM AND MENDICANTS

The institutions of the regular clergy, in contrast, feature very prominently in wills, accounts, council minutes and the commune's statutes. The constitution of 1262 records among the bodies due to receive from the commune alms or protection or both ten houses of regular monks, eight mendicant communities and six nunneries.[35] This is to omit a great number of eremetical communities (if that appellation is not too paradoxical; it is clear that 'hermits' were not necessarily solitaries). In 1307 a list was drawn up in connection with the 'alms of bread': it listed the numbers of monks, nuns and hermits in Siena or within a mile of the city due to receive a 3d. loaf. Some 900 'mouths' are recorded and the list may be worth giving in full: see table 7, p. 136.[36]

While probably not a complete record of Siena's religious, this at least provides a starting-point or minimum. The comparative numbers are significant, with three mendicant orders well in the lead and totals of nuns strikingly high at 363, while the urban and suburban anchorites are also numerous, ranking with the major houses of friars.

The 'hermits' represent an important and well-recognized feature of Siena's religious commitment. It was normal for wills to make mention of them, the most common form of bequest being one of 6d. or 1s. or even 5s., according to the testator's means, to each anchorite, male or female, living in the city or within one mile of it; more rarely the distance specified was half a mile. It was unusual to provide a total sum for distribution though a testatrix allocated 10s. specifically to the anchoresses Lucia and Palmeria, besides a general fund of 30s. for other *reclusi* at Siena or within the usual one-mile boundary. Lucia and Palmeria, who were sisters, must have been well-known characters, for they figure in another will, in which they shared equally a bequest of 20s., as 'imprisoned in cells' (*carcerate in carceribus*) outside the Camollia gate.[37]

34 Pecci, pp. 208–11.
35 *Const. 1262*, pp. 36–53. Similar lists in *Cost. 1309–10*, 1, pp. 56–64, 77–83.
36 B 120, ff. 402 and v.
37 Dipl., AGC, 17.10.1300, 13.6.1301. Other examples: ibid., 17.2.1277, 6.2.1292, 27.12.1306, 23.8.1307; Dipl., Spedale, 14.8.1249; ASS, Ms B 73, ff. 212v–13.

Table 7. *Numbers of religious*

Institution	'Mouths'
Friars Minor	99
Preachers (Dominicans)	97
Augustinian Hermits	80
'friars near Siena' (*fratelli presso di Siena*)	46
Cruxed Friars	16
Carmelites	30
nuns of S Petronilla	72
nuns of S Maria Novella	42
nuns of S Prospero	59
nuns of S Mamiliano	26
nuns of Ognissanti	21
brethren of S Giovanni	12
nuns of S Lorenzo	29
Servites	31
Humiliati	22
nuns of Vico	29
nuns of S Margherita	24
nuns of S Benedetto	21
nuns of S Abbondio	20
Cistercians ('monks of Clairvaux')	4
hermits, male and female, within one mile of Siena	89
nuns of Sperandio	20

HOSPITALS

Hospitals – for the sick, the elderly and the pilgrims – were also an essential institution of religion and charity, the practical pole of the spectrum whose spiritual extreme was represented by Lucia and Palmeria in their cells. It is difficult to keep track of them, for new hospitals were continually coming into being while others went into dissolution or were swallowed up in a constant process of takeovers. Some had specialized purposes: there was, for example a leper hospital, while certain hostels, such as those of the Hospitallers and Templars, catered primarily for the numerous pilgrims on their way to and from Rome.

Biagio di Tolomeo dei Tolomei, who was presumably childless, made a will (1299) by which he founded no fewer than four hospitals, these being entrusted, for her lifetime, to his widow who was to have powers of 'government, domination, administration and dispensation' over them all. He divided up his estate (apart from some small family legacies) between the hospitals which were to be the particular concern respectively of S Maria della Scala (Siena's major hospital), the Dominicans, the Franciscans and the Augustinian Hermits. If these four bodies had not set up hospitals as requested within one year of Biagio's death the task was to be undertaken by the Cistercian monks of S Galgano, and if that abbey in turn failed to establish hospitals within a year the onus was to pass to the Hospital of Saint James at Altopascio.[38]

A rather less ambitious founder was the notary Taurello who has already been mentioned as setting up in his lifetime (1294) the hospital of Santa Croce, with himself as its first rector.[39] Taurello built the hospital on his own land as a dwelling-house for the poor 'for the salvation of my soul and the souls of my family, both dead and alive, and for the remission of sins'. His sons and their heirs in turn were to succeed as patrons with powers to 'nominate, postulate, represent, elect, possess, place and ordain'. No man or woman might be received as an oblate or servant of the hospital without Taurello's express consent. He was clearly a man who knew exactly what he wanted and had set up a charitable institution with himself as an autocrat at its head.

An important earlier foundation was the Domus Misericordiae initiated as a congregation of lay 'oblates' by B. Andrea Gallerani, which received many privileges in the years after Gallerani's death (1251), but 'the Hospital' (without further qualification) was S Maria della Scala, close to the cathedral, which came in time to devour large numbers of other hospitals and to rank with the greatest lords and landed proprietors of the contado.[40] Its creation was connected with the cathedral chapter, but it had graduated to a position of independence and its economic and social importance was such as to make it a subject of constant interest to the commune.

Gifts and legacies to S Maria della Scala were very common indeed and many consisted of scattered plots of agricultural land. The donors of these 'parcels' often stipulated – though the condition was not always observed – that the Hospital should not alienate the plot granted it.[41] There were also testators who insisted that their monetary legacies should be converted into land. The property of the

38 Dipl., AGC, 22.1.1298.

39 Ibid., 28.9.1294; see above, p. 133.

40 G. Catoni, 'Gli oblati della Misericordia. Poveri e benefattori a Siena nella prima metà del Trecento' in G. Pinto (ed.), *La società del bisogno. Povertà e assistenza nella Toscana medievale* (Florence, 1989), pp. 1–17 (with references to sources and literature). Donors to the Misericordia often stipulated that annual payments should be made to their own relatives or to other ecclesiastical bodies out of these bequests (Catoni, p. 8). On the Hospital see Epstein, also O. Redon, 'Autour de l'Hôpital S Maria della Scala à Sienne au XIII siècle', *Ricerche Storiche*, 15 (1985), pp. 17–34, and G. Piccinni and L. Vigni, 'Modelli di assistenza ospedaliera tra Medioevo ed Età Moderna. Quotidianità, amministrazione, conflitti nell'ospedale di S.M. della Scala di Siena' in *La società del bisogno*, pp. 131–74.

41 E.g. Dipl., Spedale 14.8.1249.

Hospital and its subordinate houses was to be found in all parts of the contado, with perhaps a tendency for the highest concentration to lie to the south-east of the city, particularly along the main routes. By 1286 seven brethren of the Hospital were overseers of the estates, permanently resident at Asciano, Serre di Rapolano, Montisi, S Quirico, Corsignano, Sasso d'Ombrone and in Val d'Orcia. The general expansion of the Hospital's authority involved (to give a single instance) protectorate over the important hospital at Grosseto (1295). Purchasers and exchanges in a very active land market complemented gifts and bequests and by 1318 the Hospital's agricultural activities were organized through a system of granges (which would now be styled 'farms') comparable to that possessed elsewhere by the Cistercian order. Naturally houses and other urban property were also accumulated on a considerable scale.[42]

As the Hospital escaped the authority of the chapter it fell increasingly under that of the commune, whose arms indeed came to be placed over the doorway (1309). By then, however, it had secured almost total exemption from the commune's taxation, whilst the struggle to win exemption from that of the bishop ended with success around the same time (1307). For a wealthy institution, fiscal immunity did not imply freedom from the role of lender and the Hospital was called upon for loans in the 1270s and 1280s. The relationship was of course reciprocal; when the Hospital ran into financial crises in the following century the commune could not see this central corporation in trouble without coming to the rescue.[43]

An important source of provision of land for the Hospital was the advent of oblates: those entering as brothers, 'wishing to renounce the world and to enter the Hospital of S Maria at Siena for the salvation of our souls' made over their property 'without any exception or reservation' when they took the decision to devote themselves to the service of their brethren and the poor. The assistance given was not confined to residents of the Hospital. One of the brothers, for instance, was responsible for keeping a list of poor persons and families 'in the city of Siena, outside the said Hospital' who deserved to receive a loaf each week; the number of loaves required weekly had also to be recorded. Within the hospital discipline was very strict and any brother failing to rise for morning Mass or to perform his duties of service to the sick was punished by restriction to a diet of bread and – wine![44]

---

42 On the Hospital's territorial growth see Epstein, chapter 2.
43 Ibid., pp. 17–18, 238–41.
44 Redon, p. 30; *Statuti volgari de lo spedale di S.M. Vergine di Siena . . . MCCCV*, ed. L. Banchi (Siena, 1864), pp. 4–8, 44–5, 73.

CIVIC RELIGION

Bishops, parishes, monastic houses, mendicant orders, hospitals are all less central to the theme of this book than is the nature of the religious feelings of the Sienese. Those who took part in the procession to the cathedral on the day of the Assumption of the Virgin would not have seen themselves as participating in a 'religious' ceremony fostered by a 'political' institution, the commune. Many would have associated the occasion particularly with the confraternities to which they belonged since these religious gilds provided the framework within which the procession was organized. 'Civic religion' as exemplified by the commune's own chapel in the Palazzo – the commemorative church planned for Montaperti seems never to have materialized – is, to use anachronistic definitions, an indivisible politico-religious complex. The understanding was simply that 'Government work is God's work'.[45] The dedication of Siena to the Madonna after the victory of Montaperti, the Podestà's oath to preserve, maintain and defend the Catholic faith 'as it is held and taught by the holy Roman Church', the candles burning perpetually before the altar of the Virgin in the cathedral and the lamp 'before the carroccio of the commune . . . to the honour of God and the blessed Virgin Mary',[46] are all central to an understanding of the medieval Sienese and naturally they have their parallels in other cities.

These features of the city's life had roots in the earlier stages of the commune's development. Before the dedication of 1260 to the Virgin, the city's seal already bore a representation of 'the Madonna seated, with her son on her arm, having a rose in her right hand, on each side an angel carrying a candle and beneath her feet a dragon'.[47]

NAMES

In considering the religious feeling of the Sienese it may be well to begin where religious life itself began for them, at the baptismal font. What names did the Sienese receive? In view of the ubiquitous domination of the name 'Maria' in later times and the city's own patronage, it is a surprise to find that in the thirteenth century this was not the most common baptismal name for Sienese women. The name ranked only third or fourth in popularity, the preference in selecting names for girls being for something more worldly; the most popular feminine name in the 1280s appears to have been 'Gemma', followed by 'Benvenuta' ('Welcome'). Other names which found favour were 'Fiore'

---

45 Inscription on the facade of Parliament House, Bangalore, India.
46 *Const. 1262*, pp. 25–6.
47 *Sigilli medioevali senesi* (Museo naz. del Bargello, Florence, 1981), p. 18.

(Flower), 'Buonafemina' (Good Woman), 'Divizia' (Wealth), 'Diamante' and 'Riccha' – the last three seeming to imply, like 'Gemma' (gem), mundane if not unspiritual values! – and 'Beldì' (good day). Names from saints were rather uncommon for women; the next in order of popularity after 'Maria' which can be put in this category was 'Margherita', which ranked seventeenth, and even this could mean 'pearl', to go with gem and diamond.[48] There is a curious contrast here with the names given at this time by the notorious worldly Venetians to their ships; three quarters of these had religious names, mainly from saints.[49] Even the name 'Caterina', to become illustrious in Siena in the fourteenth century through the most famous of the city's saints, was a rare name in the thirteenth although St Catherine of Alexandria was certainly not an obscure figure in Tuscan art.[50]

Male names are less easily divisible into those with religious and those with secular connotations. 'Giovanni' (the most common name among 1285 tax-payers), 'Giacomo' (which comes fourth) and 'Pietro' (sixth) were very popular names which have Christian associations. But a great many of the common masculine names were of the type known as 'augurative', i.e. they imply wishes for good fortune. Such names usually incorporated the syllables 'buon' or 'bene': among them are 'Buonaventura' (the most common name after 'Giovanni'), 'Bencivenne', 'Benvenuto', 'Buonaccolto', 'Buonaccorso', 'Buoncompagno', 'Buoninsegna', 'Buonsignore' and 'Benincasa' (the name of St Catherine's father). Clearly the importance that can be attributed to the choice of personal names is limited, nevertheless it is interesting that these names, particularly the feminine ones, do not seem to proclaim a city totally dominated by the standards of a devout and otherworldly piety.

USURY AND INTEREST

One religious question must have haunted the lives of many Sienese, or certainly the last part of their lives. The doctrine of the Church on the subject of usury was complicated, but the basic tenet was that loans should not bear interest. Had this rule been simple in its implications and had these been heeded, Sienese finance could not have taken the form that it did and indeed the development of the city

---

48 P. Waley, 'Personal names in Siena, 1285' in *Florence and Italy. Renaissance Studies in Honour of Nicolai Rubinstein*, ed. P. Denley and C. Elam (London, 1989); O. Castellani, 'Nomi femminili senesi del sec. XIII', *Studi linguistici italiani*, 2 (1961), pp. 46–64; the ASS holds unpublished material of Prof. O. Brattö on Sienese personal names.

49 B. Z. Kedar, *Merchants in Crisis* (New Haven and London, 1976), pp. 156–60.

50 For an intended painting of her see Dipl., AGC, 18.6.1282 (will). At least three fourteenth-century Sienese depictions of St Catherine of Alexandria survive, one in an altarpiece at Boston, Mass, formerly attributed to Barna, others in a fresco by Lorenzetti in S Agostino, Siena (G. Kaftal, *Iconography of the Saints in Tuscan Painting*, Florence, 1952, pp. 226–34) and a panel painting (N 61) in the Museo Horne, Florence.

would have been very different. In reality transfers between different currencies (repayment in another currency was easy to arrange) and other practices made it possible for money to breed money. Arguments about compensation for loss, risk and the expense of time and trouble assisted the acceptance of realities which were daily ones to the Roman see, to virtually all other major ecclesiastical bodies and to the financiers of Siena and the other Italian cities. In practice loans, whether made by bankers or by other citizens or prelates, involved the payment of interest: interest payments of 10 per cent per annum and above were central to the entire system of credit on which Sienese finance and trade depended. Only with rates of interest above 30 per cent did serious doubts arise. An agreed corpus of make-believe masked the realities and normally served to persuade men that their operations were not sinful.[51]

So much for the usual situation and its acceptance. But thoughts of death and the hereafter could induce doubts and a very different attitude. This is evident from wills, for at that stage most men of affairs had something to say about making restitution 'for things wrongfully taken and illicit gains' (*pro rebus male ablatis et lucris illicitis*). The formulae vary considerably, but tend to mention 'all usuries and things taken by me wrongfully', 'usury and things taken wrongfully and illicit profits', 'usuries taken and things acquired illicitly' (or 'illicitly and in an evil way', *malo modo*).[52] Sometimes specific sums of money were set aside for restitution to those who had suffered as a result of the testator's usurious activities and in certain cases plots of land were earmarked for sale to cover such reimbursement.[53] Executors were often charged with the difficult task of making restoration of 'all usuries and everything illicitly or wrongly taken and received'. It was quite common for testators to remember particular victims and set aside money for them. The man who bequeathed 10 l. to a bank 'in satisfaction of everything acquired by me illicitly from the property of that company' was perhaps extreme in his scrupulousness, but the company was that of the Bonsignori and the will was made just a month after it had become clear that that bank was in very serious trouble (1298).[54]

Another rather extreme case was that of Giacomo di Angioliero, who was clearly a very worried man, haunted by his sins when he made his will in 1259. He wanted to be sure that 'all usuries and things wrongfully taken or illicitly acquired', as recorded in an account-book of his company, should be restored. He

---

51 This important topic cannot receive adequate treatment here. For the background see G. Le Bras in *C. Econ. H.*, 3, pp. 564–70.
52 Examples from Dipl., AGC, 7.5.1276, 28.4.1284, 6.2.1292, 22.1.1298 and Spedale, 24.2.1227, 19.9.1239.
53 Dipl., AGC, 13.12.1301.
54 Ibid., 27.9.1298.

was convinced that unfortunately 'my entire property is not sufficient to make restoration of the usury and things wrongfully taken'. All his possessions were to be sold by the abbot of S Galgano, as his executor, to assist repayment of his debts and usurious profits. Giacomo seems to have had on his conscience most of all a recent business trip to France, possibly because he had fallen ill when on that journey. In a codicil added six days after the original will he recalls twenty-five instances of extortionate loans made on this visit to Champagne and the area of the Marne, mainly to town communities and parishes. The total lent amounted to the quite considerable sum of 1,500 l. *tournois*. When he dictated the codicil Giacomo was seeing things in a slightly less gloomy light, for he now bequeathed 700 l. to his daughter Giacopina 'and if anything is left over after repayment of usuries and property wrongfully taken, I wish and order that this residue should be given and distributed for the good of my soul between religious foundations and the poor, as it shall please the abbot of S Galgano'.[55]

AMBROGIO SANSEDONI, OP

The religion of the Sienese may also be approached through the personality of the Dominican Ambrogio Sansedoni (1220–87), who was one of several Sienese of this time to have secured local recognition as a saint. For the last twenty years of his life he seems to have been the city's most influential cleric and this predominance is reflected in a comparatively full biographical record.[56]

Ambrogio was born into a very prominent banking family whose pink brick palace, with its old tower, stands near the eastern end of the Campo. The history of the bank is not well documented, but as early as 1234 a testator mentions large shares in the *societas* of the sons of Sansedoni[57] and some chance survivals among vernacular letters reveal members of the family as active in dealings in cloth in Paris and Champagne at the beginning of the fourteenth century. At that time they were anxious about threatened Sienese legislation against *grandi* but so busy at the French court that Pepo Sansedoni suggested his wife and family joining him there (1311).[58] It is probable that Ambrogio's father was a certain Guido (he was also known as Buonatacca) who had been prominent in the commune's affairs, serving as Podestà at Grosseto in 1257 and acting as ambassador to King Manfred three years later.[59]

---

55 Text in Zdekauer, *Mercante*, pp. 36–40. See also above, p. 39.
56 The main contemporary lives are in *AA.SS.*, March, 3 (1865), pp. 179–250. A useful recent work is P. Giacinto D'Urso, OP, *Beato Ambrogio Sansedoni 1220–1287* (Siena, 1986). For other Sienese saints of the period see A. Vauchez, 'La commune de Sienne, les ordres mendiants et le culte des saints. Histoire et enseignements d'une crise (nov. 1328–avr. 1329)', *MEFR*, 89 (1977), pp. 757–67.
57 Dipl., Spedale, 1.5.1234.
58 P. and P., pp. 71–96.
59 Ciacci, 2, pp. 206, 208; *BSSP*, 43 (1936), p. 17.

Ambrogio's background is reflected in his sermons. He remarks that 'sons of usurers usually follow their fathers in this occupation, as we see at Florence and Siena' and elsewhere likens calculations concerning such qualities as mercy and good manners (*curialitas*) to those involving revenue and expenditure.[60] In another sermon, on the Marriage Feast at Cana, he discusses the prohibited degrees in marriage and suggests that the reason for these being reduced by the Fourth Lateran Council (1215) was to facilitate marriage alliances between warring families. His mention of 'great peaces' (*magne paces*) which could be aided by such alliances was certainly a reference to the pacificatory movement in the Italian communes: indeed he probably had in mind the Sienese peace negotiations of 1280. Intermarriage between the major Sienese dynasties was common, hence projected alliances in the interest of internal peace could well have foundered on difficulties about existing relationships but for the relaxation decreed in 1215. Before that time the prohibited degrees had extended to sixth cousins.[61]

Sansedoni was born with a deformity, the nature of which is not clear but his arms were partially paralyzed (writing presented difficulties for him) and his face or head was 'not in proportion'. His early biographers depict his astonishing religious precocity, but not everything they say commands credence. He used to station himself by the Porta Camollia ('the gate where pilgrims from beyond the Alps enter the city') and reached an agreement with his father, whereby he was allowed to bring home five pilgrims once a week. These guests were fed, housed and given alms. The next day Ambrogio would accompany them to Mass and then take them on a tour of 'the main churches of the city'. His other works of charity included bringing food to people in the Hospital and in prison. His parents' hopes that he would acquire the tastes of a conventional young man of his class were disappointed. They had expected him to frequent 'the milieu of young nobles in the city . . . riding about on horseback and hunting with his own hounds and birds (hawks)' and eventually to marry.

Instead Ambrogio entered the Dominican order on his seventeenth birthday. He studied philosophy and theology at Paris under the great scholastic Albertus Magnus, the 'Doctor Universalis' who first adapted Aristotelianism for the Church. He himself taught at Cologne and later at Rome. At what stage he returned to the Dominican house at Siena is not clear, though this had become

---

60 T. Kaeppeli OP, 'Le prediche del B. Ambrogio Sansedoni da Siena', *Archivum Fratrum Praedicatorum*, 38 (1968), pp. 5–12 (quotations from pp. 6 and 8).

61 Dr D. L. d'Avray of University College, London, most generously gave me his transcript of this sermon and provided comments which enabled me to comprehend it. It is Siena, Biblioteca Comunale, Ms. T.iv.7, ff. 12v–15; the words quoted here are from f. 14. For the 1280 pacification, see above, pp. 120–2; for marriages between the major families, English, 'Five magnate families', pp. 186–227, 433–519.

the centre of his activities by 1267, when he consulted the council about a sum of 400 l. owed the commune by his late father.[62] and his involvement in negotiations between the papacy and his city can be traced from around that time. He is reported to have refused the offer of the bishopric of Siena (together with other forms of preferment), presumably either on the death in 1273 of his fellow Dominican Tommaso Fusconi or that of Bernardo in 1281.

It seems clear that Ambrogio was as much at the centre of Siena's religious life in these years as either of these bishops. His greatest contribution to a far-reaching religious revival – indeed a transformation – was his foundation of confraternities for both men and women, based on the Dominican house. He drew up constitutions for these gilds whose purpose was 'the observance of a Catholic life and penance for sins'. An innovation attributable to Ambrogio's influence was the introduction of the singing of 'praises'. His followers used to meet daily to sing these *laudes* 'rhythmically, in the vernacular tongue'. The opening and closing words were 'Jesu, Jesu, nostro signore' and these were inscribed over the doorways of the brethren. The movement was such a success that its influence soon spread, inspiring the *laudi* of other Tuscan cities such as Florence, Pisa, Lucca and Cortona.[63] Sansedoni's foundation seems to have been a residential one so far as single women were concerned, whereas married women were encouraged in religious observances and works of charity towards the poor and sick, and he was also the organizer of a confraternity of flagellants.

Some witnesses claimed to have seen Ambrogio levitate ('he was lifted up into the air') when preaching, though he himself said that he was unaware of this. Another had seen a dove hovering around his mouth. His charity is exemplified by the special appeal he made to the council for the release of a prisoner. The man, an Englishman named Alfred, was probably a pilgrim who had fallen foul of the law, though he could have been a mercenary captured in battle.[64]

Ambrogio's powerful presence in the city's spiritual life is also attested by his appearance in wills and these bear witness to his connections with the capitular and episcopal family, the Malavolti, and confirm their Dominican associations. In 1278 a Malavolti widow bequeathed 12 l. to the Sienese Dominican house, 3 l. to the bishop and the same sum to the family church of S Egidio 'for its decoration' (*in ornamentis*) and she ordered that the rest of her estate 'should be given and distributed to the poor and to religious fundations, as shall seem best to Brother Ambrogio of the Order of Preachers, my executor'.[65]

62 Talk by Dr U. Morandi at the Palazzo Pubblico, Siena, 18 March 1987 (quoting from CG of 25 October 1267).
63 Talk by Prof G. Varanini at the Palazzo Pubblico, Siena, 18 March 1987. The texts of the earliest Sienese *laudi* have not survived.
64 CG 12, ff. 65 and v (1268).
65 Dipl. AGC, 12.7.1278. See also above, p. 133.

He was also to supervise the distribution of linen and bedding and to have full powers over her dowry and other property. Should he be unable to carry out these responsibilities his place was to be taken by the prior of the Dominican house. The link with the Malavolti is also confirmed by the will (1286) of Mea (née Tolomei), wife of Mino dei Malavolti and daughter-in-law of the testatrix last mentioned; she allocated the sum of 300 l. to be spent at their discretion *ad pias causas* by her mother, her husband and Ambrogio or, failing him, the Dominican prior.[66]

It was inevitable that Sansedoni should be drawn into a political role, particularly in the commune's difficult relations with the papacy when seeking to escape from the consequences of its Ghibelline alignment. His intermediacy was not confined to Siena since in 1267 he received papal authorization, subject to the receipt of adequate guarantees, to end the interdict placed on another erring commune, San Gimignano.[67] Siena itself fell under interdict again after its ill-advised support of Conradin and Ambrogio was involved in the negotiations which eventually led, thanks to his intervention, to the lifting of this condemnation by Gregory X.[68] The rejoicing at this achievement was such that a celebratory horse-race (*palio*) was instituted on its anniversary, but this was later shifted to commemorate the date of Ambrogio's death.[69] His involvement in internal pacifications is mentioned by his biographers and his reference to them in a sermon has already been touched on, but no contemporary documentary evidence survives to corroborate his role.

Some of those who were outside the gates of the Dominican house at the moment of Ambrogio's death saw him ascend to Heaven 'like a bright star'. He was buried in the sacristy the following day and later his body was translated with great solemnity to a special chapel in S Domenico, but this fell into a ruinous condition and his remains had to be restored to the sacristy. Plans for this special chapel had been instituted with great promptitude, the commune granting 50 l. towards it and the same sum towards a tomb, while within a few weeks of Sansedoni's death a bequest was made to 'the fabric of the church of S Ambrogio at Camporegio'.[70] The bishop also promptly authorized the collection of miracles performed by Sansedoni, but for some reason he did not achieve formal canonization by the Roman Church. He was venerated locally as a saint, was depicted in the church of S Domenico at Arezzo in the fourteenth century, and

---

66 Ibid., 9.4.1286.

67 *AA.SS*, March, 3, pp. 244–5; there is a copy of the document in the Archivio Comunale, San Gimignano (L. Pecori, *Storia della Terra di S. Gimignano*, Florence, 1853, pp. 86–7).

68 CG 16 (May 1273), ff. 63v–66 (partly quoted in *RIS, CS*, p. 72n., but the tale about a murdered bishop, ibid., pp. 70–2, with editorial annotation, is fantasy).

69 *AA.SS.*, pp. 186–8; W. Heywood, *Palio and Ponte*, London, 1904, pp. 74–81.

70 Vauchez, p. 759 and n.; Dipl., AGC, 23.6.1288.

appears among Taddeo di Bartolo's portraits of Famous Men in the antechapel of the Palazzo Pubblico.[71]

Sansedoni's special devotees tended to be women: two of these, Genovese and Nera, are singled out in the hagiography as *devotissimae* and another became mystically aware, *in absentia*, of his death. Women were very prominent indeed in all aspects of the city's spiritual life and their role appears in some late thirteenth-century letters in Italian between members of the Montanini family, a very important dynasty connected by marriage with the Malavolti. Several of the letters are from Cristina Menabuoi, founder of S Croce in Val d'Arno. She and the other nuns write to Arrigo Montanini to congratulate him on the news that two of his sisters have decided to enter a nunnery. Another letter is from a Dominican who informs Arrigo that, though unworthy of the honour, he has been invited by the Podestà and Nine to deliver a series of sermons.[72]

SPIRITUALS AND HERETICS

A contemporary of Sansedoni who also had an important influence on the city's religious life was Pietro *pettinarius* (the comb-seller) (d. 1289). The Franciscan Spiritual leader Ubertino da Casale met Pietro and remembered him as 'a man full of God' (*vir deo plenus*). He was a Franciscan tertiary and also a brother of the confraternity of the Domus Misericordiae Pauperum whose founder was the layman Andrea Gallerani (d. 1251); Gallerani's feast, celebrated on Easter Monday, was not officially recognized by the commune till 1347.[73] Pietro seems to have been remembered, rather oddly, for his eccentric reluctance to sell his customers combs which were in an imperfect condition, but there can be no doubt about his standing in the city; it is confirmed by the will of the pious clothier Bartolomeo di Ildebrandino (1284), which was witnessed by two tertiaries.[74] Bartolomeo wished his brothers to take advice on the place of his burial (which was to be either S Galgano or the house of the Humiliati) from Pietro, who was also to be consulted about the restitution of usury and illicit or ill-gotten gains. The commune granted the Franciscans 200 l. towards a special tomb, with a ciborium and altar, for Pietro; this was even more generous than the gift made two years earlier to the Dominicans in respect of Sansedoni. His feast day continued to be celebrated, with the official participation of the commune, well into the fourteenth century. The continuance of his fame is also attested by his appearance in Dante's *Purgatorio* (XIII, 125–9) as the man whose prayers

---

71 *Bibliotheca Sanctorum*, 11, p. 631. The feast of Ambrogio Sansedoni figures in the list of holidays observed by judges and notaries (*Statuti . . . giudici e notai*, p. 101).

72 A. Lisini, *Lettere volgari del sec. XIII a Geri e Guccio Montanini (Nozze Pezzuoli-Curzi*, Siena, 1899).

73 See Vauchez; Pecci, p. 235; above, p. 137.

74 Dipl., AGC, 23.4.1284.

earned entry into Purgatory for Sapia, the 'envious' woman who had rejoiced over the defeat of her fellow-citizens at Colle (1269).

A notable feature of Sienese religion in the thirteenth century is the apparent weakness of any heretical movement, despite the continuing strength of the dualist Patarenes in some parts of northern and central Italy. There are occasional references to the condemnation of Patarenes – in 1251, 1275, 1276, 1286, 1288 and 1290 – but heretical beliefs do not seem to have presented a serious challenge to orthodoxy. The most significant case recorded was one involving three brothers of a magnate family, the Montecchiesi. In 1304 these were found guilty by an inquisitor of heretical belief and sentenced to life imprisonment and the confiscation of all their property.[75] In general the inquisitors, mainly Franciscans, who were assigned to Siena must have regarded it as a quiet posting, although their servants had special authority to wear armour.

WILLS

A good indication of how the Sienese themselves regarded the religious institutions and movements of their day is provided by testamentary bequests.

Every testator hoped to allot some money for the salvation of his soul, but the balance between beneficiaries is best illustrated in the wills of those whose means made possible a full list of legatees, hence more information is available about the religious tastes of the better-off. The Bartolomeo di Ildebrandino whose will reveals his admiration for the comb-seller provides one instance of this.[76] Much of the will (which unfortunately is partly illegible) is dedicated to the future of his wife, son and two daughters; the possibility of one or both of these becoming nuns is taken into account. Apart from his place of burial, twenty-three religious institutions receive specific bequests. The main beneficiary is the Hospital of S Maria della Scala which is to receive 25 l.[77] Gallerani's Domus Misericordiae ranks next with 10 l. The Franciscans receive 5 l. and there are small bequests to individual Franciscans – who should have owned no property! – one of them a Piccolomini. The Dominicans receive the same, other mendicant houses (Servites and Augustinian Hermits) less. Twelve nunneries were to benefit, that of

---

75 G. Severino, 'Note sull'eresia a Siena fra il sec. XIII e XIV', *Studi offerti a R. Morghen* (Rome, 1974), pp. 889–905; there is no reference to Siena in S. Savino, *Il catarismo italiano e i suoi vescovi nei sec. XIII e XIV* (Florence, 1958). See also P. Mariano d'Alatri, *L'inquisizione francescana nell'Italia centrale nel sec. XIII* (Rome, 1954), especially pp. 59, 148–9 (and Dipl., AGC, 18.5.1300). A heretic condemned in 1321 (Bowsky, *Commune*, p. 76) was said to have been involved in a Sienese heretical group for two decades. The case described in G. Sanesi, 'Un notaio usuraio processato per eresia', *BSSP*, 6 (1899), pp. 497–509, does not relate to heretical beliefs.

76 See above p. 146.

77 Unfortunately parts of this will are illegible; the references to the Hospital and the Augustinian Hermits are probabilities, not certainties.

S Prospero to the tune of 5 l., though seven of them got only 10s. apiece. The tertiaries of the Humiliati were to receive 1 l., as was a minor hospital (S Agnese) and the church of S Donato (with a gift of 5s. to each of its priests). The leper-house received 10s., as did the brethren of the baptismal church of S Giovanni. Every anchorite in Siena or within a mile – the standard provision – was to get 1s. The general tenor of this will suggests that the mendicants had by no means completely ousted the older orders, even among those who ranked as their sympathizers and admirers.

Something of the same feeling emerges in the will of the timber-merchant (he refers to a workshop, so he presumably had a carpentry business also) Grimaldo di Venture (1292).[78] Grimaldo was a tertiary of the Humiliati and it was natural that he should allocate 5 l. to that Order 'for building their church'. The same sum was to go to the Carmelites 'for building an altar in their church'. Three orders of friars – Dominicans, Franciscans, Augustinian Hermits – received 2 l. each, the Servites 1 l. Twelve nunneries are named. The fabric of the cathedral receives 1 l., the Hospital (della Scala) 15s., the bishop 5s. Four other hospitals benefit, among them the leper-house. Lest anyone should feel neglected, 6d. was to go to every church in the city – and naturally 6d. to each anchorite. Grimaldo had retained property in the contado and links there. The church at Ampugnano was to benefit from the sale of land, as was the *pieve* at Sovicille, each of whose dependent chapels was also allocated 5s. 'The poor of Grosseto' were recipients of the largest specific charitable bequest, 8 l.

A similar attitude is evident, on a rather humbler scale, in the will of Francesco di Adota (1291) a hosier.[79] He hoped for burial in the episcopal cemetery and bequeathed 1 l. to the cathedral and 10s. to the bishop. His parish church, S Pietro in Castelvecchio, received 20s. 'for adornment' and its chaplains 10s. The main mendicant orders came off best (the Preachers, Minors and Augustinians got 4 l. each), the Servites and Carmelites (2 l.) and Humiliati (1 l.) less well. Two hospitals benefited and every monk and nun (this was exceptional) as well as every 'hermit' in the city or nearby was to receive 6d. He too left money to a church in the contado.

Francesco's might be described as an eclectic will, but the preference felt for the new orders is unmistakable. Sometimes this sentiment is clearer still, the favoured beneficiaries tending to be the Dominicans. Fiore, the widow of Bartolomeo di Ildebrandino, drew up a will in 1301, seventeen years after her husband, in which fifty-four specific bequests were made to religious institutions or individuals.[80]

---

78 Dipl., AGC, 6.2.1292.
79 ASS, Ms B 73, ff.212v–13.
80 Dipl., AGC, 13.6.1301. For her husband's will see above, p. 146.

The will was made at the Dominican house, where she hoped to be buried, and legacies to this house, the fabric of its church, the prior, the Preachers' confraternity and nine named friars amounted to a total of 20 l. 10s. The Humiliati were to have 7 l. 10s., four other mendicant orders benefited, many nunneries and some monks, three hospitals and a parish church with its chaplain, several other confraternities and the fabric of the cathedral, whilst the usual terms award a donation to every anchorite.

A few years later a still more marked preference seems indicated in the will of one Fino di Maffeo, who also hoped for burial at S Domenico and special masses there.[81] The Dominicans were to receive 16 l., the next most favoured religious legatee, the hospital of S Agnese, 4 l. This will also remembers a parish church and its priest, several monastic houses and – in the usual way – anchorites. Apart from that, there was money and clothing for the poor and wax candles for various churches. Some of Fino's property was earmarked for charitable causes after his wife's lifetime and she was instructed to raise money for the poor by selling the produce of one of their vineyards, 'for my soul and hers'.

Not all the ecclesiastical legatees of the Sienese were local or even regional. In 1285 a young merchant lay dying at Brienne le Château near Troyes in Champagne; he hoped for burial in the Premonstratensian house of Basses-Fontaines and he left money to that church and to the Minors and Preachers of Brienne, as well as to eight ecclesiastical bodies at Siena.[82] Nor was the Holy Land a forgotten cause. The brethren of the confraternity of S Maria della Scala prayed for 'those who make the holy journey and gain the holy land beyond the sea' and mention of crusading in wills was common. Aldobrandino di Dietaiuto was a pious man though not a wealthy one, and one of his sons, his executor, was an Augustinian friar. He bequeathed 5s. (this was one-tenth of his total religious bequests) for 'aid to the present and future defenders of the Holy Sepulchre of our lord Jesus Christ against the Saracens'.[83] In 1277 a woman named Fina, who was probably unmarried and without close relatives, made a will before setting out on pilgrimage to Rome.[84] Considerably the largest of her numerous legacies for religious ends was 25 l. 'for the aid of the Holy Land beyond the sea when there is an expedition (*passagium*) for that purpose'. Infantino, a Sienese teacher of Latin who was a friend of Bishop Rinaldo Malavolti, made his will at Gaeta (north of Naples) in 1282.[85] Half of his estate was to be shared between his wife and various other relatives, the other half was assigned to the aid of the Holy Land. Fiore, a

81 Ibid., 27.12.1306.
82 Ibid., 5.2.1285.
83 Ibid., 19.6.1276 (with interesting inventory of property, dated 22 October 1280).
84 Ibid., 17.2.1277.
85 ASS, Ms B 73, ff. 228–9.

widow whose will has already been mentioned, left 10 l. 'for the aid of the Holy Land; I wish the prior of the convent of Friars Preacher at Siena to hold it until there is a general *passagium*, when he is to provide this sum for the said purpose'.[86] Some years later (1321) 200 Sienese cavalrymen took the cross, but the project proved abortive and these would-be crusaders never left Italy.[87]

Pilgrimage rarely features in Sienese wills, but Uberto di Viviano, a spicer, bequeathed money (the amount is illegible, but may be 10s.) for 'an honest (*legalis*) man to go on my behalf to the house of St James in Galicia'. The expectation that pilgrims would make wills before setting out is attested by the halving of the notarial charge for wills made in these circumstances.[88]

CONFRATERNITIES

One is surely nearest to the heart of thirteenth-century Sienese spirituality in the confraternities of pious laymen and women.[89] The Hospital had such gilds, both of men and women, the Domus Misericordiae had one, the principal mendicant orders (Dominicans, Franciscans, Augustinians, Servites) each had their own and there were confraternities of *disciplinati* (flagellants) dedicated to St Nicholas and to the Holy Cross. Doubtless there were others, indeed one authority estimates the number of flagellant gilds alone in the late thirteenth century at twelve. One suspects that a quite high proportion of adult Sienese, especially among the middle elements, were members, though that is admittedly a guess.

No early statutes survive for most of these gilds, though some statutes of the Dominican *laudesi* founded by Ambrogio Sansedoni are preserved in the text of an episcopal privilege (1267): these reveal that the members met to sing praises at the Dominican house daily and went in procession through the city twelve times a year. More is known about the activities of one of the flagellant confraternities, the *disciplinati* of S Maria della Scala, whose early statutes date back to 1295 and 1300.[90] This gild, 'of Siena and the contado', dedicated its statutes 'to the honour and reverence of our Lord Jesus Christ and His Mother the Virgin Mary and all the saints

---

86 Above, p. 148.
87 *RIS, CS*, p. 390. P. Pirillo's investigation of crusading in Florentine wills at this period ('La Terrasanta nei testamenti fiorentini del Dugento' in F. Cardini, ed., *Toscana e Terrasanta nel Medioevo*, Florence, 1982, pp. 57–73) shows 13 per cent of a sample of wills including legacies for the Crusade.
88 Dipl., Spedale, 3.8.1240; *Statuti . . . giudici e notai*, p. 108.
89 See G. M. Monti, *Le confraternite medievali dell'alta e media Italia* (2 vols., Venice, 1927), especially 1, pp. 126–33, 228–49; G. G. Meersseman, *Ordo Fraternitatis. Confraternite e pietà dei laici nel medioevo* (3 vols., Rome, 1977), especially 2, pp. 598–603, 649–65, 954–63, 1029–34, 1046–7, 1303; F. Dal Pino, 'I Servi di Maria a Siena', *MEFR*, 89 (1977), pp. 749–55.
90 L. Banchi (ed.), *Capitoli della Compagnia dei Disciplinati a Siena* (Siena, 1866). The statutes of the Dominican flagellants are printed by G. Prunai in *BSSP*, n.s. 11 (1940), pp. 119–56 and in Meersseman, 2, pp. 649–65.

(*Santi e Sante*) of God; to the honour and reverence of the Holy Roman Church and our father the bishop of Siena; and for the salvation and consolation of the souls of all members of the gild, who are commended to Jesus Christ the Crucified'.

The lay officials of the gild (which had its own salaried chaplain) were a prior and chamberlain (treasurer), with six councillors serving for a three-monthly period. The prior served for six months. Eighteen other brethren reinforced these officials in the task of considering applications for admission, and those surmounting this preliminary hurdle required a two-thirds vote of a full capitular gathering to achieve reception into the noviciate. Candidates had to be at least twenty years of age. The grounds for exclusion were numerous: those belonging to other confraternities of flagellants, or having belonged within the last year, were ineligible, as were former members of religious orders, anyone who had committed a sin for which he could not obtain absolution, also usurious lenders and notaries who had registered usurious transactions. The prior and councillors had power to expel any brother 'at fault' (*chi fusse in colpa*), though one thus expelled could be readmitted after an interval of a year if he sought this and an investigation found that he had mended his ways. The gild was seen as a perpetual corporation, whose property (under the care of a 'Protector'), including alms and prayers, was common to all the brethren, 'both the dead and the living'.

Each month a chapter-meeting of all the brethren was held, on which occasion a payment of 1s. had to be made into the funds (1s. 6d. by those who failed to be present). This basic subscription, though not high, must have ruled out membership for the poor. Brethren had to recite nineteen paternosters and ave Marias daily (seven of each, with five more 'in reverence for the five wounds of Jesus Christ'), besides one more of each on sitting down to a meal and on rising from it and on going to bed and rising. They had to confess at least once a fortnight and to communicate thrice a year in the gild's chapel. They had to hear the mass daily 'or at least see the holy body of Christ', and might listen to sermons 'wherever they wished'. Presence at the gild's own mass on Sundays was compulsory, as was presence at the *disciplina* (self-flagellation) each Friday; the penance for absence was the recitation of many additional prayers, but three successive absences might lead to expulsion.

The obligatory sessions of flagellation took place in the gild chapel; voluntary flagellation on other occasions was permitted. During the *disciplina* the prior led the singing of 'some praise or other holy thing, in praise of Jesus Christ' and on each occasion he had also to say five paternosters and five ave Marias for the souls of departed brethren and their relatives. When the brothers went forth in procession *a disciplina* they were to carry their banner but not on other occasions. The statutes do not make it clear how frequent were these public processions.

Maundy Thursday was a regular day for them. They required the prior's consent and each prior had the right to ordain one at least once during his tenure of office.

There was a charitable side to the activities of all these confraternities. The Hospital's *disciplinati* and in particular the prior and chaplain had to visit their sick brethren. If alms were required for the succour of sick members the prior could levy 6d. from each brother with the consent of his councillors. The associated feminine confraternity (consorority?) was to be aided by its masculine counterpart in almsgiving so that it could dispense twelve *staia* of baked bread each week to 'poor, wretched, needy and deserving (*vergognose*) persons and religious bodies'. Annually in May each of the brethren was to make a formal promise of alms either financial or in kind; these offerings were voluntary but they had to be adhered to. Should any of the brethren fall into serious distress the officials were to consult together about what help could be given. Attendance at the funeral mass of a departed brother was compulsory and each member was to say a hundred paternosters and the same number of ave Marias for the dead man's soul within the week following his death. The organization of the funeral mass was the responsibility of the prior. Brethren were urged to offer hospitality to strangers who belonged to similar confraternities.

Naturally there were also rules governing conduct. The brothers were forbidden to swear or indulge in loose talk, to gamble, to enter taverns or other 'dishonest' premises. Each Sunday 'everyone must accuse anyone offending' in these respects or otherwise 'not leading a good life' to their prior, in secret; the prior might then award appropriate penance or recommend expulsion. This provision for secret accusation was doubtless accepted without complaint by citizens of a commune which paid officials to perform the same office of secret denunciation.[91] Some of the moral clauses throw light on contemporary *mores*. The brethren were to be decently shod and clothed, short garments and pointed shoes being banned. Also 'let no one go wandering about in churches or in other dishonest places' (*ciascuno si guardi d'andare vagheggiando per le chiese, nè in altri luoghi disonesti*). Whenever they met – not merely in their chapel – they were to greet each other fraternally with the formula 'Praised be Jesus Christ', to which the reply was 'May He ever be praised and blessed'.

It would be interesting to know more about the practice, so central to some of these gilds, of flagellation. This was an activity common to many of the revivalist movements of the thirteenth century in Italy. The statutes of the *disciplinati* of the Holy Cross (which date however from the second half of the fourteenth century) give some detail about self-flagellation performed each Sunday after the mass.[92]

---

91 Above, pp. 58–9.
92 Monti, *Le confraternite medievali*, 1, pp. 131–3.

The brethren were to kneel and whip themselves 'for such time as it shall take those not performing the discipline to recite five paternosters and five aves'. Then all were to sing Adoramus, to listen to the *Jube domine benedicere* and an epistle sung by one of the brethren, and to recite seven more paternosters and aves. More flagellation followed, during which the *Jube* was to be recited again and a passage read from the Gospels, succeeded by two paternosters and aves. Then a passage concerning Christ's Passion was read and a *laude* sung. Another paternoster and ave followed, then more prayers both in Latin and the vernacular and more flagellation again. After removing their special cowls the brethren returned to the church from the vestry to hear a reading of their statutes and for the assignment of penances. The liturgical detail, slightly simplified here, is very considerable; some of the prayers were to be said aloud, others recited silently.

CONCLUSION

The confraternities constituted a momentous development in piety in the second half of the thirteenth century, perhaps even more influential among laymen than the growth of the Franciscan and Dominican movements in the first half of the century. It is striking that these innovations could be successfully absorbed within the Church, as acknowledged and indeed greatly approved institutions, in such a brief period. With so much religious enthusiasm in the air, the surprising thing is not the occasional appearance of unorthodoxy but the fact that it remained exceptional. This process of adaptation speaks well for the flexibility and good sense of the prelates and the more influential mendicants.

The city authorities may have been more disposed to caution than were the religious leaders, to judge from the reception of a petition submitted to the General Council in 1308 by the gild of the Virgin Mary.[93] The rector, Chamberlain and councillors of this body explained that it existed 'for the sustenance of the poor of the city and contado of Siena. Many good men, knights, judges, doctors, merchants and other artisans and young nobles of the city have freely and spontaneously joined this company and God has inspired them to go through the city seeking alms and to take these to the poor and wretched, the needy and modest (*verecundi*). They distribute loaves, clothing and money among these people according to their needs, giving also whatever they can obtain through legacies and in other ways. Their firm and constant rule and intention is not to hold possessions of their own but to pass on at once whatever they receive for the use of the poor. If they receive fixed property they sell this at once and hand on the proceeds to the poor.' A difficulty had arisen, in that the gild lacked a legal corporation's power to appoint representatives to act on its behalf: it needed to

93 CG 73, ff. 162–5.

become a *collegium et universitas* so that it might empower representatives to act in selling, making gifts and exchanges, transferring and alienating property, and agreeing to rents, terms and other settlements and transactions. The Council displayed no enthusiasm for the gild's work or sympathy for its dilemma. By a large majority it rejected the petition, agreeing however that the Nine should consult men learned in canon and civil law on the subject.

A fundamental and deep-seated belief in the law prevailed among Siena's rulers. They were not to be swept off their feet by petitioners' rhetoric. Ambrogio Sansedoni would have seen the matter differently and would have been found more persuasive, but he had been dead for twenty years and the gild lacked an advocate comparable to him in standing and personality. Religious enthusiasm flowed and ebbed, the conviction that only firm legal principles and institutions could check the ever-present threats to internal stability remained constant.

7 *Assumptions*

Some aspects of the ways of thought and life of the thirteenth-century Sienese may strike an observer in the late twentieth century as particularly unexpected or particularly surprising. Which these routines, suppositions or attitudes are, depends, naturally, on the viewpoint or expectation of the observer, hence it is not entirely correct to label what surprises us as 'assumptions' or presuppositions. However, since they are important features of Italian medieval civic society and were taken for granted by the medieval Sienese as aspects of their way of life which would not have required explanation or justification to their own contemporaries, it may be acceptable to consider them under the title given to this chapter. It will comprise two main sections; first the advanced bureaucratization of the commune (and the city's other institutions) and the very striking degree of intervention in all aspects of life that this made possible; secondly, the emphasis given to display, pageantry and visual aspects of authority and government.

BUREAUCRACY

The strength, extent and ramifications of Sienese bureaucracy have already been indicated in connection with the commune's institutions. The insistence that the chancery should retain copies of all letters despatched and preserve all relevant deeds, while also adding copies of them to the cartularies of privileges, sets the tone for an intensely literate mode of government characterized by a spectacular consumption of paper, parchment and ink. Typical was the insistence that every transaction of the Chamberlain and the four Provveditori had to be recorded in writing, that at least two of the latter were to be present whenever that Chamberlain made or received any payment, that both copies of the accounts must be checked in full by all these officials every month and the terms of their oaths of office be read by them at least every two months. Typical too were the precise measures concerning the keys to the commune's coffers: one of these was the senior Provveditore's, the other, which was dissimilar and therefore complementary, was in the care of his colleagues. The system generated a mass of written records, since all Biccherna accounts were kept in duplicate, the Chamberlain and the Provveditori having separate copies. And to write of this as a 'duplicate' method is to understate greatly the amount of writing done since the surviving volumes of Biccherna records are clearly neat copies made up at the end of six-monthly periods of office, not records made at the time of the transactions themselves. The same is true for the notarial records of Council meetings: the proceedings were noted in rough during the sessions, then written up formally for acceptance as correct records, much as minutes of meetings nowadays.[1]

The consumption of paper by the commune's judicial institutions is equally striking, since the detailed depositions of all witnesses in the city's very busy courts were recorded in full, and this involved writing out in Latin the statements of many witnesses concerning what might be quite minor disputes over property, for instance, and cases of theft and violence, which were then read back at full length to the witness in the vernacular.[2] This technique incidentally implies considerable linguistic expertise.

Correspondence, accounts, minutes and the other forms of record mentioned come nowhere near the total body of written material generated and accreted by the commune. Numberless inventories, for example, were compiled, and statutes promulgated and recorded in several copies. It is hardly surprising that purchases of paper and parchment should have ranked as significant items of expenditure in the Biccherna volumes. Paper, though something of a novelty, compared favourably in price with parchment, the latter costing, per quire, about 5s., the price of some forty sheets of paper. From the earliest surviving volumes (from 1248) the deliberations of the General Council were recorded on paper, whereas parchment was used for the main series of the Biccherna accounts (the *Entrata e Uscita* volumes) until 1302,[3] after which paper gradually came to be used.

A few examples will give some notion of the scale of the purchases. In January 1278 six reams of paper were bought (2,880 sheets) for 20 l. 5s. In 1281 twenty-eight quires (a quire was four sheets folded in eight leaves) and six sheets of parchment for use by the Fifteen *gubernatori* and the Biccherna cost 6 l. 5s. 10d. The following year 136 quires and thirteen sheets of parchment were bought for the Biccherna and for copies of statutes and judicial records, while around the same time a considerable purchase of paper was made, amounting to 229 (mainly small) bound volumes and 5,358 sheets at a cost of at least 14 l.[4] Literate men were not in short supply, but the cost of their labour was of some significance. A notary who in 1282 made a copy of new statutes which covered five quires and four sheets received 52s., while another whose work amounted to about eight quires was paid 3 l. 18s.[5] The ubiquity of notaries could also be exploited to assist

1 Above, pp. 52, 59; *B.* 16, pp. vi–vii.
2 See the surviving records of the Podestà's court, Podestà 5–9 (1298) and the Capitano del Popolo's, Capitano 4 (1302).
3 B 116.
4 B 71, f. 21; 80, f. 74; 82, ff. 115v, 138v.
5 B 82, f. 139.

the flow of information to the authorities; for example, any instance of a will containing bequests in favour of the commune had to be reported by the notary who had drawn up the will. It is an indication of the commune's frequent calls on notaries that their gild forbade them to haunt the entrance to the Palazzo.[6]

The multiplicity of bureaucratic employment offered by the commune, mainly part-time, has already been stressed.[7] Fiscal valuers, for example, required the assistance of professional surveyors. In 1293 Giarino 'of the abacus' (*de abbacho*) was employed for twenty-two days, with two assistants, to plot out the vegetable-gardens planned for Castelfranco di Paganico, a new foundation in the southern contado: at 14s. a day the bill came to 15 l. 8s.[8] Naturally bureaucracy bred its own dependents. Three officials had the duty of negotiating the rents paid by the commune for the property it hired to house the Fifteen, the Podestà and his retinue and various other officials. The remuneration of these three, at 5s. each, was no very considerable item, but they could not get by without their very own messenger, which brought the total cost of their functions to 16s.[9] Officialdom also required an array of equipment, such as the measures, weights and scales needed in the regulatory process for the sale of salt, wine, oil and flour. Identical weights and measures had to be held at every place within the contado. Each barrel manufactured by a Sienese cooper had to be sealed with the commune's official seal.[10]

There was a danger that those in charge of the practicalities of civic life might try to skimp on all this and get by with a minimum of *papasserie*, but it was made difficult for them to cut corners. Officials concerned with roads, bridges, fountains and woodlands must have felt the temptation most because their workers were usually illiterate, but they were specially adjured to keep all their paper-work, including financial accounts, in neat copies for retention in the office ('sì che sempre nel detto officio sia copia di quelle cose le quali si fanno'). In all respects a high degree of literacy was assumed. A chained copy of the commune's statutes was kept available for public consultation, even if the right of access to this was presumably a formality in the case of a vast majority of the female population and a considerable majority of the males also.[11] A full inventory of the commune's arms and warlike stores had to be read aloud and checked over in detail every quarter by the Chamberlain and Provveditori, while new military ordinances

---

6 *Cost. 1309–10*, 1, p. 105: *Statuti . . . giudici e notai*, p. 83. Wills were normally drawn up shortly before the testator's death. But this clause could have caused difficulties when a testator made an unexpected recovery or was merely (for example) setting out on a long journey.

7 Above, pp. 58–9.

8 B 109, f. 145v.

9 B 82, f. 159.

10 *Const. 1262*, pp. 110–12.

11 *Cost. 1309–10*, 2, p. 136; *Const. 1262*, p. 181.

continued to be promulgated in imposing numbers.[12] As the recent archival records reached constantly increasing dimensions, a decision that fiscal assessments had to be burned after payment had been made was perhaps a consolation to harassed officials.[13]

What has been said of the commune's bureaucracy and its assumptions concerning literacy could equally well be said of the administration of all the other institutions claiming the loyalty of the Sienese. Certainly it is true of commercial firms, of gilds and hospitals, indeed it applied to every form of religious activity except that of the stubbornly solitary hermits. Yet the commune itself, by its expectations as well as its administrative vigour, achieved an unchallengeable hold over the lives of its citizens.

REGULATION

Nothing was so private a matter that it lay beyond the reach of the commune. Such a concept as 'the liberty of the individual' could have little meaning in a society where men might be instructed to wear their hair short at the back 'so that at least part of their neck is visible'.[14] Within the domestic sphere, legislation laid down that a woman might not bequeath more than a quarter of her estate to anyone other than her own children, while many other statutes governed dowries, wardship and family relationships. A woman was permitted to separate from her husband if five reliable men supported her claim that she was in danger from his violence or that of his relatives, and in such circumstances the husband had to give her adequate financial support. Should the need arise, a son could be compelled to provide food for his father. A legal guardian had to be nominated for anyone recognized to be mentally defective or even an incorrigible spendthrift (*prodigus*).[15]

At night it was illegal not merely to be outside but to leave a door open.[16] Watchmen of the guard were permitted to frequent brothels during the curfew if not on duty so long as they did not consume food on the premises. Gambling was a civic monopoly and source of profit and so was subject to considerable restrictions: it was totally prohibited within an area three miles outside the city and in Siena could not take place before spectators except in the commune's own casino, while at Christmas all gambling was forbidden. Fines were common both for gambling illegally and for illegal presence as a spectator.[17] Another leisure

---

12 *Const. 1262*, p. 125; *B.* 15, p. 188 (a notary copies forty-seven new clauses *de ordinamento equorum et balistarum*, 1254).
13 CG 65, f. 94 (1304). This was not an unusual measure. The Biccherna volumes analysed in chapter 2 were not fiscal records in the strict sense.
14 Zdekauer, *Vita privata*, p. 45.
15 *Const. 1262*, pp. 213n, 214, 237, 242–3.
16 *Cost. 1309–10*, 2, p. 364.
17 Ibid., 2, pp. 245–7: B 104, ff. 7, 15v; 116, ff. 6, 20v; 120, f. 39v.

activity, visiting the baths at Petriolo, Macereto or Vignoni, was under communal control to an even greater extent. The commune farmed out the rights to these places but still fixed maximum charges for rooms, mattresses and so on, and closely regulated the sale of food there, one of the Podestà's officials having a special responsibility for the bathing establishments. Gambling was forbidden there but certain games such as chess were permitted. Men and women had to bathe separately.[18] Hunting, which was both a leisure pastime and an important source of food, was also regulated closely. It was illegal to snare or shoot pigeons, to take quails between April and June, to set bait for birds within eight miles of the city and to net them anywhere.[19]

Education, though certainly not a communal or lay monopoly, was also a matter for the civic authority in Siena, as in the other Italian cities. Though a papal privilege to a 'university' (1252) seems to have been ineffectual, the commune already recruited and paid teachers of commercial arithmetic and of law and Latin (thus contributing to the preparation of future notaries and administrators) as well as of medicine. Teachers of law and Latin were exempted from military service, and the latter were even excused duties as night watchmen (lest they confuse their irregular verbs, on the sleepy morning after?). A Sienese who was teaching Latin at Arezzo was tempted back by an offer of a salary higher than the Aretines were paying, together with tax exemptions. The 1274 statutes offered special protection to scholars and teachers, and in 1275 it was decided to set up a *studium generale* (general school) of letters. No doubt news of this led to an Englishman writing from the papal court to seek employment as a teacher of logic; he seems to have secured an annual salary of 50 l. (1279), twice the basic pay (assigned notionally for their lodging) to the teachers of other subjects.[20] Educational expansion meant seeking out pupils as well as teachers; it was suggested that six was the minimum number for the establishment of a viable law school. At this time Siena was not successful in setting up a widely recognized 'centre of excellence' in education, but by the early fourteenth century a good deal had been achieved. There were then five teachers of Latin ('grammar') and logic (subjects in the *trivium*, the liberal arts course) and law, also two doctors of natural sciences (*scienze di fisicha*) who were well rewarded at 90 florins per annum.[21]

---

18 D. Barduzzi, *Provvedimenti per le stazioni termali senesi nei sec. XIII e XIV* (Siena, 1899): CG 51, f. 31: *Cost. 1309–10*, 2, p. 81; see also above, p. 114.

19 *Cost. 1309–10*, 2, pp. 265–7.

20 *Const. 1262*, p. 410n; *Cost. 1309–10*, 1, pp. 103–4; 2, p. 158: *B.* 5, p. 85; 8, p. 109; 9, p. 97; 103, f. 107v; 118, ff. 299–305v: CG 20, f. 79r and v; 22, f. 29r and v, Alleg. E; 23, f. 20v: P. Nardi, 'Comune, impero e papato alle origini dell'insegnamento universitario in Siena (1240–1275)', *BSSP*, 90 (1983), pp. 50–94.

21 B 118, ff. 299–305v; 120, f. 368. I am indebted also to an unpublished paper by Dr P. D. Denley on the early history of the *studium*.

The Sienese could be – and were – compelled to plant fruit trees. Their building work was affected by the compulsory uniformity of size of bricks and tiles and by the compulsory wage-scales of masons and woodworkers. A little more surprising perhaps is the commune's right of compulsory purchase, not only in connection with town-planning (new open spaces etc.) but also in the interests of landowners themselves. The owner of a plot bordered on three sides by the land of another owner could be compelled to sell out to that neighbour.[22] This measure must have been responsible for much long-sighted scheming and a great deal of ill-feeling.

The close regulation of economic life is the most explicable aspect of Siena's *étatisme*. The supply of grain was crucial to the city's existence and its regime's stability, and it was natural that there should have been communal granaries for use in years of shortage. Connected with the same matter was the control of mills and milling. Detailed regulations governed the location of mills and gave intending millers rights of compulsory purchase in appropriate sites. The construction of fishponds was encouraged and the import and sale of fish regulated. Any purchase of food within two miles of the city by stallholders for resale was forbidden. Baking and the sale of wine were closely regulated and kilns subject to frequent inspection. Horses and pack animals for hire had to be officially valued.[23]

Did the commune really possess the means to enforce this all-pervading legislation? The statutes certainly testify to the councillors' belief in their commune's authority. There was no shortage of messengers and criers to make known its will; apart from the regular four messengers and three criers, a body of sixty Sienese was permanently on call to undertake any necessary mission.[24] Obviously there was defiance and violence. To evade the law by escape into the wilder parts of Tuscany was common, yet so was the contrary, law-abiding, decision to purchase pardon at a bargain price. Certainly the people of the contado often felt the authority of Siena as a grim reality. It has already been mentioned that when subject communities fell into debt their people were even forbidden to visit a doctor in Siena.[25] The system of spies and officially empowered denouncers no doubt added to the commune's formidability. The use of this governmental technique was ruthless. If a man offered a bribe to an official and it was accepted, he was rewarded, if he proceeded to denounce the accepter, by being granted a quarter of the fine levied on the corrupt official.[26]

22 *Cost. 1309–10*, 1, pp. 474–5; 2, p. 65 (for the application of this clause v. CG 61, ff. 111r and v), pp. 547–8.
23 *Const. 1262*, pp. 309, 353–4: *Cost. 1309–10*, 2, pp. 66–72, 309–10, 367–8, 389–90, 402–3; CG 61, ff. 51v–5: *B.* 17, pp. 109, 121, 175. See also S. De Colli, 'Lo statuto degli "ufficiali sopra i mugnai" (anno 1281)', *BSSP*, 64 (1957), pp. 153–81.
24 *Const. 1262*, pp. 113–14.
25 CG 48, ff. 50–9 (see also above, p. 109).
26 *Cost. 1309–10*, 2, p. 432.

SUMPTUARY LAWS

Sumptuary legislation, which is a feature of all the Italian communes, provides a characteristic instance of their ubiquitous control. As with many other aspects of that control, it was much dependent on the institution of 'secret' denouncers; within each contrada the Podestà had to have one of his *secretos exploratores et accusatores bonos et legales* to watch out for offences against sumptuary laws.[27] These laws should almost certainly be seen as part ethical and religious, part economic, in their motivations (not that contemporaries would have accepted this distinction). There was a primitivist vein of puritanical distrust of individual display and conspicuous expenditure in the outlook of many, but that attitude on its own might have been less influential in law-making had it not been supported by the reasonable doctrine that private fortunes needed to be safeguarded at a time when capital formation was scarce and such consumption withdrew capital from productive activity.[28]

The laws were concerned both with apparel and ornamentation generally and with major social occasions. Maximum lengths were laid down for women's skirts and in the case of unmarried women they were never to have trains. The embellishments which could be used to decorate clothing were very precisely limited: they could be only of silk or gold and could be worn by women on the breast or hands or on the patterned parts of sleeves and the front of mantles. Men were allowed ornamentation also on the shoulder and neck of leather garments. Women were not to wear crowns on their heads, but the less ostentatious silver 'garlands' or circlets were permitted if they weighed less than two ounces and these might even be gilded 'in the usual way' so long as they did not have pearls in them also. Women were allowed pearl buttons, up to the number of five and worn on the breast, and silver girdles weighing not more than twelve ounces.[29]

The dubbing of a knight was the occasion of a major gathering, yet it was not to be marked by gifts, except of plain cloth; presents of gold and silver money were prohibited, nor could the entertainment involve the new knight sending round a *giullare* (*jongleur*) or jester. The most detailed social regulations were those relating to weddings. No more than twelve men might be present at the betrothal ceremony and no more than seven female relatives of the groom could call on the

---

27 C. Mazzi, 'Alcune leggi suntuarie senesi del sec. XIII', *ASI*, 4th s., 5 (1880), pp. 133–44; *B*. 28, pp. 140–1. There is also much sumptuary legislation in S. Mengozzi, 'La "Charta bannorum" di Ubertino dell'Andito, Potestà di Siena nel 1249', *BSSP*, 13 (1906), pp. 381–456 (especially pp. 449–54).

28 See C. M. Cipolla in *C. Econ. H.*, 3, pp. 419–21.

29 Mazzi; *Cost. 1309–10*, 2, p. 378.

new bride. The groom might not give presents to the bride's relatives, nor she to his, nor his female relatives to her. At the betrothal both parties had to swear an oath of adherence to these provisions (here considerably abbreviated and simplified). Only relatives and close neighbours could be involved in the celebrations. Restrictions concerning women's clothing were not lifted for these occasions, and ladies' dresses were not to be *décolleté*, i.e. *frascollati de la forcella del petto in giù*. Again, payments to *giullari* were regulated.[30]

Similar decrees applied to funerals, the other major 'rite of passage'. Women were not permitted to attend burials of men, nor more than six of them the burial of a woman. The size of the group accompanying the widow from her house to the interment was limited to twelve men and twelve women. The duration of the formal lamentation in front of the house, which could not begin until a bell had been rung, was also restricted. Those who might take part in this and who might then sit in the house and later make visits of condolence were defined and limited. Women other than the widow were not to wear mourning for more than a fortnight.[31] Such regulations governing the commemoration of death, though normally, and probably rightly, regarded as coming under the heading of 'sumptuary' measures, were not primarily economic in their motivation. A very important factor in all these measures was clearly a generally accepted notion that all forms of display should be subject to direction and restraint.

DISPLAY

The commune's concern with display and the visual aspects of life was not merely negative or passive. A major occasion for civic pageantry was the feast of the Assumption, more particularly after the city's devotion to the Virgin Mary had been strengthened by the victory of Montaperti. Since the German cavalry, whose share in the battle had been crucial, had invoked the aid of St George, that saint also was specially commemorated, at least for some years, by a civic procession with candles to his church on his feast day (23 April).[32]

But the major feast continued to be the Assumption (15 August), when representatives of the contado communities bore wax candles to the cathedral as a symbol of their subject status. The feast was to the Sienese what 'Empire Day' was to the British in the early twentieth century, a day for celebrating overlordship. On the eve of the feast the people of Siena, in their contrade, processed to the cathedral, attendance being compulsory. On the following day ceremonies

---

30 *Const. 1262, Cont., BSSP*, 2, pp. 142–3: *Cost. 1309–10*, 2, pp. 312–15, 405.
31 *Const. 1262, Cont., BSSP*, 2, pp. 315–17; *Cost. 1309–10*, 2, pp. 318–23.
32 *Const. 1262*, pp. 54–5.

associated with the city's overlordship took place, and, at least from 1310, there was a horse race, with a first prize (*palio*) of 50 l. Evidence of an August *palio* goes back as far as 1238, so the legislation of 1310 concerning the race should be seen as a re-establishment, or perhaps an attempt to set it on a firm annual basis. The race certainly did not take place in the Campo; the 1310 *palio* was run from the village of Fontebecci to the cathedral. Music also played an important part in the festivities of 15 August and it was sometimes necessary to reinforce the city's own musicians by borrowing those of neighbouring communes (as witness the payment made to San Gimignano's trumpeters in 1295). A tight-rope walker seems also to have participated in the entertainment, to judge from a payment made to a juggler, 'for the hire of a rope'.[33]

Easter was the other principal occasion for festivities. Dramatic spectacles were presented in the Campo on Good Friday. In 1257, for instance, the Crucifixion was enacted, as well as 'a play of the Marys'. From 1307 another *palio* was run every year on 20 March, to commemorate the death, twenty years earlier, of the Dominican Ambrogio Sansedoni. Around that period the gild of judges and notaries observed fifty-five annual religious feasts as days on which their members were not to work.[34] The readiness with which other circumstances became opportunities for festivity illustrates even better than these regular occasions the Sienese enthusiasm for pageantry. Notables, officials and armies had to be formally welcomed, and leave taken of them. In 1281, for example, a gathering of 'barons and magnates' took place in Siena, perhaps in connection with the *podesteria* of Count Guido Selvatico. This must have been an important Guelf occasion and trumpeters were sent to meet the *baronibus et magnatibus viris, pro honore communis*.[35] Siena's Podestà for the first six months of 1306, Andrea, a feudatory from Massa Fermana in the Marche, was clearly a man who relished pageantry. He had the band of trumpeters, with their piper and tambourine player, accompany him for a formal meeting with a colleague who was taking up appointment as Podestà of Lucca. In Andrea's time the eight trumpeters were frequently in demand, for the first *palio* in honour of the blessed Ambrogio Sansedoni, for the procession to celebrate the news of the Florentine capture of Pistoia (10 April 1306), for the arrival of the new Capitano and his entry into office, for his predecessor's departure and for the dubbing of knights. The

---

33 On the patronage of the Virgin see H. C. Peyer, *Stadt u. Stadtpatron im mittelalterlichen Italien* (Zürich, 1955), pp. 48–55; Heywood, *Palio and Ponte*, pp. 62–6: *RIS, CS*, p. 310; B 112, f. 98.

34 *B.* 17, p. 102; Heywood, pp. 68–81; for Sansedoni see above, pp. 142–6; *Statuti . . . giudici e notai*, p. 101.

35 B 80, f. 135.

following year a Sienese contingent of cavalry and foot was dispached to aid Florence and took its leave at a ceremonial parade in the Campo.[36]

On such occasions the commune's *carroccio*, its cherished civic emblem, was present as the focus of patriotic pageantry. All the principal independent Italian cities had their own ceremonial waggons (*carrocci*).[37] There is no contemporary representation of Siena's, or any means of learning much with certainty about its appearance, though it was brightly painted and dominated by a banner at the top of a tall mast. It may have been drawn by horses or by horses and men rather than the more conventional oxen. The mast bearing the banner could be lowered when necessary: it was twenty-six *braccia* long and attached to another, fixed, mast which enabled the Sienese standard to dominate the scene from a great height, no doubt a factor of particular importance when the waggon was borne into battle.[38]

Something of the veneration felt for the *carroccio* is conveyed by the instruction (in the 1262 statutes) that a lamp should burn day and night in its presence. This ceremonial waggon usually accompanied the Sienese army on campaign with an escort of infantry. Brought back in triumph from the victory of Montaperti, four days later it stood in the Campo to preside over the submission of the men of Montalcino (*in campo Fori ante conspectum victoriosi carroccii civitatis Senarum*). Nor was its role confined to affirmation of the city's external authority, for thirty years earlier the organization of the Popolo had promised obedience to the commune, its members swearing an oath 'at the *carroccio*'.[39]

Pageantry constituted a substantial element in the commune's expenditure. The pay of a trumpeter, which rose from 1 l. to 2 l. per month, was by no means to be despised, particularly since this seems to have been a retainer, augmented by a sum of 2s. for each occasion on which the trumpeters performed.[40] But it was the appeal to the eye rather than to the ear which cost money. Musicians, messengers, town-criers, all had to be arrayed in clothing which bore the commune's arms. The messengers (*balitores*) of the Court of Wardship (Curia del Placito) had to have a cloak or waist-band coloured half-red, half-yellow; the commune's musicians were to have the commune's arms on their uniform. In 1282 the Fifteen decided that the attire of their doorkeeper reflected unfavourably on their prestige and 9 l. 2s. was laid out on procuring him a much smarter uniform and cloak. At the time of the military crisis of 1260 the alliance between Siena and King Manfred's representative Count Giordano was given visual emphasis; when

---

36 B 118, ff. 173, 222–4, 249, 287; 120, ff. 253v, 322v, 344v.
37 See H. Zug Tucci, 'Il Carroccio nella vita comunale italiana', *QFIA*, 65 (1985), pp. 1–104.
38 The account by the chronicler Montauri (*RIS, CS*, p. 203) dates from the fifteenth century.
39 *Const. 1262*, p. 26; *B*. 13, p. 178; *CV*, 2, n. 628 (pp. 846–52); the payment to a notary who *stetit et scripsit iuramenta populi quando iverunt ad caroccium* is *B*. 2, p. 207.
40 B 56, f. 30; 113, f. 155; 118, ff. 173, 222, 293.

the trumpeters went out to welcome the Count's arrival they were dressed in tunics specially designed for the occasion, bearing the Count's arms as well as the commune's. Even routine expenditure on such clothing was heavy. The criers had to have new suits of red or green each year. The clothing allowance for one year (1305) for three criers (*bannitores*) came to 44 l. 12s. 4d., 42 l. 10s. of this being for material (38 *brachia* of cloth at 35 l., and 7 l. 10s. for leather), the remainder being the charges of the tailor (36s.) and the cutter (6s. 4d.).[41]

The normal beneficiaries of the commune's high sartorial standards were its own officials, but special rewards of clothing were made to bearers of good news. Messengers reaching Siena with news of the birth of a son to King Manfred, and of a victory at Lucca (1263), of 'good news from Ravenna' (1274) and from Pavia (1275), and the victory in the contado at Rigomagno (1281) all received gifts of cloth. Of these the bearer of dynastic news benefited more handsomely than those whose news was military, but he had come further. Whereas the usual outlay on such an occasion was around 10 l. or less, the messenger from Manfred's court received garments to the value of 39 l. 9s. A period of multiple good news could be an expensive time. In 1306 five messengers reached Siena with favourable tidings from Bologna, Lucca and Florence and gifts of apparel to them cost 60 l. 16s. 6d.[42]

Banners were another costly item. The Biccherna volume recording these gifts to messengers registers a total expenditure of 337 l. 3s. 10d. on banners in a half-year period. The following year 69 l. 3s. 4d. was spent on two silk pennons and two standards (one for cavalry, one for infantry) for the force to be despatched to Florence. These were large but not unprecedented bills. In 1278 there occurred one of many campaigns against the recalcitrant population of Sticciano; the army was furnished with eighteen new flags and four new banners, at a total cost of 80 l. Often elements within the army required their own banners. The gift of a banner might even help to induce one contado community to serve against another, while Guelf affiliations had also to be affirmed with appropriate standards. The carroccio of course had its own flag; when Conradin came to Siena in 1268 a purchase was made of white silk for a new one and for a first prize for the celebratory horse-race, at a cost of nearly 500 l. A few years before that the victory of Montaperti had been celebrated by buying an entire new set of standards and banners.[43]

41 B 56, f. 18v; 82, ff. 102v–03; 118, f. 225; 'Breve 1250', pp. 71–2; *Cost. 1309–10*, 1, pp. 112–13; *Const. 1262*, p. 115.
42 B 37, f. 33v; 56, f. 18v; 61, f. 7v; 80, f. 90; 118, f. 229v.
43 B 118, ff. 228v–9; 120, f. 369; 73, f. 49; 59, ff. 55 (Monticiano against Prata), 46 (36 l. 5s. 6d. for three standards of the Guelf Party); 42, f. 93v; 35, f. 20 (1262). The distinctions between 'pennons', 'flags', 'banners' and 'standards' are problematical: the vocabulary used here is that of the Biccherna notaries.

VISUAL ART

It was an assumption that a Sienese official, like Dogberry, should have 'every-thing handsome about him'. The commune had its own gold cup, its deeds were preserved in painted chests, and the volumes of statutes and accounts were illuminated and bound in covers which constitute one of the most notable surviving forms of medieval Sienese art. The books and their bindings, now greatly admired, were a much less considerable budgetary item than the banners and tunics. A notary's fee for copying and illuminating (not a specialist's job in this instance, it would seem) the statute of the Fifteen was merely 1 l. The sums paid for painting Biccherna covers varied from 8s. per volume (in 1277 and 1281) to 1 l. (in 1306). In these early volumes, the covers (most of which have unfortunately migrated from Siena) usually depicted the Chamberlain or the coats of arms of the Provveditori. More elaborate scenes – to judge from the covers which are still extant – begin around 1320, with the portrayal of the Chamberlain kneeling before the local saint, St Galganus.[44]

Painting on the outside of chests (*cassoni*) was another inexpensive job – the painter of a *cassone* to be kept at Giuncarico received a mere 6s. 6d. (1292)[45] – but murals were a different matter. In 1289 Master Mino painted the Virgin and other saints on the walls of the council-chamber in the temporary Palazzo del Comune adjacent to the new Palazzo, and was paid 22 1.[46] Visual art in the Palazzo was minatory as well as religious, hence the portraits of convicted forgers displayed there.[47]

The great series of decorative programmes in the new Palazzo was not embarked on in the period considered here, the main fourteenth-century elements being Simone Martini's *Maestà* in the Sala del Mappamondo, scenes of military virtues, subject places and famous men, and that great allegory of civic life, Ambrogio Lorenzetti's incomparable frescoes in the Sala of the Nine. In the following century these were to be joined by Taddeo di Bartolo's series of famous Romans and saints and by Spinello Aretino's cycle of the life of Alexander III, the Sienese pope.

The Simone Martini *Maestà* (1315) bears an inscription in which the Virgin, the city's patron or tutor, reminds the councillors of her delight in good counsel (*buon*

---

44 See *Le Biccherne* (Rome, 1984). B 82 f. 99 (payment to a notary *scribenti statutum et minianti statutum xv*); 67, f. 29; 79, f. 25 (both 8s.); 103, f. 69 and *Le Biccherne*, p. 66 (both 10s.); 118, f. 307 (2 l. for volumes); *Le Biccherne*, pp. 78–9; for a list of the covers now untraced but known to have existed, ibid., p. 387 (a list which could be supplemented from the Biccherna volumes).

45 B 108, f.146.

46 B 101, f. 74v.

47 *Cost. 1309–10*. On this topic see G. Ortalli, *La Pittura infamante nei sec. XIII–XVI* (Rome, 1979).

consigli), while the Christ-child carries a scroll with the words *Diligite iustitiam qui iudicatis terram* ('Love justice, you who are judges of the earth' – *Wisdom*, I, 1).[48] The tradition of didactic civic art, which was to reach its noble zenith in Siena with Ambrogio Lorenzetti's paintings in the Palazzo, had already been established in the thirteenth century.

Pageantry and visual display were justified and encouraged as stimuli to civic patriotism and pride, and the expense involved was willingly borne in the cause of promoting that spirit. That at least is what modern writers seem to imply. But have they rightly analysed cause and effect? Would it not be more accurate to see display as the *expression* of patriotism? The citizens of a great medieval commune required no consciously instilled 'image' to provoke strong feelings about their home city. It had formed them, it provided the familiar surroundings of their lives, its historical traditions were known to them from childhood, its enemies were known to them as their enemies. They had their domestic enemies too, but altruistic public spirit needed no conscious, cynical inculcation.

The bequests to the commune which notaries were required by law to report were not figments of a hopeful imagination but realities.[49] In 1290 one Bonacorso spent twenty-four days in the contado collecting customs dues. On his return he found that the payment he had received for the expenses of his military escort was actually 24 l. more than he had spent, and he returned that sum because 'he did not wish to keep it' (*quia noluit eos retinere*). A few years later a Franciscan friar paid 5 l. 16s. 6d. into the Biccherna 'saying that he had received them from a person who told him that he had had them wrongly, from the commune of Siena' (*disse che lli aveva ricevuti da una persona che lli disse che lli aveva ricevuti dal comune di Siena come non doveva*).[50]

A Sienese chronicler said that the Campo of Siena was thought 'the most beautiful piazza, with its beautiful and abundant fountain and beautiful and noble buildings and shops around, of all the piazze in Italy'.[51] He was neither propagandizing nor echoing propaganda. He was reporting his own and others' pride in the appearance of the city to which they fully belonged. For such men the pageantry of patriotism was the natural vocabulary of visual expression.

---

48 See N. Rubinstein, 'Political Ideas in Sienese Art: the frescoes by Ambrogio Lorenzetti and Taddeo di Bartolo in the Palazzo Pubblico', *JWCI*, 21 (1958), pp. 179–207.

49 B 107, f. 22 (3 l. 'a Guidone Pieri de Faenza quos reliquid communi Sen' in suo testamento').

50 B 103, f. 26; 116, f. 129 (1302).

51 *RIS, CS*, p. 550.

8 Revenue

The emphasis of this chapter will be on the relative importance of different forms of revenue and on how Siena's fiscal system affected the citizens. The commune's fiscal institutions and their functioning at this time and later have been depicted very thoroughly in William Bowsky's pioneering *The Finance of the Commune of Siena 1287–1355* (1971).[1] The view offered here, less detailed and less institutional, also differs in that it attempts a more general assessment of the commune's fiscal policies and their impact. One feature common to Bowsky's approach and mine is the cautious treatment of quantitative matters, necessitated by the nature of the surviving source material.

Some general points need to be clarified about the commune's fiscality before considering the revenues under the various forms in which they were gathered. The institution central to revenue-collecting activities was the Biccherna and the principal surviving source for the subject is the series of volumes of the Entrata and Uscita (Revenue and Expenditure) of that office which, with some gaps, go back to 1226.[2] From the later thirteenth century, however, the organization of indirect taxation by a separate office (the Gabella) achieved increasing independence, and money received by it is not recorded, or only indirectly reflected, in the Biccherna volumes. It is fundamental that the concept of a 'budget' is absent from the philosophy of the medieval communes. Fiscal policy was hand-to-mouth and consisted of a series of reactions to the city's constantly changing financial situation. By far the greatest single item of expenditure was warfare, essentially a matter for extremely short-term planning, and many forms of revenue, some of them seasonal, were also irregular and could fluctuate violently in the course of a year.

Urgent decisions were the norm, and so fiscal activity was open to experimentation and less subject to tried methods and conventions than many other aspects of the commune's policy. There were times when Siena's financial affairs were to a large extent (though not formally) placed in the hands of a single company or banker, although it is most unlikely that such an expedient would have recommended itself as a principle. There were obvious dangers in accepting very

---

1 Clarendon Press, Oxford (Italian edition: *Le finanze del Comune di Siena, 1287–1355*, Florence, 1976).
2 See above, pp. 59–60.

large loans from one bank or individual and even in allocating to one the payment of very large sums to soldiers.[3] At times politically rash measures had to be adopted under pressure, but this did not mean that the system itself was casual or designed to incorporate bold experiments. Indeed it was cognate with the rest of the commune's administrative machinery in that the approach was painstaking and cautious. Considerable attention was devoted to detail and the citizens themselves made a great contribution in time and energy to the conduct of fiscal business.

DIRECT TAXATION

Early in 1274 the rather insecure regime of the Thirty-six, neither whole-heartedly Guelf nor whole-heartedly 'popular', gave much thought to the commune's financial situation. Three direct taxes had been levied since the return of the Guelfs in 1270, but the return from these had been disappointing, possibly because the rich were being assessed too benevolently. A Council-meeting on 16 February decided that the Podestà should summon a special meeting of sixty of the nobler citizens and magnates (*de nobilioribus et magnatibus civitatis*). Any absentees were to be fined 5 l. and those who attended were not to be permitted to leave the meeting until proposals had been agreed that would raise a sum of at least 12,000 l. At this extraordinary meeting (17 February) it was decided that a loan of 10,000 l. should be raised, with the proceeds of indirect taxation as security for the creditors, and that both city and contado should again be assessed for a direct tax which, it was hoped, would produce 5,000 l. in the contado alone.[4]

These proceedings were typical in that the decision to levy a direct tax (dazio) could never be a matter of routine: justification by exceptional circumstances was always required, and partly for this reason its occurrence was very irregular indeed. In times of military crisis it was a frequent eventuality, but otherwise it was rare. That much is clear, though the loss of the records of assessments (which were destroyed as a matter of routine so that each set of assessors should begin their task with open minds) means that there are very serious gaps in the documentation. Probably many levies of such dazi have left no trace, while surviving indications that remain in conciliar and Biccherna records are incomplete and often puzzling, partly through long delays in payment. Five or more dazi were exacted in the city between 1286 and 1291, yet such are the gaps in the evidence that only one can be traced between 1291 and 1310.[5]

---

3 B 40, ff. 2v–15 (1267, loans by Ranerio Bistugi); 43, ff. 26v–7, 108, 111 (1268, payment of troops and tax-farming, Ventura Ubertini and Berizello Bonricoveri); 107, ff. 12v. 16v (1292, loans by Truffino Frederighi).

4 CG 18, ff. 55–8.

5 Bowsky, *Finance*, pp. 310–12. That dazi were frequent, although traces of their levy have infrequently survived, is also suggested by references to eleven dazi in the period *c.* 1231–43 in the 'Ricordi di una famiglia senese' (*ASI*, App. , 5 (1847), pp. 5–76).

In principle each levy involved a new assessment (*allibramento*). The statutes stated clearly that 'no dazio or loan may be imposed or collected on any past assessment' (*per libram actenus factam*).[6] Does this mean that even the most urgent of them was in all circumstances preceded by the elaborate process of fresh assessment? The compulsory burning of assessments once they had ceased to be current (a measure which dates back at least to 1292, and probably earlier) should have helped to ensure this. But sometimes a new tax was levied before collection of the previous one had been completed, and then the 'old' assessments must have been available. It seems quite clear that the three dazi of 1285 were all based on the same *allibramento*,[7] and the constitutional rule may have been ignored on other occasions.

By the 1250s – and probably considerably earlier – all the machinery existed for an elaborate assessment. In 1257 forty-five men (fifteen from each terzo) were appointed *ad allibrandum* in the city, *burgi* and *subburgi*, and the same number for possessions outside the city. Their tasks included the measurement of houses and open spaces (*platee*). At least 200 l. was required for the pay of these officials. In that year there were two *dazi*, one of 5 per cent, one of 8 per cent, the collectors being paid by results at the rate of 1s. in the *lira*, i.e. 5 per cent of the sum received.[8]

The planning of the *allibramento* was a complicated matter and could be a controversial one. On 13 December 1286 a reinforced meeting of the General Council discussed a proposal for a new *libra*. In addition to the usual councillors, the governing Fifteen and the customary reinforcement of 120 (*de radota*), there were present representatives of the knights (*milites*), the merchant and cloth gilds, and the city regions (*contrade*). Thirteen speeches were made (two councillors spoke twice) and eleven different formulae put forward for the basis of the fiscal assessment. The councillor who carried the day – he was the twelfth speaker – proposed that a further meeting of the reinforced Council should consider two schemes, one for totally separate assessment of possessions and movable property, the other involving a formula in which these two elements were taken into account jointly. Three days later the Council met again to make its choice. This time there were seven speakers, three of whom had not contributed on the 13th, and it was one of these – in the twentieth speech of these two sessions – whose opinion eventually prevailed. Movable and immovable property were to be

---

6 *Const. 1262.* p. 138.
7 *Cost. 1309–10*, 1, p. 250; Bowsky, *Finance*, p. 70; Waley, 'Project'.
8 The use of the military obligation as a basis for forced loans in the 1230s (below, p. 174) suggests the possibility that a *libra* assessment was not in existence at that time: B. 17, pp. 11, 13, 33, 79–80, 99, 166, 190–203, 207.

assessed separately, in both the city and the contado, and the main basis of the assessment appears to have been estimated market values.[9]

In the hope of ensuring that the officials making the assessment should be unbribable it was normal to insist that they should be recruited among men assessed above a certain minimum, thus of course ensuring also a certain class bias in their selection and outlook. This minimum might however be as low as 25 l. (1289).[10] It has already been mentioned that the number of assessors made them expensive and subtracted appreciably from the proceeds of the tax. In 1282 some sixty men took part in the work, each putting in an average of about seventy days, making a total of 4,240 man-days, at a rate of 2s. per day.[11] The sum paid out to *allibratores* thus came to about 425 l. Calculation of the total yield of each dazio is difficult, partly on account of the delays which ensued. No dazio was ever formally wound up, it would seem, and small amounts continued to dribble in over a long period despite the penalty for late payers – often payment of an additional $33\frac{1}{3}$ per cent, the *tertium plus*. Since the dazio was a reaction to a financial crisis, and often a military one, prompt payment was as crucial as full payment.

A further complication in calculating the yield is the arrangement whereby sums of money owed by the commune to tax-payers could be set against the tax due. As it was common for the city to be tardy in the repayment of loans, what appears as tax evasion by a citizen may represent a payment excused one of the commune's many creditors, while even payments apparently made may represent credit given in the same circumstances.

On occasions the total yield of a direct tax was quite low. In the first six months of 1286 the revenue recorded in the Biccherna account amounted to about 99,000 l. Of this a little under 4,800 l. was derived from a dazio of 15d. in the lira, in the terzo of Camollia only. The remaining 95 per cent of the Biccherna revenue in this period came mainly from loans.[12]

The dazi of 1285–86 were not very productive in terms of their contribution to the commune's total income but they did perform the function of drawing large sums of money from the very rich and presumably of being known to do so. Equality in taxation was rightly seen as a crucial aspect of policy and this was why heavier assessments for the wealthier elements had been central to the programme of the Popolo in the 1250s. Very large tax payments by wealthy families,

9 CG 32, ff. 35–8v. For the basis of the assessment see Cammarosano in *SM*, s. 3, 12 (1971), pp. 306–7.
10 CG 37, f. 56v.
11 B 82, f. 111v; 83, f. 114r and v.
12 B 92, ff. 1–67.

such as those made by some of the Salimbeni and Gallerani in 1282 and again in 1285, may have been notional sums deducted from the commune's own liabilities to banking firms; on the other hand it is not ruled out that there was an element of political punishment in the assessments implied by such payments.[13]

Direct taxation was at least as characteristic of the commune's policy in the contado as in the city, indeed there were occasions when a dazio was levied in the contado only. Of the six recorded in 1286–1310 two were contado taxes, but each of these was in a year when there was also a tax in the city itself (1288, 1291). Direct taxation in the contado went back certainly to the 1250s and probably earlier. In 1254 a dazio in the contado was intended to produce the very considerable sum of 25,000 l.[14] Payment was made to Siena through the subject communities, on whom pressure could be brought to bear, so that this was in the constitutional sense a form of indirect taxation, a manifestation of indirect rule. The proceeds could be remarkable. In the first six months of 1282 over 21,000 l., more than a quarter of the Biccherna income for this period, was derived from a dazio of 20 per cent in the contado, and two years later a similar tax, at 6¼ per cent, yielded about 16,500 l.,[15] the apparent disparity suggesting that a fresh assessment had been undertaken in the interim.

The task of Siena's own assessors in the contado was presumably not to produce an assessment in detail but to evaluate the means of each community as a whole. To tap the wealth of the nobles of the contado was a much more difficult matter. Certainly the Ardengheschi, for example, owed dazio payments to the commune by the terms of an agreement reached in 1257, but such families tended to flout obligations of this sort.[16] The commune persevered in claiming, occasionally with success. A number of back payments in 1286 included 432 l. 11s. 8d. from Aldobrandino of Sinalunga in respect of six unpaid dazi, 322 l. 18s. 4d. from Fazio di Cacciaconte and his five brothers in respect of five, and rather smaller sums from a number of other contado nobles, in some instances relating to as many as thirteen or fourteen dazi.[17] The last figures, unless the commune was exaggerating its claims, which seems improbable, indicate that dazi must have been levied in the contado on many occasions in the thirteenth century.

There was a large disparity in the city too between the revenue aimed at and that actually received. The 1262 statutes contain many clauses about tax evasion, which

---

13 For these dazi see above, pp. 33, 81 and Waley, 'Project'. For the 1282 payments, B 83, f. 31; for 1285 (when some Salimbeni paid 2,740 l. 6s. 2d., some Gallerani 853 l. 14s. 5d.), B 88, ff. 143, 149; 90, ff. 183v, 185, 320.

14 *B*. 15, pp. 14–15, 125, 140, etc.

15 B 82, ff. 83–93; 85, ff. 12v–17v.

16 P. Angelucci in *I Ceti dirigenti dell'età comunale nei sec. XII e XIII* (Pisa, 1982), p. 138: for Ardengheschi tax debts to the commune in 1282, B 83, f. 28v.

17 B 93, ff. 6–12v.

reveal that much of the money due from levies of the 1250s had not been received. Each month a report was to be made on progress in securing payments, the names of defaulters were to be read out in Council every two months, non-payers were to lose all civil rights and were threatened with imprisonment and the destruction of their property.[18] No doubt the peripatetic way of life of many bankers and merchants made it harder to collect taxes from them. The three dazi of 1285 and surviving records of payments towards them help in assessing the extent of evasion, though vagaries in the spelling of names and other such difficulties make it impossible to calculate precisely the number who made payments towards some, but not all, of these levies. A sample suggests that perhaps as many as 20 per cent failed to pay a dazio in 1285, though doubtless the reason was not always evasion. Even the statutes of 1262 had to excuse those who were held as prisoners of war or 'were unable to pay', while the vernacular constitution mentions those unable to pay through *povertà o necessità*.[19] Evasion presented greater difficulties for a resident citizen than for a notionally subject feudatory.

LOANS

The dividing line between direct taxes and forced loans was a narrow one, though voluntary loans were a quite different matter. A general forced loan was levied on the basis of the *libra* assessment, i.e. that used for direct taxes.[20] *Gabella* (indirect tax) assessments were also used in calculating the share of forced loans allocated to communities in the contado. The revenue from gabelle was commonly earmarked to guarantee repayments of loans, so that all these fiscal institutions interacted. It was normal for sums owed by the commune to lenders (both capital and interest) to be deductible from tax obligations, whilst a dazio might be levied in order to make possible the repayment of a loan.[21]

Propositions of the sort set out in the preceding sentences are clear enough, but it is much more difficult to treat such matters quantitatively. The sums recorded in official documents are often misleading since they might be intended to mask the payment of rates of interest disapproved by the Church as usurious. Bowsky notes cases in which the sum actually lent was half that stated in the records; obviously such instances throw out all calculations about repayment whether the interest only or both capital and interest are stated incorrectly.[22] As with direct taxation, the Biccherna volumes on their own are a very inadequate source of information about loans.

18 *Const. 1262*, pp. 140 ff.
19 Waley, 'Project', p. 181; *Cost. 1309–10*, 1, p. 256.
20 *Const. 1262*, p. 83, *Cost. 1309–10*, 1, pp. 258–9
21 Bowsky, *Finance*, pp. 170, 176–7.
22 Ibid., p. 190; see also the comment of Isaacs in *RSI*, 85 (1973), p. 38.

A forced loan, in its most common form being based on the *libra* assessment, was defined as, for example, one of '25 soldi per cent'. In the later thirteenth century rates, possibly based on different systems of assessment, commonly varied between 3¾ per cent and 12½ per cent.[23] In the 1230s the cavalry obligation had been used as a basis for a forced loan,[24] but it was natural that this system should be dropped when a general tax assessment was available on a topographical basis for the entire city, as well as for the Masse and contado. It was thus possible to assign an appropriate share of the load to each to the terzi and within these to the regions, or libre, to which the obligation and the task of collection were passed on. The same system of sub-contracting the administrative burden was applied *mutatis mutandis* to the communities of the contado.[25]

Not all forced loans were 'general': sometimes those who had to lend were specified, though this did not happen frequently. Some of the loans were aimed as politically punitive measures, as in 1268, a time of military crisis, when a forced loan of about 7,000 l. was levied on Siena's Guelfs. The wheel of Fortune turned, and in 1275 it was the Ghibellines who were the victims of a compulsory loan, the *prestancia Ghibellinorum*. A levy of the intermediate period (autumn 1270), a *prestantia . . . imposita specialibus personis* may well come into the same category, but no further definition is provided of these 'special people'. These punitive loans provide support for Professor Isaacs' suggestion that forced loans were usually unwelcome measures resorted to in times of famine or military crisis.[26]

Occasionally those who had to lend compulsorily were selected on other grounds. In 1291 sixty-six men had to lend 25 florins each, twenty-two 'from the wealthier citizens' of each terzo. The ninety men chosen to lend a total of 4,000 l. in the same year, to judge from their familiar (banking) names and the considerable sums provided were selected according to the same criterion.[27]

The total sum envisaged when loans were levied tended to be sizeable: the product involved was rarely below five figures, and though 8,000 l. was the sum required in 1282, it could be as high as 30,000 l. or even 45,000 l.[28] The role of the contado, though spasmodic and apparently confined to forced loans, could be very considerable, as has been indicated.

The fiscal measures of 1289 and 1292, both years of heavy military expenditure,[29] illustrate the commune's reaction to financial crisis. In the first six months

---

23 B 40, f. 21 (1267); Bowsky, *Finance*, pp. 329–30.
24 *B. 4*, pp. 6–26.
25 E.g. B 83, f. 6v (Campagnatico owes 1,200 l. of a total loan from the contado of 20,000 l., 1282).
26 B 43, f. 24v; 61, f. 3; 46, f. 3; *RSI*, as cited in n. 22 above.
27 Bowsky, *Finance*, p. 330; B 106, ff. 109–111v.
28 B 82, ff. 54–7v; 103, ff. 41v–50; 107, ff. 56–124v.
29 Bowsky, *Finance*, table 9 (p. 186).

of 1289 the revenue passing through the Biccherna reached the not particularly high figure (no gabelle payments are included) of about 65,000 l. Some 23,000 l. of this was derived from forced loans in the city and nearly 6,000 l. from one in the contado. Rather over 5,000 l. each was loaned by two banking companies, the Tolomei and Bonsignori. Another loan totalling 13,000 l. was raised from fifteen individual financiers, the largest element being 4,000 l. from two members of the Montanini family (one of whom, Gerio, was later a partner with the Bonsignori).[30] The same pragmatic approach was in evidence three years later. In the first half of 1292 Biccherna revenue ran at a similar level (62,000 l.): almost 40,000 l. of this was provided by two general compulsory loans mainly from the city, about 500 l. from the Masse, a few odd payments from contado communities, and a mere 75 l. 18s. 10d. from contado nobles. As before, the voluntary loans from financiers amounted to a good deal less: one Truffino Frederigi, a money-changer (*campsor*), loaned rather over 13,500 l., to be repaid from the gabella proceeds, and some smaller sums, totalling about 800 l., were loaned by three other financiers.[31]

In both 1289 and 1292 loans played a much larger part than direct taxation, possibly to a greater degree than was usual even in a crisis. The term 'voluntary loan' covers, of course, a wide spectrum of borrowing varying from large loans from banking companies like those just mentioned, to the rarer instances of quite small individual loans. Though there are a few small sums among the eighteen loans repaid in the summer of 1282,[32] the accepted doctrine must have been that there was little point in borrowing piecemeal in Siena, where bankers were so numerous. Usually the commune needed money in a hurry (late lenders, like late tax-payers, were liable to penalties) and the prospects of lenders securing rapid repayment were not good. What rates of interest did this imply? Loans from bankers normally involved a rate of between 15 per cent and 20 per cent per annum.[33] This seems a handsome rate of remuneration and conflicts with a recent authoritative view that in the course of the thirteenth century the commercial rate of interest in the main Italian cities was falling from 20 per cent to 10 per cent and even below that.[34] Clearly the bankers were doing well for themselves, yet it must be said that forced loans were often remunerated at the same rate and in very exceptional circumstances of retarded payment they might

30 B 99, ff. 10v, 11v, 31–2: English, pp. 58, 87.
31 B 107, ff. 12v, 15v, 54, 56–136v, 138. For Truffino see also B 106, ff. 109–111v.
32 B 36, ff. 1–14; 40, ff. 2v–17v; 76, f. 31v; 93, f. 1v; 95, f. 26v; 96, f. 71 (bankers' loans); 82, ff. 143v–4v.
33 B 76, f. 31v (15 per cent); 82, ff. 143v–4v (15–20 per cent); 88, f. 189v (15 per cent); 118, ff. 278v, 285v (15 per cent, 18 per cent).
34 P. Spufford, *Money and its Use in Medieval Europe* (Cambridge, 1988), p. 262.

attract higher interest still. By the second decade of the fourteenth century the rate was less generous,[35] but the prodigality of the previous period is another argument in favour of the view that the regime of the Nine, in its beginnings at least, was a compromise with the wealthy bankers, not a domination over them.

INDIRECT TAXATION

Indirect taxes, not levied directly on the basis of an assessment, were generally designated as 'gabelle' and from the later thirteenth century tended increasingly to be administered by an office independent of the main financial machinery of the Biccherna, a development connected with the growth of the tax-farming system.

The gabelle took an almost infinite number of forms. Some of the most familiar included payments of customs on goods entering Siena and, less regularly, at other places.[36] Sheep passing through Sienese territory on their way between the summer grazing-grounds high in the Garfagnana and the winter pastures nearer the coast were charged at the considerable rate of 22 l. per thousand. In the autumn of 1268 these amounted to 25,500 sheep, and Siena's 50 per cent of the proceeds (it is not clear who got the other 50 per cent) brought in 280 l.[37] Most productive were taxes on food and on articles and processes connected with it.[38] Grain, flour and bakery were all subject to the gabella, so were wood, beasts of burden and the barrels and casks made to contain food; the most important of these taxes were those on bread, meat, and particularly, wine. At the beginning of the fourteenth century the miscellaneous 'eight gabelle' were normally farmed at more than 5,000 l. a year, the wine gabella at over 6,000 l., meat at 600 to 800 l., bread at 500 l. The commune's monopoly (*dogana*) in olive oil and salt completed the fiscal control of foodstuffs, the all-important salt monopoly being based on a notional rather than an actual amount for the consumption of the commodity. The commune's occasional marketing of grain and fish, though not a tax, must have been a source of profit.[39]

Another gabella was levied on all forms of contract, commercial (including sales) and otherwise; this placed a heavy responsibility on notaries who alone could officially record contracts.[40] Evidence about the yield of this impost in the period considered is scanty, and it must have been difficult to collect. Finally, a gabella was charged on all salary payments to officials. The rate for posts held by

---

35 Bowsky, *Finance*, pp. 172–3, 180–1.
36 *Const. 1262*, p. 413.
37 B 43, f. 10v.
38 Bowsky, *Finance*, pp. 140–51, with useful tables.
39 Ibid., pp. 56–60; *Cost. 1309–10*, 1, pp. 278–9.
40 Bowsky, *Finance*, pp. 151–7.

Sienese elsewhere was one-sixtieth of the salary; for offices held in Siena the rate in the first decade of the fourteenth century was a great deal higher, at 5 per cent, though this seems to have been halved soon afterwards.[41]

The surviving evidence on the productivity of gabelle is sporadic, but it requires consideration. There is little of it for the early period. In 1255 various sources of indirect or miscellaneous revenue were farmed by or mortgaged to a consortium of financiers, some of them members of the Scotti bank; these included tolls, monopolies (the *dogana*), the profits of the commune's chancery, various meadows, woods and mills, and the revenues of two towns in the contado, Asciano and Selva. The value of these receipts (presumably for one year) was put at 22,560 l.[42] Some twenty years later a gathering of the General Council gave special consideration to the commune's financial situation. It was recommended, *inter alia*, that gabelle should on no account be farmed or mortgaged. The belief then (1278) was that the gabelle proceeds which were to go direct to the Podestà's officials (*Curia*), would average 5,000 l. a month over the next five months.[43] About a decade later, however, the total product of the gabelle was apparently below 22,000 l. in a year. Bowsky's figures suggest that in the early fourteenth century the yield was higher, the taxes on commodities alone averaging over 12,000 l. per annum.[44]

The indirect taxes should be thought of as producing the revenue on which the commune was believed to be capable of managing in that ideal but extremely rare period, a year of peace. One can hardly speak of an 'average' year, but in February to June 1306, a time of quite low military expenditure, indirect taxation seems to have accounted for about 80 per cent of the commune's revenue. In a more difficult and unsettled period (the second half of 1274) it yielded a mere 30 per cent.[45]

The farming of indirect taxes had the advantage of ensuring in advance a known revenue, but if the farm was sold for some years the commune was unable to benefit from any circumstances which might increase a tax's profitability. In the records it is not always easy to distinguish the farming of a tax from pawning or mortgaging, though in principle the latter left it open to the mortgagee to draw all the proceeds of the tax until the debt to him was extinguished; from the commune's viewpoint it was a much more open-ended commitment than farming. Farming was probably favoured by the wealthier elements who, as

41 Ibid., p. 117: *Cost. 1309–10*, 1, pp. 122–3.
42 *B*. 16, pp. 56 ff, particularly 125 and 128. For the affiliations of Pietro Scotti and Orlando Renaldi, see Roon-Bassermann, pp. 89–90.
43 CG 22, f. 9.
44 Bowsky, *Finance*, pp. 140–51, 165.
45 B 118; 57, ff. 6, 33v. See figure 1, p. 183.

Bowsky points out, saw themselves as the likely beneficiaries of the institution. Other interested parties could also become farmers, as when the butchery and bakery gabelle were farmed to the gilds related to these trades.[46]

Farming inevitably led to disputes when the farmers found that unforeseen circumstances had landed them with a deficit and the case was aggravated when the commune could be accused of having failed to honour the conditions agreed upon. Some characteristic instances illustrate this type of controversy. On 31 December 1298 the Council debated the petitions of three farmers. One had, with colleagues, purchased the gabella and toll of the newly-founded settlement of Castelfranco di Paganico, and as there was a great shortage of salt in the region he had been permitted to take some there. His complaint was that he was now being asked to pay tax on this salt. The second complaint came from one Buoso Azzolino, who had purchased the gabella of all mills in the contado and of the market at Monteriggioni. His takings had suffered as a result of hail damaging the vineyards. The third complainant had with his colleagues bought the revenue for five years of Sasso d'Ombrone and Monteverdi and discovered that the revenues and grazing rights of Monteverdi had been usurped by the commune and people of Paganico.[47]

A row in May 1303 was a more serious affair. The men involved, one of them a member of the Pagliaresi, a *casato* dynasty, were people to be reckoned with. Their complaint was that they had purchased the gabella of all mills in the city and contado for one year, but a number of parties who were not *de facto* subject to the commune had failed to make any payment and 978 l. still remained to be paid by the recusants. When the petitioners attempted to collect the money themselves they were actually thrown into prison and also incurred expenses to the tune of 150 l. They claimed that by the terms of the contract made with them the commune should have given assistance in collecting the money, but had entirely failed to do so. The matter produced a lengthy debate and eventually, by 176 votes to 54, the Council recommended a compromise, The petitioners were to receive some compensation, but it was not to exceed 270 l.[48] No doubt the history of taxation has always been a history of compromises.

OTHER REVENUES

Many other forms of revenue besides taxes and loans contributed to the commune's funds. Some of them, deriving from the possession of property, have already been touched on, since rents from lands and buildings could be farmed

46 Bowsky, *Finance*, pp. 121–8, 134–43 (see also the comments of Isaacs, p. 34).
47 CG 54, ff. 90–1v (also 55, ff. 78–9); for another example, Bowsky, *Finance*, p. 134.
48 CG 62, ff. 128v–132v.

and mortgaged. The mortgaging, pawning or offering as security of woods, mills and water-rights have been mentioned: some of the woodland was valuable, the Selva del Lago yielded 1,080 l. in six months of 1288. Rights over pasture were also leased out. Under the general heading of 'rents' should be placed revenues from mining rights, but deposits of the prized minerals (silver and copper) were meagre by this period. Income from them was small, as it was from the few urban rents of houses (in the second half of 1298 these brought in 67 l. 5s. 6d.) and, more surprisingly, from the lease of stalls in the Campo (at 2 l. per annum each these yielded 28 1. 9s. in one six-month period).[49]

The profits of justice – to which may be appended the barely perceptible revenue from chancery dues – were more considerable, not because their volume was large as a matter of routine but because the occasional windfall or campaign to extract past fines or a proportion of them and offer *rebannimentum* at bargain prices could be very lucrative.[50] Small fines did not add up to a lot. In 1294 167 men were condemned because four years previously they had failed to take the oath of obedience to the Capitano del Popolo; at 10s. a head, even with a 1/3 addition for late payment, the proceeds were around 100 l. only.[51] Of much greater significance were the fines paid by Salimbeni and others in 1273 (at least 2,000 l.) and by Remaneto, an exile from Castiglione d'Orcia, in 1280 (4,650 l.).[52] As for offers to settle long overdue fines by part-payment (*compositiones*), these were usually accepted readily. In 1255 a Council-meeting discussed a number of such offers, which tended to be of around one-third of the fine imposed. Two men who had exported grain illegally and made an attack on officials offered 35 l. in lieu of their 100 l. condemnation, and another, who had attacked his brother-in-law, 30 l. in lieu of 100 l. It was agreed *nem. con.* that all these offers should be accepted.[53] There is something almost pathetic about this eagerness to grasp part-payment. In 1303 three brothers from Asciano petitioned the Podestà ('you who are the head of the light of the city and contado of Siena') alleging poverty with such success that a fine of 9,000 l. from seventeen years before was commuted for a payment of 75 l., less than 1 per cent of the original sentence.[54]

In troubled times the confiscated possessions of political rebels could also provide healthy sums: in the spring of 1282 forty-seven payments of rent from such property yielded a total of just under 1,000 l.[55]

---

49 B 36, f. 1 (pasture); 80, f. 30v (Campo); 97, f. 54v (woods); 114, f. 124 (houses). Bowsky's material on rentals (*Finance*, pp. 61–6) is largely from a later period.
50 Above, p. 70.
51 B 110, ff. 69–88.
52 B 76, f. 13v.
53 CG 4, f. 43v.
54 CG 62, ff. 93–4v (voting favoured this decision by 243–9).
55 CG 17, f. 100; B 76, f. 13v; 82, ff. 74–6.

Payments of an agreed annual tax (*census*) were due from the bishop of Volterra in respect of the Montieri mines, and from the Aldobrandeschi counts. The former amounted to 215 l. per annum, the latter to a mere 62 l. 10s.[56] Various forms of permit or licence were also sold, though these too were inconsiderable sources of revenue. The fee paid on achieving citizenship was 1 l., which in 1295 was raised to 5 l. The usual price of a licence 'to bear defensive arms' (to wear armour) was 36s. Permits for the export of grain (*tratte*) achieved some importance in the fourteenth century, but there is no evidence that they produced income in the thirteenth.[57]

Cavallata, an ambiguous word, was often used to denote a money payment made to the commune in lieu of cavalry service. The military obligations of the Sienese will be discussed in the next chapter, but at this juncture it is worth remarking that money commutation for service was frequently levied both in the city and contado in a compulsory form, that is to say on these occasions the person or community paying was not offered the alternative of actually performing cavalry service. In 1263 *cavallata* was levied at the rate of 40 l. per horse on those of the city who owed service. For a man like Orlando Bonsignori, whose due was seven horses, this was a weighty tax.[58] In the contado the *cavallata* could entail payments by some 200 communities and bring in more than 7,000 l. (1277).[59]

The most consistently productive aspect of the military obligation in financial terms was probably the condemnation of those who failed to respond to the commune's call. Sometimes this facet of military service was taken into account at the time of the decision to summon the army. In April 1272 a full-scale call-up of Sienese aged between eighteen and seventy was agreed, and the penalties for absence were set extremely high. Absentee cavalrymen were to be fined 50 l. for the first day, with an additional 5 l. for each subsequent day missed. The equivalent amercements for infantrymen were 25 l. and 2 l. Some years later (1304) these fines, which applied to the contado as well as to city-dwellers, were fixed by legislation. Those who could not report because they were absent from Tuscany at the time were not excused but were to be fined on a scale determined by their tax assessment; this sliding scale began with a 1 l. fine for those assessed at 50 l. or less, rising to 10 l. for those assessed at more than 400 l.[60]

On that occasion the military obligation was enmeshed with the commune's general fiscal organization, and the same principle could apply in other ways. In 1291 certain contado communities had been guilty of not sending infantry levies

56 B 36, f. 12; 39, f. 31; 90, f. 19v.
57 Bowsky, *Finance*, pp. 53–6; B 99, ff. 1–4.
58 B 36, f. 12.
59 B 65, ff. 3–5; 67, ff. 4v–5v, 8–9v, 12r and v.
60 CG 15, ff. 68v–9: Bowsky, *Commune*, pp. 139–40; *Cost. 1309–10*, 2, p. 472.

required of them for a campaign in the Maremma. It was decided in Council that they should be compelled to pay in entirety the fines to which they had been condemned but that 75 per cent of the sum thus raised would be set against their gabella obligations (the grain, flour and wine taxes) for the following year. A similar notion of barter secured for Campagnatico a diminution of gabella payments as a reward for the participation of their levies in a successful engagement near Grosseto (1297).[61]

When a subject town, or a number of them, defied a call to arms, the ensuing fines could be a significant source of revenue. In 1263 several communities failed to send contingents to participate in campaigns at Radicofani and Campiglia; their condemnations yielded over 1,500 l. Some thirty years later S Quirico was fined 750 l. for a similar misdemeanour, though the town eventually escaped with a much smaller payment (100 l.)[62]

Sums derived from individual cavalry absentees were usually low, especially when men merely arrived late or departed early, but the consequences were financially rewarding if absence was on a dramatic scale. In the summer of 1281 some 450 Sienese owing cavalry service absented themselves either totally or for part of a campaign and the resulting fines yielded about 3,500 l.[63] It may have been something of a status symbol to pay fines for days of unauthorized absence. The highest fine in 1281, of 30 l., came from an Ugurgieri, and aristocratic or plutocratic names predominate among the other fine-payers.

Sometimes those who owed the service of more than one horse failed to provide the total due from them. In 1281, 206 people paid fines for a total shortfall of 115 horses, yielding a sum of about 2,300 l.[64] These figures all testify to the importance of the fines on absentee cavalrymen. One unusual transaction may also bear witness to the regularity of this source of income. In 1267 the banking company of Bonsignori paid into the Biccherna 198 l., being the money 'of the absentees' (*absentium*) paid 'on account of their absence at the time of the army sent to the abbey of S Antimo'. Rather than being the outcome of an agreement between the body of absentees and the Bonsignori bank, this must surely represent a farm purchased by the bank, to be recouped from the absentees themselves![65]

CONCLUSIONS

The receipt of funds by the Biccherna was necessarily a spasmodic process. Sometimes the revenue increased greatly as a Chamberlain and Provveditori

---

61 CG 41, f. 56; 52, ff. 62, 74–5, 86v–7. For use of a similar technique see also CG 49, ff. 64–5v.
62 B 37, ff. 7–15v; 109, f. 16v.
63 B 80, ff. 10–21v.
64 B 82, ff. 48–53v.
65 B 41, f.4.

neared the end of their six-month term of office, and one is probably justified in imagining officials anxiously seeking to hand over an apparently flourishing concern. Some examples of this may be cited. The Biccherna officials for the second half of 1268 received 3,400 l. in revenues in the first three months of their tenure, then 56,300 l. in October–December. In 1266 about 12,300 l. was received in January–April, 27,600 l. in May–June; and in the following year the revenues of the month of June (about 15,000 l.) were higher than those for January–May inclusive (12,800 l.).[66]

The revenue recorded in the volumes of the Biccherna *Entrata e Uscita* is very far indeed from constituting the commune's total income. The proceeds of indirect taxation came to be excluded from them as a matter of routine, being channelled through the office of the Gabella. The records also give misleading answers to questions concerning direct tax payments actually made. In some cases payments may appear because they were credited, i.e. excused in order to be set against the commune's indebtedness to the taxpayer, in others payments of tax may have been recorded – through myriad forms of fiscal bargaining and ingenuity – under other categories. Disparities in the account-books between receipts and expenditure were normally very small indeed, and most commonly the books appear to balance precisely. In rare instances the Biccherna officials passed on small balances to their successors, very seldom indeed do they confess to having spent more than they had gathered (in December 1290, most exceptionally, a deficit of some 4,000 l. was admitted).[67] A statement that a fine of 250 l. had been received, one-third in currency (*chontanti*), two-thirds in promissory notes (*cartta*) (1302) is another reminder that there could be notional elements in the Biccherna accounting.[68]

After these warnings it should be clear that the stated totals of the Biccherna volumes have very serious defects as sources of quantitative information concerning the finances of Siena. The totals alleged none the less merit discussion. In the sixty years beginning in 1248, there are surviving volumes recording totals of revenue and expenditure (which are normally identical or very close) for sixty-five of the 120 half-years terms of office.[69] Up to about 1280 the figures for a full year tended to run at between 20,000 l. and 40,000 l., though there were some years (1251, 1261, 1268, 1274) in which they were a great deal higher. The disparities are very striking indeed. The total figure for 1268 (about 147,000 l.) was not surpassed until 1307. From the 1280s onwards there was in general a

---

66 B 39, 40, 43. See also Bowsky, *Finance*, p. 46.
67 B 103, ff. 53, 109v.
68 B 117, f. 53.
69 See figure 1, p. 183. The gaps happen to be spaced in such a way that it has not been possible to give totals which apply to the 'modern' (i.e. January to December) year.

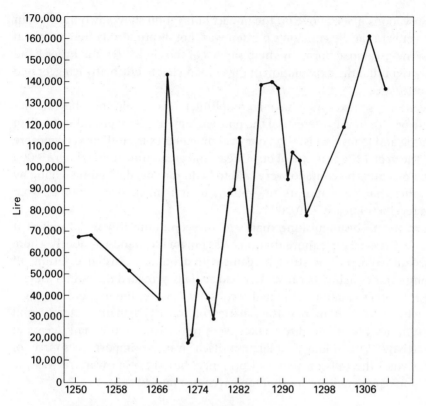

1 *BICCHERNA TOTALS (12-MONTH TOTALS).*
Totals are those for the twenty-four 12-month periods for which figures survive, to nearest 1,000 lire.
Source: Bicherna volumes, ASS.

marked rise to totals of 90,000 l. per annum or above, with occasional dips (to 67,500 l. in 1284 and again to 76,500 l. in 1295). Although the figures for 1286, 1288 and 1289 (years of war) came quite close to the total for 1268, it took fifty years for this to be clearly surpassed.

These increases should be seen as in part the consequence of a general tendency towards inflation of the Sienese currency, not merely of higher receipts and spending in real terms. Between the 1270s and 1310 the Sienese *lira* weakened by a factor of more than one-third in terms of the Florentine florin (the rate of exchange being around 35s. to the florin at the beginning of this period and 53s. at the end). Moreover the period of maximum deterioration in the rate of exchange (1282–1302) coincides in general with that of the marked rise in the Biccherna budget.[70]

70 P. Spufford, *Handbook of Medieval Exchange* (London, 1986), pp. 50–1. See the remarks of Isaacs, pp. 26–9.

The observations made above on the impact of taxation show my doubts about Bowsky's verdict that the contado's burden was 'not disproportionately heavy in relation to the fiscal load borne by the residents of the city'.[71] On the other hand he is surely right that the exploitation of the contado has been greatly exaggerated by some historians.

Whatever Sienese taxes may have accomplished, it is certain that they did not redistribute wealth in the interests of the poorer elements. Bankers did well out of fiscal farming and loans, whilst the poor paid direct taxes from their very meagre earnings. The year 1302 was one of dear bread and great hunger, in which 15,000 people of Siena and the contado were said to be in dire need, yet alms-giving by the commune that year appears to amount to not much over 1,000 l., from Biccherna receipts of nearly 120,000 l.[72]

To return to the distinguishing marks of the commune's financial policy, it should be emphasized once more that this was pragmatic, hand-to-mouth. There was a constant willingness to strike bargains with debtors, for instance, letting off subject communities lightly because they had actually provided the military levies they owed. Indirect taxation remained a constant feature, the background, as it were, roughly sufficient to pay the salaries of the city's many external and domestic officials. Loans and direct taxes were resorted to in the many years of military activity. The military obligation itself was an important source of revenue, beyond the calls on personal presence, but above all warfare was the main occasion of expenditure. To that topic we must now turn.

---

70 P. Spufford, *Handbook of Medieval Exchange* (London, 1986), pp. 50–1. See the remarks of Isaacs, pp. 26–9.

71 Bowsky, *Finance*, p. 255.

72 CG 61, ff. 133v–6; B 116; 117, especially ff. 369v–72v. For a rather more generous attitude to the poor in 1295 (a gift of 1,000 florins) CG 48, ff. 50–5v.

9 *Expenditure*

The money collected by so many and various means was expended by the commune principally on the assertion of its powers against recalcitrant subjects and hostile neighbours. Certainly the payment of officials was a major routine item and the general expense of administration and bureaucracy, contributions to religious bodies and the extension of the commune's rights were all significant costs. Yet armies and policing usually accounted for a considerably greater sum than all other forms of expenditure combined and it seems likely that there was no year in the later thirteenth century in which this was not the case. Military exigencies had done much to form the commune's institutions and self-awareness and they remained of paramount importance. The obligation to serve in the field was as fundamental as that of serving in the council-chamber and the notion and reality survived of a citizen army, reinforced rather than diluted. Overlordship in the contado could be asserted only with the support of armed force. To survive as a power in the turbulent world of the Tuscan cities Siena had to garrison its own territories and appear potentially threatening to those of its neighbours. Meanwhile the politics of the peninsula drew it into a still wider military network.

It will however be convenient to start with the cost of official salaries, normally the principal non-military item. An analysis of the expenditure recorded in the Biccherna volume for the second half of 1257 suggests that about 8 per cent of the total for that period went on 'routine' salaries (omitting extra payments for special tasks). Of the approximately 3,500 l. paid in salaries about a quarter went to the Podestà (900 l.) and the same to the Capitano del Popolo. Other important payments were to watchmen and guards (674 l.), to fiscal officials (330 l.) and judges (315 l.) Messengers were numerous but their fixed pay in this period came to little over 100 l. These figures have obvious deficiencies – for example judges, tax-gatherers and messengers, in addition to their salaries, received payments based on work accomplished – but they help to assess the commune's ongoing financial commitment to salaried officers.[1]

Consideration of expenditure later in the century suggests that the salaries offered to the major external officials were soon to rise greatly. By the 1290s it

---

1 Based on *B*. 18. For the inadequacy of the Biccherna volumes as guides to the total finances of the commune see above pp. 181–4.

was normal for the Podestà to receive around 3,000 l. or even more for his six-month tenure. In 1296 his salary was 3,700 l., the Capitano's 1,200 l. Some deductions must be made for amounts paid by the Podestà to his own subordinates. Nevertheless it appears that by this time something like half the regular outgoings on salaries was received by this one official. The Capitano's salary had increased also, but his share of the total remained about the same.[2] The large sum paid to the Podestà may be connected with Siena's position within the Tuscan Guelf world, or one that she sought to assert, for to offer a high salary to the city's leading official was to emphasize the city's own eminence.

The Podestà's salary rise should be seen also as part of a general increase of expenditure on diplomacy within the Guelf alliance. In 1291, when the Podestà was already on a salary of 3,000 l., Siena had three lawyers permanently retained as advocates at the papal court at a salary of 25 l. each per annum. No doubt they had other business and this retainer would not have been their sole income. The conduct of diplomacy by emissaries was another growing expense. In the same year of 1291 an ambassador despatched to Perugia remained in receipt of salary and expenses for almost four weeks. A few years later a single mission to Boniface VIII's court cost over 400 l. in salaries. Yet another expensive aspect of the Tuscan diplomatic fabric was the appointment of a special councillor to accompany the commander of the Guelf cavalry tallia. This representative of the commune received when on duty a salary of 2 l. a day, which in one half-year period involved a payment of 219 l.[3]

Payments of this sort towards the Guelf alliance, a kind of military-diplomatic insurance policy, illustrate the difficulty of drawing distinctions between military and other expenditure and thus of calculating military expenses as a percentage of the total. Naturally there were also purely domestic items such as the alms paid regularly to ecclesiastical, particularly mendicant and monastic, institutions and, in famine years, money and food given to assist the hungry. Perhaps the greatest outlay, together with official salaries, on non-military (or not directly military) purposes was on the purchase of lands and rights in the contado. This forward policy was indeed written into the constitution in the form of a commitment to 'increase the city and jurisdiction of Siena . . . buying or otherwise acquiring castles in whole or part and acquiring rights'.[4] Money thus spent was after all capital investment on which direct returns could be expected, a form of expenditure calculated to strengthen the commune's finances.

2 Bowsky, *Finance*, p. 316 (app. 4); B 113, ff. 159–61v.
3 CG 42, f. 32v; B 104, ff. 72, 91, 98v; 114, f. 219.
4 Bowsky, *Finance*, pp. 26–30; *Cost. 1309–10*, 2, p. 503.

THE CONDUCT OF WAR

Despite the expense of administration, diplomacy and territorial aggrandisement it remains true that the commune spent most of its money on armed strength. Force was displayed and war conducted in many different ways. The Sienese had no hesitations about how their aggressive strength might be deployed. As a councillor explained, defining the intentions of a proposed campaign against Arezzo (1290), this should be *ad depopulationem et destructionem inimicorum et rebellium existentium in civitate Aretii et exterminium ipsorum finale*: the aim was depopulation, destruction, extermination[5] – with no half-measures or mealy-mouthed pretexts! But an all-out assault was exceptional and the clash of arms in a full-scale trial of strength a rarity, whereas campaigning and manoeuvring were virtually an annual routine. In a period of fifty-seven years (1251–1307), there were only two years of complete peace; in forty of those years campaigns were conducted by troops of the Sienese commune, and in fifteen other years men were under arms in preparation for fighting.[6]

The launching of a campaign required preparation and indeed clauses in the constitution insisted on delay. Even when the necessary three conciliar meetings had given approval, much had to be settled about the size and nature of the force needed, stores and armaments, measures required concerning pay, rewards, compensation, fines for absentees and special powers during hostilities.[7] The process of reaching and approving these decisions could last three or four weeks, even in an atmosphere of urgency. Clearly exceptions were sometimes made. When news reached Siena (9 December 1286) that the recently departed Podestà and his entourage had been set on within a few miles of Siena, the cavalry and infantry forces of the city and the zone where the assault had taken place were called to arms at once (*incontinenti*). The Council's proposal was to summon every available man without delay in opposition to an insolent band of robbers. Unfortunately there is no record of exactly what ensued in these very exceptional circumstances.[8]

Clashes on a considerable scale in the open field were very rare; they occurred at Montaperti (1260), Colle (1269) and Pieve al Toppo (1288). The element of risk when on campaign was normally not great and the pleasure of manoeuvring in the country in agreeable weather must often, for those on horseback, have been

5 CG 39, f. 64v.
6 Based on *RIS, CS*, pp. 54–89, 192–236, 255–312 and B and CG for these years. It should be noted that there are no surviving Biccherna volumes for the two hypothetically peaceful years, 1299 and 1305.
7 E.g. CG 30, ff. 26–34 (7–31 October 1285); see above, p. 51.
8 CG 32, f. 33r and v.

considerable. Military activities for the Sienese were normally confined to Tuscany, so that home was not distant, though exceptions were not unknown. Service in the Alban Hills (in Boniface VIII's campaign against the Colonna, which did involve some fighting), in Apulia, in Liguria and in Romagna, was the lot of some Sienese contingents.[9]

The norm was garrison duty. The Sienese held fortresses scattered over their territory, often with quite small bodies of men; these were seen as observation posts capable of holding out briefly against attack while assistance was summoned. Presumably they were also places of retreat for the rural population, who were the main victims of the persecutory mode of warfare which then prevailed. In a normal year the Sienese would have some seven, ten or even eleven places garrisoned, each of them by no more than a dozen men, so often a hundred men were involved in all, though that number would sometimes be multiplied by two or three. In 1266, with Ghibelline Siena under much pressure, the garrison at Monteriggioni was increased to forty, while there was a force of about 350 at Grosseto. Monteriggioni was the invariable northern bulwark against Florence, the other usual strong points being, to the south-east Monticchiello, and in the Maremma Montelaterone, Montorsaio and Campagnatico. The last two were in part the property of the Sienese commune, the former purchased in the 1250s, the latter in the 1280s and 1290s.[10]

It is misleading to think of a thirteenth-century soldier as a man whose sole task was to fight or overawe the forces of the enemy. There was a total lack of distinction between military and police functions,[11] and in practice an armed Sienese was quite as likely to be overawing Sienese subjects suspected of reluctance to pay their taxes or of intent to sell grain illegally outside the contado as he was to be facing the commune's external foes. It seems to have been a matter of routine – at least in years of poor harvest – to set up a force to police the boundaries in the hope of deterring Sienese *comitatenses* who might smuggle their grain across the border to get better prices in a market uncontrolled by their suzerain. Sometimes it was also thought advisable to use armed men to serve as a guard for those engaged in sowing.[12]

Raiding was the characteristic form of military activity, and defensive tactics consisted primarily in attempting to absorb raids with the minimum of damage. Though they participated in successful Guelf campaigns against Arezzo, the Sienese were quite often on the defensive; they suffered raids as well as inflicting

---

9 See above, p. 124.
10 Based on B (for 1268, B 42 and 43). For the places mentioned see also *Repertorio*, pp. 18, 27–8, 104–6, 129–30; on the *castra* see also Redon, pp. 27–30.
11 Bowsky, *Commune*, p. 123.
12 E.g. CG 3, ff. 91v–92v; 5, f. 19; *B*. 26, pp. 37–8; 118, f. 217v (see also B 67, f. 33).

them. It is difficult to know how many armed men they placed in the field at times of maximum effort, partly because they often called men for very brief periods, i.e. a few days only. When they had recourse to both Italian and transalpine mercenaries, in the heyday of the Guelf alliance, it is likely that as many as 1,000 horsemen were sometimes on the payroll. Occasionally infantry from the contado, also employed for engineering tasks, were called in very large numbers. The campaign against Arezzo in 1292 may have used 3,000 men, but even this was no more than half the force that the Florentines could call out.

CAVALRY SERVICE

The obligation of the wealthier citizens to serve in the community's cavalry force was common to all the independent Italian cities and the militia system was in force in Siena long before the period covered by this book. Indeed it was characteristic of the communes that military institutions were evolved early and did much to shape the financial and other governmental ones. They involved the appointment of many officials and commanders. In each Sienese terzo the cavalry force had a *dominus*, also a standard-bearer who had two counsellors, a banner-bearer and four captains; the infantry had a similar force of officers. There were also six men chosen 'to distribute horses', i.e. to select those who should bear the *cavallata*, or cavalry obligation, within the city, and the same number for the same office in respect of the contado.[14]

The men drawing up the city's list had a delicate task. It was far from easy to determine who was capable of undertaking the upkeep, care and handling of a valuable war-horse. The list rapidly lost its utility if not kept up-to-date, and while exclusion from it would be felt as a slight by an enthusiastic equestrian, inclusion was a mixed blessing. When a man died who had had the obligation of keeping and raising a horse, the heir might be a woman or there might be no heir; it was often long before the succession was settled, and there might be a lengthy period of provisional co-inheritance. Families and *consorzerie* with jointly owned wealth also complicated matters, and there were usually some horses 'owed' with no able-bodied person to ride them ('more horses than riders', as an official complained),[15] for instance when those owing mounted service were children or elderly or in poor health. Also a continuous process of partition of the cavalry obligation was inevitable as inheritances were divided in succeeding generations.

The consequences of all these factors show clearly in a list of 1288 recording

---

13 B 79 and 80; Bowsky, *Commune*, pp. 146, 158; *Florentine Studies*, p. 96.
14 CG 9 (1260), ff. 35v–6, 96.
15 *B.* 13, p. 154.

ninety-eight horses due.[16] Of these, fifty were owed jointly and, more seriously, only twenty-one of them constituted an obligation shared equally between brothers or joint heirs; twenty-nine were owed by more complicated combinations of relations or *consorzi*. The wealthy would only contribute to the full extent of their means to the city's mounted strength if some Sienese were allotted the obligation of providing more than one horse. This development added the complications of multiple obligation – which necessarily involved service by a substitute rider – to those of shared obligation.

In principle at least, the person who owed service of one or more horses received payment to cover the upkeep of his steed. Stabling and fodder were expensive items and a man receiving an allowance on this account (20 l. per annum in 1252, 27 l. in 1275, 30 l. in 1288) was not necessarily making a profit or even breaking even.[17] But this subsidy was an expensive institution which often lapsed when there was no military urgency, and it was unlikely to be paid throughout an entire year: those summoned for service always received pay, whereas the routine payments for maintenance were spasmodic. Compensation was invariably offered for horses injured or killed, and for this purpose it was necessary that an agreed valuation should be placed on every animal beforehand. The maximum and minimum valuations authorized in 1275 – 70 l. and 40 l. – were large sums,[18] and very considerable amounts were paid out under this heading – no doubt war-horses were subject to many ills – despite the precaution of fixing maxima. The obligation to provide a substitute rider (*equitator*) when the person involved could not serve in person, either because he owed service of more than one horse or for some other reason, has already been mentioned.

The *cavallata* was thus a costly matter for the commune, though it was also one absolutely central to the city's military means. The expense of the maintenance allowances had always to be weighed against military exigencies, and this may account for a tendency to aim at a reasonably low figure when deciding on the size of force to be raised. The rather patchy evidence which survives suggests that it was normal to levy a *cavallata* of between 200 and 300 horse.[19] It may be that to seek more than this number of equestrians in thirteenth-century Siena would have been unrealistic and that the contrast with contemporary Florentine obligations – which were two or three times this number – is an index of the demographic disparity between the two cities. Yet there were times when the Sienese set their sights higher, aiming at a force of 500 or 600 horsemen, so that

16 B 97, ff. 126–9.
17 *B*. 13, p. 150; CG 20, ff. 36v–7v; 35, f. 24.
18 CG 20, f. 37.
19 Examples: *B*. 13, pp. 49–58 (270); 33, ff. 30v–5 (c. 200); CG 15, f. 27 (200); 18, ff. 144v–9v (246); 20, ff. 36v–7v (200); B 121, ff. 312–18 (285). For Florence see *Florentine Studies*, pp. 94–5.

the principal constraint may have indeed been financial. A proposal in 1292 to raise the levy from the agreed level of 300 to 380 seems an indication that at least that number of local horses and riders could be found.[20]

It was very unusual to call out the city's entire militia force *en bloc*. Each terzo had its own *cavallata*, divided into troops of twenty-five, while the contado also had a threefold division, each region being linked to one of the terzi. Most common was the summons of one terzo at a time, hence, for example, the reference to the campaign 'when the *Camollenses* were in the army against Torri di Maremma'. The decision as to which terzo should serve was sometimes reached by drawing lots.[21]

It has already been mentioned that fines for non-performance of military service were a significant source of revenue. Since it was realized that absentees would be numerous, special penalties were often discussed and fixed before a campaign was launched. The fine for the first day of absence was set very high, thereafter a gentler level prevailed. There was a constant struggle to deal with problems which confronted the *cavallata* system in the forms of youth, age, sickness, absence abroad and the joint obligations of *consortes*. If the obligation fell on a minor, his guardian became responsible. If a member of a *consorzeria* was unable to reach agreement about sharing with his fellows, he nevertheless had to make a down payment of money to the commune. A neighbour was held responsible for stabling the horse of someone who was away. The sick and elderly had to maintain a horse even if they were unable to ride it. These were among the clauses of the lengthy ordinances promulgated in a Council meeting in 1275,[22] yet the ingenuity and firmness displayed simply could not make these problems disappear.

No subject discussed in Council was more contentious than the cavalry obligation and none more certain to arouse protests of injustice, often from men who did not rank among the Council's more familiar voices. The most common complaint was that the obligation was levied on the wrong people. In one characteristic discussion (January 1285), one speaker wished multiple obligations to be dropped (i.e. nobody should owe more than a single horse), while another wanted an end to all dues of less than one horse. Someone else wanted a total levy of 500 instead of the 300 proposed. Such debates were numerous. There were calls for the abolition of all partial obligations except for a simple 50/50 division. Some wanted a change to a system of money commutation in the case of women and minors. Apart from fractional dues, the biggest problems were set by those who ingeniously used their 'due' horse for the performance of paid service by their retainers or who alleged exaggerated or even false claims for compensa-

20 B 36, f. 76v; 97, ff. 126–41v; CG 43, f. 42.
21 *Const. 1262*, p. 66n; B 80, f. 20v; CG 16, ff. 80–1.
22 CG 20, ff. 36v–7v.

tion. The use of retainers was a particularly vexed question and it was illegal for a *famulus, serviens, familiaris* or *domicellus* to have responsibility for a *cavallata* horse, no doubt because of the suspicion that his loyalty might lie with his master rather than with the commune. Again and again there were complaints of 'injustice and iniquity in the *cavallata*' and of the burden falling on the wrong people. To quote a typical speech, 'the balance should be equal'.[23]

Three petitions heard in a single conciliar session (November 1306) illustrate well the difficulties of administering the cavalry obligation.[24] The first petitioners were two brothers, members of the Tolomei family, who claimed that they had been assessed at two horses but fined in respect of three. The next, Imiglia, widow of the prominent banker Orlando Bonsignori, stated that though she had made payment (of 12 l. 10s.) for the notional quarter share of one horse owed by her, she had somehow been fined for non-payment, the fine amounting to 21 l. 10s. (50s. for the first day, 5s. for each of the seventy-six following days). Lastly a man who had lived for more than twenty years in France complained of the condemnation in respect of his due of a three-quarters share; in his absence, he claimed, arrangements for payment had been made and carried out. All three petitions were successful. Evidently Sienese bureaucracy had its shortcomings.

Another subject of controversy was the date from which the *cavallata* year should be reckoned, and a more serious one was the question of service by those whose loyalty was suspect. In 1272 the Ghibellines set a particularly awkward problem: since they comprised a fair proportion of the wealthier citizens it would have been absurd to exempt them all from cavalry service, but it seemed paradoxical to expect them to serve the Guelf cause to which the Sienese had recently been converted. The obvious solution was to force them to pay but forbid them to participate in person and this was adopted.[25]

Sometimes men volunteered to appear in the lists of the *cavallata* obligation. There were periods when it was in fact run as a voluntary system, though payments were made for the maintenance of the volunteers' mounts. To serve on horseback was, after all, an honour, an indication of social distinction. Substitute riders were inevitable in many cases: in 1261, at the height of Ghibelline Siena's triumphs, bodies of Sienese cavalry sent to aid Pisa and oppose Arezzo comprised eighty-nine and 188 respectively; of these forty-eight in one group and 154 in the other were substitutes. Twenty years later fifty-seven *cavallata* horsemen went on service in the contado to Grosseto and Civitella in the Maremma of whom only eighteen were serving in person. When the Guelf alliance drew the Sienese into

---

23 CG 29, ff. 36–7; 35, ff. 21–3v; 43, f. 42; 64, ff. 83–5v; 65, ff. 118–22v.
24 CG 69, ff. 96–101v.
25 B 65, ff. 118–22v; 51, f. 7; CG 15, f. 27.

somewhat notional participation in a papal war in Romagna (1281) eighteen men of the *cavallata* were summoned for service there, but all of them sent substitute riders.[26]

Mercenary horsemen supplemented the native Sienese cavalryman but did not replace him, and there was no continuous process of declining participation. Many later instances occur of large-scale cavalry service performed in person. Because payment was made to the 'holder' of the horse, not its rider, the records often fail to specify how many rode in person – this applies, for example to the 500 cavalry who served against Arezzo in 1288 and to the 285 called in the summer of 1307 – but in 1313 more than 150 of the *cavallata* certainly served in person for over a month at Colle, and such participation continued for long afterwards.[27] Why, indeed, should there have been a decline, unless one accepts some general theory of natural human enervation? There was no general retreat to the office and counting-house, away from the countryside. There were always young men who enjoyed spending part of the summer on horseback, as later generations could testify from experience in the yeomanry regiments and their equivalents. The tendency for *cavallata* rates of pay to decrease in the late thirteenth century also suggests a relatively plentiful supply.

INFANTRY SERVICE

The infantryman's obligatory service, which involved his own modest weapons as well as his personal presence, was a much more straightforward matter. As with the cavalry due, the organization was by terzi, with everything on a larger and simpler scale. Many in the city owed service as crossbowmen and had to keep their own crossbows, each of which was worth about 1 l. 10s., though there were also more elaborate crossbows, quasi-artillery weapons which cost much more and were not individually owned.[28] In 1253 all three terzi sent crossbowmen for an average period of only about one week; 783 men served, under two commanders.[29] The numerous crossbowmen received the same pay as other infantry, much below that of their mounted colleagues. The rate varied considerably – from 1s. to 4s. a day – with no tendency to a general increase in the second half of the thirteenth century; it is not clear what governed these variations.[30] There were also infantry who served as *pavesarii*, carrying large shields which cost rather less than 1 l. each.[31]

---

26 B 33, ff. 30v–5; 80, ff. 103v–4, 124–5v.
27 B 97, ff. 126–9; 121, ff. 312–18; Bowsky, *Commune*, pp. 145–6.
28 *B*. 26, p. 91; 27, ff. 62, 65, 83r and v (cost of crossbows).
29 *B*. 14, pp. 131–56.
30 See table 8, p. 194.
31 B 35, f. 18 (cost of shields: 10 l. 2s. for fifteen).

Table 8. *Rates of pay for Sienese infantry*

Year	Rate per day	Source
1250	4s.	*B.* 10, pp. 56–60
1251	3s. 6d., 4s.	*B.* 11, pp. 48–62; 12, pp. 26–66
1253	1s. 6d. (c)	*B.* 14, pp. 131–56
1257	1s. 4d. (some c), 1s. 6d.	*B.* 26, p. 29
1258	1s., 1s. 4d.	*B.* 27, p. 139
1259	1s. 4d.	B 30, f. 13v
1261	1s., 2s. (c)	B 33, ff. 27v–8, 35v–8, 52–6v
1263	1s.	B 36, f. 30
1267	1s. 2d., 1s. 6d. (c)	B 40, f. 11v
1268	3s. (some c)	B 43, ff. 40–3v, 89
1273	3s.	B 55, ff. 27–8v
1276	2s.	B 65, f. 38
1281	3s. (c), 3s. 4d., 3s. 5⅓d.	B 80, ff. 60 and v, 69v–71v, 97v
1282	2s., 2s. 4d., 2s. 8d., 4s.	B 82, f. 100v; 83, ff. 85v, 88v, 91
1289	3s. (c)	B 101, f. 75

(c)=crossbowmen

Summons of infantry were normally piecemeal affairs and it does not seem possible to estimate the total potential force available. A *levée en masse* was a constitutional possibility but not a historic reality. Even when a notional general call-up was proclaimed (as in April 1272, for all Sienese aged between eighteen and seventy), the purpose of the levy was probably financial, the imposition of fines for absence, as much as military. The penalties for not performing military service were not merely financial; defaulters were ineligible for office or membership of the main council.[32]

THE CONTADO'S MILITARY SERVICE

The contado's military service obligations differed in various ways from those of the city and this was particularly true of cavalry service. Certain subjects had specific military dues laid down in the terms of their subjection or relationship. The Pannocchieschi owed personal horsed service to the commune as citizens, whereas the men of their lordship could not be compelled to serve 'this [i.e. the Sienese] side of the monastery of San Galgano'. The town of Montalcino owed Siena full service on horse and foot, while Montepulciano owed infantry service only (1294). When the Sienese called the foot of one of the city's terzi,

32 CG 15, ff. 68v–9; *Const. 1262*, p. 142n.

Montepulciano had to send 200 men, if two terzi were called, 400, and in the unlikely eventuality of a total call-up, 500.[33]

Nobles of the contado were not eligible to receive *cavallata* payments, their obligation coming into a separate category.[34] Their cavalry potential was considerable since many had retinues prepared to serve on horseback, but obedience was a quite different matter. In 1252 Siena called on Count Aldobrandino (Aldobrandeschi), the Ardengheschi counts 'and other nobles of the contado' for cavalry contingents; this was successful in the case of the Count of Elci and Rosso of San Lorenzo (probably one of the Ardengheschi), but apparently not in that of the others named. A few years later (1257) two men were despatched to ride through the contado 'to summon cavalrymen to be sent to Florence to serve the Florentines'. The levy of a *cavallata* of one hundred in the contado on 1275 shows that the contribution made by the subject territory to the commune's cavalry strength was sometimes a quite important one.[35]

In the contado as in the city the pattern of military organization had been established before the mid thirteenth century and particularly in the course of the bitter struggle with Florence in 1229–35. The contado infantry, as mentioned above, had a triple division in that each terzo of the city was associated with a particular section of the contado for the purpose of military liability, hence a reference (for instance) to representatives sent *per comitatum Terzerii Civitatis* 'to send men and communities to the army at Torniella' and payment to a man *quando iviit per comitatum Terterii Civitatis* 'to present lists of crossbowmen and archers'.[36]

The basis of the summons could be different for different parts of the contado, for example in 1272 the entire eligible male population in the area between the rivers Merse and Ombrone were called as infantrymen, whereas elsewhere the summons on this occasion was restricted to five men per thousand tax-payers (*allibrati*). One of the five was to be armed with bow or crossbow and all were to come with rations for at least a month.[37] With planning on such a scale it is scarcely surprising that as many as 3,000 contado infantrymen should be in the field simultaneously. In 1304 lists of *comitatenses* liable for infantry service were drawn up – the outside age-limits on this occasion, more realistically than in 1272, were twenty and sixty – and the level of fines for absence proclaimed. The penalty was to fall both on the individual and on his village or community, the former paying 1 l. for the first day and 10s. a day thereafter, the community 3 l.

33 *CV*, 3, pp. 846–52, 992–8, 1387–93.
34 *Const. 1262*, p. 66n.
35 *B*. 13, pp. 36, 116; 17, p. 181; CG 20, ff. 36v–7v.
36 *B*. 16, p. 64; 34, f. 28.
37 CG 15, f. 69.

and 1 l. The community was also responsible for paying the troops it provided – periods of actual service, as opposed to readiness, were always paid – and the sums thus disbursed were deductible from the community's tax obligations to Siena[38]

A common use of contado infantrymen was for engineering and pioneer operations. In 1306 seventy-five men from Asciano found themselves employed in destroying the fortifications of Rapolano. Sometimes they were sent further afield, even as far as Liguria in the Guelf campaign of 1273, but presumably this was avoided when possible and peasant soldiers were always regarded as potential deserters, particularly at the time of the grape harvest.[39]

Conscripts and other soldiers were offered not merely pay but medical treatment and compensation for various misfortunes, and doctors accompanied the army on campaign. Sienese wounded who survived the attentions of their medical officers were brought back to the city and if necessary received hospital treatment. The outcome of a conciliar discussion about the extension of these advantages to German mercenaries (1260) is not recorded, but it is likely to have been favourable.[40] The attitude illustrated by the *mendum* (compensation) clauses in the laws of the medieval communes[41] is evident also in some other forms of liberal treatment. Siena offered five years free of taxation to the son of any soldier killed on garrison duty, and full pay for the entire period of his captivity to any mercenary taken prisoner (1267).[42] That such offers may have been inspired by temporary difficulties in recruiting rather than humanitarian motives does not make them less interesting.

MERCENARIES

Since men serving by virtue of an obligation were paid for the period of their service, and quite often for the upkeep of horses when not serving, the difference between them and mercenaries does not lie in the receipt of pay. Nor, since mercenary troops were sometimes recruited in Siena or its contado, is the distinction one between locals and men from elsewhere. The line can only be drawn between those called to arms on account of an obligation and those who enlisted by choice. It might indeed be clearer if mercenaries were styled 'volunteers'.

Ambiguities of nomenclature often make it difficult to know what was the basis of service of the Tuscan *masnadieri* who made up the small garrisons of the

---

38 Bowsky, *Commune*, pp. 146, 148, 158.
39 B 118, f. 250v; 55, f. 22; CG 3, f. 41.
40 B 101, ff. 62, 88v; *Const. 1262*, p. 95; *Cost. 1309–10*, 1, pp. 95, 304; CG 9, ff. 126v–7.
41 *Const. 1262*, pp. 165–7.
42 CG 12, f. 46.

fortified places in the contado. *Masnadieri* were members of a *masnada* (band, troop: the Old French word is *mesnie*, the English *meinie*). The *masnadieri* 'de Castillione Senense et de Campili et de Titinano' (1252) may be *from* these three places or *at* them (which is probable), or quite possibly both. A list of Sienese who served at Campagnatico for some weeks in the summer of 1257 is clearer: these men *iverunt ad soldos pro comuni* (went for pay, on behalf of the commune), they were *milites* (cavalrymen) and also *soldanerii* (mercenaries). Their pay was 5s. a day, that of their commander 12s. They came from all parts of the city and must have been recruited from men who were short of a summer-time occupation or down on their luck. Two were members of grand Sienese families, Selvolesi and Codenacci, others gave their occupations as tailor, doublet-maker and tile-maker.[43]

The man recruited as a volunteer mercenary in Siena itself was a comparative rarity by the mid thirteenth century. In the second half of the century the principal development in Italian military organization was the growth of small companies, mainly of cavalry, raised and commanded by a leader who was styled the 'constable'. These constabularies, the prototype of the great mercenary companies of the fourteenth and fifteenth centuries, were recruited from many parts of Italy and beyond, the principal regions of ultramontane supply being within the present states of France, Spain and Germany. In the 1230s the mercenaries who fought on the Sienese side against Florence were recruited *ad hoc* in their own regions. At that period there do not seem to have been bodies of men seeking continuous service together through negotiation of new contracts. In those campaigns most of Siena's mercenaries had been from central Italy (Tuscany, Umbria, the Marches) and some from further north (Liguria, Lombardy, Emilia). Genoese crossbowmen were already renowned and were numerous. Frenchmen and Germans were very rare indeed.

By the 1250s all this had altered. Imperial campaigning had brought many Germans to the peninsula in the 1240s. Siena had Germans on the pay-roll in the early 1250s, the groups then being *compagnie* and *capitanerie* (in the Biccherna accounts). In the following decade the commanders cease to be referred to as *capitanei* and become *conestabiles*.[44] The crystallization of their constabularies is a gradual process, one sign of it being the negotiation of contracts between the employing communes and the commanders to cover the conditions of service. Few of the early contracts (*condotte*) have survived, but the date of those which have serve to establish the chronology of this development. The earliest ones at

---

43 *B*. 13, p. 35; 18, pp. 80–1, 99–100.
44 *B*. 12–14. For constabularies see *Florentine Studies*, pp. 84–94 and Waley, '*Condotte* and *condottieri* in the 13th century' in *Proceedings of the British Academy*, 61 (1976).

Siena relate respectively to the employment of eighty-seven Umbrian cavalry for two months and forty-five Bolognese cavalry for the same period, the former agreed at Spoleto on 27 September 1253, the latter at Pistoia ten days later.[45] The terms covered pay, compensation for horses and the possibility of taking prisoners and of being made captive. Some years after this Siena had eight constabularies, averaging round forty or rather fewer, in its employ and most – possibly all – of the constables were Germans.[46]

The heyday of the Guelf tallia system in the 1280s saw the full acceptance of the constabulary as the normal unit for mercenary recruitment. The Biccherna volume for the first half of 1280 records nineteen constabularies on the strength varying in size from seventeen to sixty-one men, though most of them numbered between twenty and forty. Some of the constables were from Spain and southern France (Pedro of Navarre, William the Catalan, Bertrand of Fourcalquier), others locals from Montevarchi and the Maremma. In the second half of the same year the number employed had fallen to thirteen, nine of these being companies already used in the January to June period.[47]

The principal advantage of the constabulary system from the commune's viewpoint must have been ease and continuity in recruitment. To send out men to likely places such as Spoleto and Genoa to search for individuals willing to enlist had been intensely time-consuming. The constable was the essential middleman, both recruiting officer for the commune and commanding officer. Moreover continuous employment could lead to the foundation of a tradition of familiarity and even loyalty, thus removing or at least weakening the standard criticism of the mercenary, that he was fickle and uncommitted to any cause. André of Villejuif (presumably a Frenchman) was in Sienese employment as a constable intermittently for eleven years (1286–96), and two local leaders of constabularies served even longer, Naldo of Foiano (San Lorenzo a Merse) between 1280 and 1295 and Neri of Staggia between 1290 and 1311.[48] The existence of the Guelf military alliance meant that a constable could have a long career without necessarily remaining on the roll of a particular commune. William the Catalan, for example, was in Sienese service from 1277 to 1286 and thereafter with the Bolognese (1288–90) and Florentines (1290–92).[49]

Though the occasional proto-company of crossbowmen is encountered and

---

45 Dipl., AGC, 27.9.1253 and 7.10.1253.
46 B 38, f. 17; 40, f. 55 (the 1267 payments suggest twenty-five as the number of some constabularies).
47 B 76, ff. 36–61; 78, ff. 26v–45.
48 B 76, 78, 80, 94–7, 99, 101, 103–4, 106–14; Bowsky, *Commune*, p. 152.
49 For William, *Florentine Studies*, pp. 88–90 and 'Condotte and condottieri' (cited above, n. 44), pp. 16–18.

infantrymen serving as mercenaries were quite common,[50] the constabulary was normally a body of cavalry. Twenty-five seems to have been considered a manageable number for a unit of Sienese horsemen[51] and the constabularies also numbered twenty-five or a multiple of that number, frequently fifty, sometimes one hundred. Obviously their usefulness to the communes as means of recruitment was enhanced if the company was a large one. When the Sienese had the system in full working order they were sometimes paying more than a thousand mercenaries in the course of a year (1281),[52] though few of these were kept on the strength for more than a few weeks. At this period the rates of pay of cavalry mercenaries tended to fall – at least in terms of purchasing power – which suggests that there was something of a buyer's market.

Apart from the wandering foreign companies of horsemen – Germans in the 1250s and 60s, Provençal and French in the 1270s and 80s – there were many bodies of Italian mercenary troops. These tended to come from those regions where rural lordship remained the prevailing social pattern, and lords still had bodies of horsed retainers or 'clients'. The Counts of Sarteano are the outstanding instance of a 'feudal' family to which Siena regularly turned as a source of cavalry in many successive generations. As early as 1266 it was suggested that a Count of Sarteano should be employed together with two subordinate commanders. The same dynasty can be found in the service of Florence and Perugia, and probably other employing communes could be traced.[53] Another zone of seignorial survival was Latium and in particular the southern Campagna. In 1281 Siena employed Pietro of Anagni and Giacomo 'of the Campagna' who between them had one hundred horsemen, Andrea of Sezze with forty-one and altogether in that year at least seven constabularies from the Campagna.[54]

The mercenary companies brought with them new problems of control. It was natural that the commune should have appointed, from a quite early date, officials with special responsibility for mercenaries, since questions must have arisen about terms of recruitment, valuation of horses, claims for compensation, involvement in internal dissensions and so on. The office of three *domini masnate* seems to have been a permanent one, but this did not prevent the periodical appointment of special officials concerned with mercenaries (*super soldatis et militibus soldatis*).[55] A close eye was presumably kept on mercenaries claiming implausible sums in respect of injured horses. There were regular parades (*mostre*)

---

50 E.g. B 80, ff. 60r and v (50 crossbowmen), 69v–71 (200 crossbowmen etc.), 87 (122 infantry).
51 Above, p. 191.
52 B 79, 80.
53 *Florentine Studies*, p. 93; *'Condotte* and *condottieri'*, pp. 20–1; CG 12, f. 32v.
54 B 80, ff. 23, 56, 62, 65v, 68v, 75, 78v, 81v, 88, 93v, 96–7.
55 E.g. B 92, f. 73; CG 36, ff. 51–72; Bowsky, *Commune*, p. 155; *Cost. 1309–10*, 2, pp. 524–5.

at which the men and their horses underwent inspection, a precaution against the notorious tendencies of armies to draw pay and rations for non-existent individuals ('dead souls').

By 1286 (and probably sooner) the constables had been compelled to provide pledges, through Sienese guarantors, for satisfactory service; when one of them deserted (*aufugit a servitio comunis*) in that year his four guarantors had to pay over the considerable sum of 94 l. each. The fund from which this payment was made had probably been deposited by the mercenaries with the landlords on whom they were billeted, to judge from earlier arrangements. Six years later another constable, Oddo of Romagna, was at fault and this time the pledge forfeit amounted to 294 florins divided equally between six local guarantors.[56] The mercenaries were also liable to deductions for duties evaded or inadequately performed. In 1295 the officials concerned with the *masnada* levied a fine totalling 666 l. 17s. 10d. on various constables and their horsemen 'for services not performed' (*pro servitiis non factis*).[57] Two clauses in the vernacular constitution deal with the general political control of mercenaries. They had to be billeted near the centre of the city and were forbidden (1306) to bear on their harness, shield or helmet the coat of arms of any Sienese citizen or *comitatensis*.[58]

The problem of maintaining authority over the companies could also be tackled in another manner, by the appointment of an overall commander. Although the Podestà was regarded as the 'natural' commander of the commune's forces, it was never easy to combine that role with his normal administrative and judicial functions. The appointment of a commander for a particular campaign was presumably seen as a way of securing better control of the troops (such a captain could be given a special temporary jurisdiction over his men)[59] as well as procuring the tactical and strategic advantages of a single command, preferably in the hands of an experienced leader. The office of Captain of War (which at first was always for a single campaign only) makes its appearance in the north Italian communes in the 1270s and spread to Tuscany soon afterwards. Siena, like Pisa, appointed its first Capitano di Guerra in 1289. The man in question was an Umbrian, Marquis Oddo of Valiana, brother of the marquis Guiduccio who had commanded Perugia's mercenary forces in 1282. In 1289 Oddo's own troop was quite small, but when he was re-employed in 1291 his men were organized in three constabularies and numbered about a hundred. This innovation remained an isolated experiment for some time but further brief appointments were made

56 B 92, f. 41v; 108, f. 52v; Dipl., AGC, 27.9.1253.
57 B 112, f. 77.
58 *Cost. 1309–10*, 2, pp. 239–40, 514–15.
59 E. Casanova, 'Ordinamenti militari senesi del 1307', *ASI*, fifth s. 24 (1899), pp. 1–12.

in 1300 and 1302, and in later decades the Capitano di Guerra was to secure a much wider field of authority.[60]

The growth of the constabulary system must be considered in association with that of the military and diplomatic nexus which might be styled the 'tallia' system. The *tallie* offered the nascent companies the prospect of prolonged employment, which itself favoured increased cohesiveness. As early as 1254 Siena, under attack from Florence, had a share or military contribution agreed with its allies (*tallia comunis Senarum*).[61] The later development of the Guelf diplomatic network has already been mentioned.[62] By the early 1270s Siena was paying regular contributions to finance an agreed proportion of the alliance's cavalry force, and on occasions sent contingents to serve in campaigns as far afield as Liguria (1273) or Romagna (1281). William the Catalan's lengthy career in the service of Siena, Bologna and Florence illustrates the military consequences of the Guelf alliance. The tallia system could result in Siena having financial responsibility for as many as 380 horsemen out of a total cavalry force of 1,500 (1292), as well as the city being required to despatch cavalry to campaign on behalf of Florence and Charles of Valois against Pistoia (1302).[63] The fabric of this Guelf alliance survived to make possible the very large armed forces which confronted Henry VII's imperial army of 1310–13.

THE COST OF WAR

It would be misleading to discuss military expenditure in terms of men alone, though the cost of constructing and maintaining fortifications and of supplies, weapons and ammunition fell much below that of soldiers.

Fortifications were a commitment of the highest importance. The condition of the contado's garrison fortresses was a compulsory subject for regular discussion in Council and that this was no mere matter of routine is shown by its consequences in February 1291. The outcome of this agenda item on that occasion was the decision that a 'merchant' accompanied by a notary should be sent on a tour of inspection of the fortifications throughout the contado, to investigate the condition of the walls and other defences as well as the supply of military stores. They were to furnish a written report to the Eighteen (predeces-

---

60 B 99, f. 95; 101, ff. 87, 89v, 150; 106, ff. 114v, 158; 493, ff. 29v, 30v, 64; 495, ff. 72v, 76, 81, 85 (there are some inaccuracies in Bowsky's reference to Oddo, *Commune*, p. 46, the date being misprinted as '1298'); for the later history of the captaincy of war see Bowsky, *Commune*, pp. 46–54; for Count Guiduccio see A. I. Galletti in *BDSPU*, 71 (1974), pp. 92, 98.

61 Above, p. 115; *B*. 15, p. 135.

62 Above, pp. 119–25.

63 CG 43 f. 42; B 116, ff. 272, 306, 356–7v; 117, ff. 235, 245, 269v. For the wider context of this development, see P. Contamine, *La Guerre au Moyen Age* (Paris, 1980), pp. 205–6.

sors of the Nine), in which particular attention was to be paid to stores which were missing and appeared to have been stolen. The Eighteen would then take any necessary action.[64]

A clause in the constitution required the appointment of three officials to be responsible for the custody of the contado strongholds, in particular Montepulciano, Castiglioncello del Trinoro, Rocca d'Orcia and Grosseto. The Chamberlain and Provveditori had to keep an inventory of arms and stores held in each of these places.[65] Everywhere the upkeep of defensive works was an obligation falling on local residents, but their labour was bound to be inadequate when schemes were ambitious. The construction of a new keep at Monticchiello (on Siena's eastern frontier, near Montepulciano) was a task undertaken in the 1250s at very considerable expense. Around the same time 2,000 blocks of stone were purchased for construction work at Campagnatico, a major stronghold in the Maremma.[66]

After the triumph of 1260 and a victorious siege in the following year it was decided to strengthen Montepulciano, so often a menace to Siena in the past; it was now to become an outlying bulwark of Sienese power. This involved the construction of a new defence system and hence much destruction, since a fortress was to be erected in what had been the very centre of the town. In a short period the cost of labour alone on this project ran to 1,350 l. and houses and open spaces in the zone marked out for military 'development' had to be purchased.[67] The treatment of Montepulciano was less harsh than that of Montalcino, where the destruction was general but apparently not motivated mainly by strategic intentions. A similar measure was passed with reference to Mensano, though in that instance self-interest eventually prevailed over rancour and the place escaped demolition through the decision to build a fortress there.[68]

The foundation of new towns in the Maremma was also essentially a strategic matter and often an expensive one, though the costs were spread over a very lengthy period. The authorization of the expenditure of 600 l. on the walls of Castelfranco Paganico in March 1300 was exceptional only in that it related to a short-term scheme which was part of a campaign to hasten the completion of this place and Roccalbegna.[69]

The constitution collected and translated into the vernacular in 1309–10

---

64 CG 41, ff. 60–1.
65 *Const. 1262*, p. 374.
66 *B.* 26, pp. 78, 101, 120, 139, 151, 167; 29, p. 39 (for these places see also *Repertorio*, pp. 27, 129–30).
67 B 33, ff. 40v, 42v–3, 59, 90; 35, f. 26; *Repertorio*, pp. 100–3.
68 B 35, f. 23; *Const. 1262*, pp. 186–8, 385; *Repertorio*, pp. 31–2. For Montalcino see above, p. 107.
69 CG 57, ff. 85v–6.

includes detailed measures concerning military equipment and stores. Weapons and tents were the responsibility of three *signori della Camera* (an office paid in wartime only) who had to be men with a minimum tax assessment of 200 l. Purchases were to be made by the Biccherna officials, who had authority to spend up to 1,000 l. on weapons, ammunition and shields. Two officials were responsible for tracing lost crossbows. Four contado fortresses (Monticchiello, Roccalbegna, Campagnatico and Sant'Angelo in Colle) were designated as places for storage of food supplies – biscuit, salt, beans and vinegar – and other stores such as rope, crossbows and bolts. Each garrisoned fort had to have its own inventory, besides a general inventory in two copies to be held in Siena. The stocking of these strongholds was allocated to yet more officials, the three *Fornitori*, who had also to be men of substance, of a minimum assessment of 3,000 l., no doubt so that they should be less subject to the temptations arising from their task.[70]

The big marquees or pavilions used on campaign (they may be seen in the famous painting of Guidoriccio in the Palazzo) were valuable objects which must have required supervision and repair. One of the tasks of the Chamberlain was to check their condition and that of the commune's crossbows at least once a quarter.[71] Although men called for service were expected to bring rations with them, it was normal to provide an army on campaign with food, and when the arrival of a cavalry force was expected fodder would also be purchased or distrained in the contado.[72] What is striking about these aspects of the commune's administration, as with many others, is the vast effort dedicated to carrying out the city's business, in human skill, time and labour, as well as in financial resources.

MILITARY DEVELOPMENTS

The commune's military organization also requires consideration in terms of development and change. The period between the first appearance of communal militias and that of fully-formed mercenary companies has been seen as a crucial one in the evolution of specialized infantry.[73] The Sienese evidence does not support this contention. As mentioned above, crossbowmen were very numerous in Siena's own citizen armies in the 1250s. Sometimes they were accompanied and presumably protected by infantry with large shields, *pavesarii*,[74] but this was not an innovation. Italian crossbowmen played an important part in Palestine much earlier, for instance at Jaffa in 1192, so that in an era of predominantly

---

70 *Cost. 1309–10*, 1, pp. 219–20.
71 'Breve 1250', p. 24.
72 CG 15, f. 69; *B*. 30, p. 143; 61, f. 1.
73 See, e.g., Pieri in *RSI*, 50 (1933), pp. 597–609.
74 B 33, ff. 35v–8; above, pp. 193–4.

defensive fighting the crossbow had achieved pre-eminence in Italy long before the mid thirteenth century.[75]

The small troops of mercenaries whose advent and crystallization did indeed provide an important element of novelty in this period, who brought change and heralded far greater changes, rarely included archers or any type of infantry.[76] In the vast majority of cases they were simply an assembly of horsemen, accustomed to use their steeds, no doubt, for moving around the countryside, on patrol or in pursuit of work, rather than in a mounted charge. They will have been armed with swords, but not necessarily with lances. Indeed these men may well never have practised a charge, still less performed one in battle. The role of the horse was to provide transport for them and their possessions, perhaps also to inspire awe when raiding or on police duties.

The cavalry obligation persisted as a fundamental aspect of the city's military, social and financial way of life. Armed men needed the mobility which the horse provided whether they were raiding and threatening 'enemy' peasants, enforcing fiscal or agrarian measures in their own commune's countryside, or merely on the watch as a garrison or patrol. In an engagement the horse could assist pursuit or facilitate escape, but confrontational occasions such as Montaperti were totally exceptional and armed men were normally recruited with the intention of avoiding them rather than of gaining glory on the field of battle.

---

75 See P. Contamine, *La Guerre au Moyen Age* (Paris, 1980), pp. 166–8; J. F. Verbruggen, *The Art of Warfare in Western Europe during the Middle Ages* (Amsterdam-NY-Oxford, 1977), p. 194.
76 Two instances: *B.* 14, pp. 120, 182 (crossbowmen and archers, 1253); 121, ff. 243v, 260v (cavalry and infantry in a Catalan company, 1307).

10 *Continuity and change*

Throughout this book examples have been selected to illustrate Sienese actions and preoccupations from laws, council minutes and other sources for the period between 1250 and 1310. A topical approach, with no chronological organization, involves the implicit assumption that the period possessed a fundamental unity and that generalizations about attitudes and activities are valid for the whole of it. This telescoping of two generations, which must have some distorting effect, cannot stand without some justification being offered.

CHANGE

How would emphasis on continuity and denial of significant development or innovation have struck a contemporary?

A convenient vantage-point might be 9 June 1311, which was a great day in Siena's history. Duccio di Buoninsegna had completed his painting for the cathedral's high altar, the supreme masterpiece usually known (since the central scene portrayed the Virgin 'in Majesty') as the *Maestà*. The huge altarpiece, comprising some seventy panels, was borne to the cathedral from Duccio's workshop outside the Stalloreggi gate, *con grandi divotioni e procissioni*.[1] Shops were closed for the day as the bishop and clergy, officials of the commune, citizens, women and children and a band of musicians all accompanied the painting on its journey. Prayers were said and the city's Protectress and Advocate was begged to preserve it from all danger and evil and to keep and increase in peace and well-being Siena and its area of jurisdiction.

For the elderly at least, it must have been a day for reflection as well as rejoicing. Some would have recalled the city's dedication to the Virgin before Montaperti, fifty-one years earlier, and for a very few memories would have gone back as far as the lifetime of Frederick II (d. 1250), father of that battle's co-victor, King Manfred. When they looked back to the Siena of their young days did they see it as a very different place and society?

The Duomo to which the *Maestà* was taken had progressed in grandeur in recent decades. A campanile had been built, other work was going ahead and

---

1 *RIS, CS*, p. 313 (chronicle of Agnolo di Tura del Grasso).

before long a new baptistery would be planned. Work on the commune's palace was in full swing.[2] Yet one unhappy aspect of life would have occurred to any reflective Sienese. The dedication of the city to the Virgin in 1260 had preceded military triumph over the Florentines. That triumph, however, had had no durable consequences and by 1311 it must have been accepted by most Sienese that Florence's briefly interrupted predominance in Tuscany was likely to be permanent. The ephemeral glory of 1260 perhaps magnified the later humiliation, so strongly felt, of being outshone by Florence.

This story went back much further; Siena and Florence had clashed in a great trial of strength in 1229–35 and thenceforth were pitted against each other in a struggle for domination which was bound to condemn the loser to bitterness. Other Tuscan cities – Lucca and Pisa in particular – had had their hours of greatness earlier. Lucca, Pisa, Arezzo and Pistoia all experienced the shadow of Florence yet none of these had challenged so directly, seemed so close to victory and felt so keenly the outcome. The Sienese were obsessed by the notion that they could equal Florence in strength and magnificence and the work on the Palazzo and cathedral was connected with that belief. The two generations who lived through the times dealt with in this book had suffered a profound disappointment.

The contrast between 1311 and 1250 would have seemed most melancholy to those closely involved in finance. Around the middle of the thirteenth century the Sienese bankers were leaders in the business of the papal court and in the conduct of finance and commerce at the fairs of Champagne. Such primacy depended on the confidence of the world of trading and money, as well as on good fortune. Techniques and expertise counted for much also, but here the Sienese had no monopoly. The political developments of the 1260s caught the Sienese banks at a disadvantage in comparison with the Florentines and this was due to ill fortune as well as ineptness. The circumstances were such that the Sienese financiers surely perceived themselves as losing ground, particularly at the papal court, through the very success of the Florentines. It was a case not of comparative loss of position but of direct gains by the Florentine companies at Siena's expense, first at the Curia, then in dealings with the most powerful monarchy in Europe, the French.

The lengthy agony of the Bonsignori bank was the most evident sign that things had gone wrong for Siena's financiers.[3] No company had been more closely associated with the papacy, yet by the pontificate of Boniface VIII (1294–1303) the Bonsignori were doing no papal business and were falling into grave trouble,

---

2 Above, pp. 12–15. For the chronology of the architectural work see now A. Middeldorf Kosegarten, *Sienesische Bildhauer am Duomo Vecchio* (Munich, 1984), pp. 22–34.

3 Above, pp. 34–5.

dragging with them the other Sienese banks whose credit generally and dealings in France in particular were involved. Meanwhile a saying was attributed to the pope himself which must have caused bitter offence if it reached Siena: the ubiquitous Florentines, he was supposed to have said, ranked with earth, air, fire and water – 'a fifth element'.[4]

It did not require the bankruptcy of a single company or unpalatable papal *mots* to bring it home to Sienese financiers that the Florentine companies had gained an unchallengeable predominance. It was brought home to them every day by the rate of exchange between their own pound and the Florentine florin, dealing in exchange being a crucial part of their work. The Florentines launched their silver coin, the *fiorino*, at a time when parity prevailed between the two currencies (1252), but the Sienese pound weakened over the ensuing decades. In 1270, 32s. 6d. Sienese was required to purchase a florin, by 1277 the rate had deteriorated to 38s. 6d. For a few years the rate tended to alter slightly in Siena's favour, but by 1292 it had weakened to 40s. and by 1302 to 50s. In 1311, shortly before the procession to the Duomo, the florin fetched 53s. 4d. Thus its strength had nearly tripled *vis-à-vis* the Sienese currency in the period covered in this book. A senior banker with a reasonably good memory would have been able to draw the graph (figure 2, p. 208) which plotted the decline of the Sienese pound. A very similar fate had befallen the Pisan pound (parity in 1252, 54s. to the florin in 1311), whilst the mint of Lucca had lost most of its importance over the same period, as well as its currency declining in terms of the florin – but this would have been small consolation to the Sienese.[5]

The year 1311 found Henry VI in Italy (but not yet in Tuscany); thus imperial authority stood in the background as it had done in the mid thirteenth century. On the earlier occasion imperial alliance had brought disillusionment; by the time of Henry VII, although a handful of magnates were banished as Ghibelline sympathizers, Siena's rulers no longer took such an alliance seriously as a card to be played.[6] Florentine might, in fact, was accepted as the first factor in Siena's foreign policy.

CONTINUITY

Despite the melancholy decline in his city's standing in Tuscany, a Sienese might have decided in 1311 that the unchanging factors in its character predominated over the shifting ones. Duccio's altarpiece would in itself have been a reminder of continuity. The painter's long career – he had practised his art for more than

4 P. Villari, *I primi due secoli della storia di Firenze*, edn 3 (Florence, n.d.), p. 331.
5 P. Spufford, *Handbook of Medieval Exchange* (London, 1986), pp. 39–51. Figure from p. 50, by kind permission of Dr Spufford.
6 *RIS, CS*, p. 313.

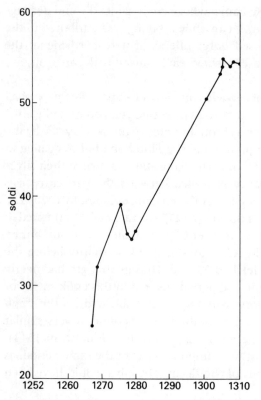

2 *FLORENTINE FLORINS IN SIENESE SOLDI AND DENARI 1252–1310.*

thirty years before completing the *Maestà* – was rooted in Sienese tradition. The massive work of carpentry which made the altarpiece possible and the technique of the gilt background are equally characteristic of Siena. Disputed attributions are a prominent feature of art-historical scholarship confronted by Duccio and the Sienese art of his time and this in itself is evidence of his centrality within a continuous tradition. Two superb paintings now in Britain help to make this point. A triptych of the *Crucifixion* in the Royal Collection bears the attribution 'Duccio', though Professor John White would ascribe it to the painter's circle. The single-panel *Crucifixion* formerly in the collection of the Earls of Crawford and now in the Manchester Art Gallery is equally controversial; Professor Stubblebine attributes it to Duccio's pupil Ugolino. Professor Deuchler sees neither painting as coming from Duccio's workshop. Nor is there agreement over the role to be assigned to Duccio himself in the painting of the *Maestà*. The disagreements of the experts make it clear that by the late thirteenth century there was a type of Sienese painting which might be the work of Duccio himself or of his assistants or circle. Differences of opinion about chronology confirm the point that there was an enduring Sienese artistic tradition.[7]

More central to the general question of continuity and change is the social and economic structure of the population. It has been shown[8] that men often exerted political authority in the city for lengthy periods, unaffected by revolutions in its external alliances and by such fundamental internal changes as the emergence of a 'popular' organization and the promulgation of anti-magnate legislation. An enduring oligarchy of landed financiers from a few very wealthy families, allied with certain other prominent figures, mainly trained in the law, characterized Siena throughout the period covered in this book. This basic fact favoured a fundamental continuity in outlook and policy and weighed heavily in the balance against any tendencies towards change from within.

If oligarchy showed a singular power of survival, this was not in the continuance of oligarchy as a socio-political form (a form that in a city–state is more or less inescapable), but rather in the continuity of individuals and families as the city's power-wielding patricians. The main reason for that is to be found in the weakness of those elements which might have been expected to penetrate from below and to transform the earlier oligarchies, a process which occurred in varying degrees in most of the greater Italian cities. Thus one returns to the lack of Sienese industrial development and the related weakness of gild organization. The failure of the Popolo to achieve lasting institutional successes is the measure of the exceptional strength and endurance of Siena's oligarchy.

The dominance of these families was not maintained through any formal monopoly of authority. Indeed a constitutionally formalized monopoly would have made its preponderance more vulnerable. In the period before the Nine, from the 1250s to 1280s, there were many wealthy landowning financiers who rarely held civic office or spoke in council. The fact of their abstention did not limit the general domination of their dynasties and those allied to them. The same situation prevailed under the Nine: members of the named *casati* families being ineligible for election to the Nine, they exerted their influence through the other offices of the *ordini* – in the Biccherna, the Mercanzia and the Guelf Party or *milites* – or through the commune's many other institutions, diplomatic, military, fiscal and so on. With estates, clients, familiars, servants, ecclesiastical office and patronage, not to mention money and borrowing power, they had no need for personal participation in the often routine preoccupations of the Nine. Certainly

---

7 See J. White, *Duccio, Tuscan Art and the Medieval Workshop*, (London, 1979); J. H. Stubblebine, *Duccio di Buoninsegna and his School*, 2 vols. (Princeton, 1979); F. Deuchler, *Duccio* (Milan, 1984). Useful for recent work on the subject is M. Davies (rev. D. Gordon), *The Early Italian Schools. Before 1400* (National Gallery, London, 1988), pp. 13–24.

8 pp. 90–3.

the period of the Nine cannot be seen as a time of control by 'middle elements', holding power at the expense of a superseded oligarchy of landed financiers.[9]

Thus one of the reflections of a Sienese in 1311 would have been, with respect to the city's ruling group, 'plus ça change, plus c'est la même chose' – whether he rejoiced in this, as a beneficiary, or deplored it. The following two decades – still 'under the Nine' – were to reveal a yet more marked persistence of magnatial strength. The Tolomei fought a private war with the Salimbeni in 1315–16; 'they had great enmity', says the chronicler, 'and the Nine could do nothing to make peace between them'. In 1318 Sozzo and Deo dei Tolomei were involved in a conspiracy against the Nine, but were condemned and driven out to the contado.[10] This pattern of great families withdrawing in defiant self-sufficiency to their estates was to continue through the rest of the decade and the 1320s.

In 1323 the commune determined to despatch a mixed force of cavalry and infantry in support of the Florentines against Castruccio Castracane, lord of Lucca. The commune's own horsemen sent 200 cavalry, i.e those owed through the militia obligation. Apart from these, eight noble families combined to add a joint body of horsemen, numbering 215, to which the Salimbeni contributed forty-six, the Piccolomini thirty-six and the Tolomei twenty-four. The commander of this amalgamation of private armies was a Sansedoni, a relative of the Dominican Ambrogio.[11] Nothing could have symbolized more clearly than this cavalry force the continuing domination of Siena's great families.

How well the wealth of the landed dynasties held up through the fourteenth century is another matter. One great landowner, the Hospital, ran into periods of acute difficulty in the 1340s and 1350s.[12] Meanwhile the city remained dependent, for the continuance of its main business and for tolls, on the agricultural market at a time when Florence, in total contrast, was already the base of a powerful textile industry.

CONCLUSION

The city's continuing dependence on the south Tuscan countryside is the most important of continuities. Those combinations which have been noted in wills remained the norm throughout the population: plots of agricultural land, woodland, animals, a house and warehouse or workshop in the city.[13] Duccio the

---

9 For this paragraph see chapter 4 above. For an expression of the same view see Marrara, particularly pp. 254–61.

10 *RIS, CS*, pp. 364–5, 372–3.

11 Ibid., p. 406. For Ambrogio Sansedoni, see above, pp. 142–6.

12 Epstein, p. 246.

13 Above, pp. 20, 39–40.

painter was no exception and possessed land near the river Tessa.[14] The 'Tavola delle Possessioni' of 1317–18 shows some two-thirds of the taxed population owning rural property. The richest, those whose total property was assessed at above 5,000 l., had on average over 85 per cent of the value of their holdings in rural wealth.[15]

Had Sienese domestic accounts and journals survived for this period it would be clear that this was taken for granted at the time. One rather unsatisfactory volume of *Ricordi* – unsatisfactory mainly because it is accessible only in an incomplete and quite unreliable edition – must be pressed into service: this is the book of domestic records and financial accounts kept in Italian between 1231–43 and 1261–62 by Moscada, widow of Spinello di Mattasala, a member of the Lambertini family. These *Ricordi* document a well-to-do household reliant largely on the receipt of rents in kind. They leased out a mill to the prior of San Vigilio, the rent consisting entirely of grain which was due at the rate of 13½ *staia* each month. More grain, flour and wine were received as rent from holdings in the Sienese countryside and grain rendered as rent was often resold. The family derived income also from workshops and other urban premises; they leased out rooms to a cooper and a brooch-maker. The sale and resale of foodstuffs was a constant feature of life at almost all levels of the population. Moscada's expenses include (1242) a very considerable purchase of must (new wine) from Tolomeo di Giacomo Tolomei della Piazza, one of the founders of the Tolomei financial house, a transaction which confirms yet again the versatility of Siena's 'bankers'.[16]

Early Sienese wills incorporate disappointingly few household inventories, but one rare survival among them lists the contents of the quite humble home in the *popolo* of S Giovanni of Aldobrandino di Dietaiuti (1280). Though a man of modest means, Aldobrandino had felt some anxiety on his deathbed about having engaged in usurious transactions; he states no occupation. At the time of his death his chattels comprised two chests, one cupboard, a bed with bedding, some benches and casks – and, of course, grain and wine.[17] It is not certain that grander households would have contained great quantities of furniture and other possessions, but the tables portrayed in the *Feast at Cana* and *Last Supper* panels of the *Maestà* altarpiece bear handsome table-linen, plentiful earthenware vessels for wine (and a cask), other vessels and goblets, a few knives.

---

14 White, *Duccio*, pp. 191–2.

15 G. Cherubini, *Signori, Contadini, Borghesi* (Florence, 1974), pp. 231–311, particularly pp. 253, 257.

16 See 'Ricordi di una famiglia senese', *ASI*, app. vol. 5 (1847), pp. 5–76. The manuscript is Ms 136 (A.IV.27) of the Biblioteca Comunale, Siena. Comparison of the manuscript with the published text shows that much is omitted and that much that has been printed is incorrect: see also G. Garosi (ed.), *Inventario dei Manoscritti della Biblioteca Comunale di Siena*, 2 vols., Florence, 1978–80, 1, pp. 292–5. A correct edition of this manuscript is much to be desired.

17 Dipl., AGC, 19.6.1276 (copy, with inventory dated 22.10.1280).

Some of the evidence suggests that Siena with its numerically weak middle class, should be treated as an instance of 'two nations', with the grand land-owners, in control of the city's destinies, on one side of the divide, the agricultural labourers, servants, grooms and carters, water-carriers and so on, on the other. Not everything fits in with this suggestion, however. In particular the flourishing religious confraternities, felt at the time to be particularly characteristic of Siena, are in conflict with it. An example of contemporary pride in these institutions is the legacy of a lady who bequeathed the sum of 3 l. to be divided between all the confraternities of the city.[18] Membership of these bodies, flagellants and the rest, extended from the rich to the rather poor, and only the distinctly poor would have found themselves debarred by the expense involved. The religious gilds brought together in a common activity those elements coming between the highest and the lowest, an accomplishment which would have been insignificant or impossible had the shape of Siena's social body really comprised an extremely slender 'hour-glass' waist. Even if the intermediate class was less significant quantitatively than might be expected, its role in the city's life was an important one.

There was a good deal to engage the loyalties of the Sienese – family, *contrada*, church and confraternity – apart from the strongly-felt pull of the city's own personality. In spite of discomfort and hunger and the occasional violence of dynastic strife, Siena in the thirteenth century had much to offer, affording its population varied forms of satisfaction, social and individual.

18 Dipl., Spedale, 2.4.1304 (text in English, '5 Magnate Families', pp. 333–6).

General index

Index of
personal names

Index of places